Jessica Huntley's Pan-African Life

BLACK LITERARY AND CULTURAL EXPRESSIONS

Bloomsbury's **Black Literary and Cultural Expressions** series provides a much-needed space for exploring dimensions of Black creativity as its local expressions in literature, music, film, art, etc., interface with the global circulation of culture. From contemporary and historical perspectives, and through a multidisciplinary lens, works in this series critically analyse the provenance, genres, aesthetics, intersections and modes of circulation of works of Black cultural expression and production.

Series Editors
Toyin Falola and Abimbola A. Adelakun, University of
Texas at Austin, USA

Advisory Board
Nadia Anwar, University of Management and Technology,
Lahore, Pakistan
Adriaan van Klinken, University of Leeds, UK
Alain Lawo-Sukam, Texas A&M University, USA
Nathaniel S. Murrell, University of North Carolina, Wilmington, USA
Mukoma wa Ngugi, Cornell University, USA
Bode Omojola, Mount Holyoke and the Five College Consortium, USA
Nduka Otiono, Carleton University, Canada
Bola Sotunsa, Babcock University, Nigeria
Nathan Suhr-Sytsma, Emory University, USA

Volumes in the Series:
Wole Soyinka: Literature, Activism, and African Transformation by Bola Dauda and Toyin Falola
Social Ethics and Governance in Contemporary African Writing: Literature, Philosophy, and the Nigerian World by Nimi Wariboko
The Birth of Breaking: Hip Hop History from the Floor Up by Serouj 'Midus' Aprahamian
Literature of the Somali Diaspora: Space, Language and Resistance in Somali Anglophone and Italian Novels by Marco Medugno
Jessica Huntley's Pan-African Life: The Decolonizing Work of a Radical Black Activist by Claudia Tomlinson
Chinua Achebe: Narrating Africa in Fictions and History by Toyin Falola
The Epic Poetry of Mazisi Kunene by Dike Okoro (forthcoming)

Jessica Huntley's Pan-African Life

The Decolonizing Work of a Radical Black Activist

Claudia Tomlinson

BLOOMSBURY ACADEMIC
NEW YORK • LONDON • OXFORD • NEW DELHI • SYDNEY

BLOOMSBURY ACADEMIC
Bloomsbury Publishing Inc
1385 Broadway, New York, NY 10018, USA
50 Bedford Square, London, WC1B 3DP, UK
29 Earlsfort Terrace, Dublin 2, Ireland

BLOOMSBURY, BLOOMSBURY ACADEMIC and the Diana logo are
trademarks of Bloomsbury Publishing Plc

First published in the United States of America 2024

Copyright © Claudia Tomlinson, 2024

Cover design: Eleanor Rose
Cover image: Portrait of Jessica Huntley, 2003 © Robert Taylor

All rights reserved. No part of this publication may be reproduced or transmitted in any form or by any means, electronic or mechanical, including photocopying, recording, or any information storage or retrieval system, without prior permission in writing from the publishers.

Bloomsbury Publishing Inc does not have any control over, or responsibility for, any third-party websites referred to or in this book. All internet addresses given in this book were correct at the time of going to press. The author and publisher regret any inconvenience caused if addresses have changed or sites have ceased to exist, but can accept no responsibility for any such changes.

Whilst every effort has been made to locate copyright holders the publishers would be grateful to hear from any person(s) not here acknowledged.

Library of Congress Cataloging-in-Publication Data
Names: Tomlinson, Claudia, author.
Title: Jessica Huntley's Pan-African life: the decolonizing work of
a radical Black activist/Claudia Tomlinson.
Description: New York: Bloomsbury Academic, 2024. | Series: Black literary and cultural expressions; vol. 5 | Includes bibliographical references and index.
Identifiers: LCCN 2024008182 (print) | LCCN 2024008183 (ebook) | ISBN 9781501394553 (paperback) | ISBN 9781501394560 (hardback) | ISBN 9781501394577 (ebook) | ISBN 9781501394584 (pdf)
Subjects: LCSH: Huntley, Jessica, 1927-2013. | Political activists–England–London–Biography. | Guyanese–England–London–Biography. | Anti-imperialist movements–Guyana. | Publishers and publishing–England–London. | Great Britain–Politics and government–1945- | Great Britain–Social conditions–20th century. | Guyana–Politics and government–1803-1966.
Classification: LCC DA591.H86 T66 2024 (print) | LCC DA591.H86 (ebook) | DDC 323.0942092–dc23/eng/20240219
LC record available at https://lccn.loc.gov/2024008182
LC ebook record available at https://lccn.loc.gov/2024008183

ISBN:	PB:	978-1-5013-9455-3
	HB:	978-1-5013-9456-0
	ePDF:	978-1-5013-9458-4
	eBook:	978-1-5013-9457-7

Series: Black Literary and Cultural Expressions

Typeset by Integra Software Services Pvt. Ltd.
Printed and bound in Great Britain

To find out more about our authors and books visit www.bloomsbury.com and sign up for our newsletters.

*This book is dedicated to the memory of Jessica Huntley,
her vision and her struggle on behalf of humanity.*

CONTENTS

List of Figures xi
Acknowledgements xiv
List of Abbreviations xv

Introduction 1

1 Growing Up, Rising Up 9
2 Raised to Resist 21
3 The Emerging Activist 27
4 National Freedom and Women's Emancipation 43
5 'Bound with the Chains of Colonialism and Imperialism' 51
6 Struggles in Male Ranks 59
7 An Old Fight in a New Place 71
8 Finding a Foothold in Activism in Britain 89
9 Becoming West Indian in Britain 99
10 'A Political Act', Bogle L'Ouverture Publications' Early Work 111
11 'A New Alternative in Publishing' 125
12 'To Re-Write Our Own History': A Black Publishing Strategy 133
13 Growing a Pan-African Publishing Tradition 141

14 'The Atmosphere Was Electric in the Shop': Bookshop Activism 159

15 'Matriarch of the Movement for Black Rights in Britain, the World' 177

16 Fighting for Decolonization in Independent Guyana 187

17 Publishing Activity in Bogle L'Ouverture's Later Period 199

18 The Bookshop Goes Back Home 205

Appendix: Oral History Interviews 211
Bibliography 214
Index 221

FIGURES

3.1 Jessica and Eric Huntley's wedding in 1950. Courtesy of the Huntley Collection, London Metropolitan Archives 38

7.1 Jessica Huntley seated at the WIDF Conference in Hungary, 1958. Courtesy of the Huntley Collection, London Metropolitan Archives 73

7.2 Hectorine Carroll in Guyana with grandsons Karl Huntley, Chauncey Huntley and son Munroe Carroll preparing to travel to England, 1961. Courtesy of the Huntley Collection, London Metropolitan Archives 87

8.1 Eric and Jessica with Karl and Chauncey outside 110 Windermere Road, Ealing, circa 1965. Courtesy of the Huntley Collection, London Metropolitan Archives 95

8.2 Jessica Huntley with baby daughter Accabre, circa 1968. Image courtesy of Accabre Rutlin, the baby in the picture 96

9.1 Jessica Huntley with Angela Davis at the Keskidee Centre in London, 1974. Photograph credited to Amit Francis. Courtesy of the Huntley Collection, London Metropolitan Archives 110

10.1 Founding members of Bogle L'Ouverture Publications at Windermere Road, with Jessica Huntley and baby Accabre Huntley, circa 1969. Courtesy of the Huntley Collection, London Metropolitan Archives 112

10.2 Poster by Bogle L'Ouverture Publications advertising prints with original artwork by Ras Daniel Heartman, circa 1971. Courtesy of the Huntley Collection, London Metropolitan Archives 118

10.3 Jessica Huntley with Walter Rodney at Windermere Road, circa 1967. Courtesy of the Huntley Collection, London Metropolitan Archives 122

11.1 Cover of *The Groundings with my Brothers*, illustrated by Errol Lloyd (1969). Image reproduced with kind permission from Errol Lloyd 129

12.1 Jessica Huntley with Andrew Salkey, author, editor and founding member of Bogle L'Ouverture Publications, circa 1980. Reproduced with kind permission from Jason Salkey 138

13.1 Jessica Huntley in 'Creation for Liberation', a film to celebrate ten years of Bogle L'Ouverture Publications (1979). Reproduced with kind permission from Ray Kril 153

13.2 The Black Parents Movement, circa 1978, featuring Jessica Huntley, third left and John La Rose, second left. Courtesy of the Huntley Collection, London Metropolitan Archives 155

14.1 The front room at Coldershaw Road, 1974, Jessica Huntley with Andrew Salkey (right) and Errol Lloyd (left). Courtesy of the Huntley Collection, London Metropolitan Archives 161

14.2 Opening day at Bogle L'Ouverture Bookshop, 20 November 1975. Reproduced with kind permission from the Salkey Estate 166

14.3 Jessica Huntley seated in Bogle L'Ouverture Bookshop, circa 1976. Courtesy of the Huntley Collection, London Metropolitan Archives 167

14.4 Bogle L'Ouverture Bookshop full of children and young people, circa 1976. Courtesy of the Huntley Collection, London Metropolitan Archives 169

14.5 Sistren Theatre Collective visit the bookshop, pictured with Jessica Huntley (1983). Courtesy of the Huntley Collection, London Metropolitan Archives 170

14.6 Eric Huntley at Bogle L'Ouverture Bookshop following a racist attack, circa 1978. Courtesy of the Huntley Collection, London Metropolitan Archives 173

15.1 Jessica Huntley with John La Rose at the First International Book Fair of Radical Black and Third World Books, 1982. Courtesy of the George Padmore Institute 178

15.2 Jessica Huntley with Maya Angelou, approximately 1980, at a book launch in London. Courtesy of the Huntley Collection, London Metropolitan Archives 180

18.1 Jessica with sculpture by George Fowokan Kelly at the LMA, 2007. Reproduced with kind permission from George Fowokan Kelly 207

ACKNOWLEDGEMENTS

My thanks firstly go to Professor Hakim Adi for his advice and guidance in this research. I am very grateful to Professor Kennetta Hammond Perry for her interest and encouragement of this project. I would also like to thank Eric Huntley, Accabre Rutlin and Chauncey Huntley, and the Huntley family for their encouragement and support with this project. Karl Huntley must also be mentioned as this is also his story. I am grateful to the many contributors to this book, those who contributed interviews, information and documents. Thanks to those who were particularly committed to this research: Errol Lloyd, Richard Small, Professor Ewart Thomas, Ngugi wa Thiong'o, Waveney Bushell, Anne Johnson, George Fowokan Kelly, Michael La Rose, councillor Grace Quansah, Dr Margaret Andrews, Linton Kwesi Johnson, Nigel Westmaas, Eusi Kwayana and Valerie Bloom. Dr Diane Bebbington, Professor Gus John, councillor Michelle Simmons-Safo, Ato Roberts (son of Ras Daniel Heartman), Howard Hill-Esbrand, Claudia Coulter, Ray Kril, Jason Salkey, Dr Masood Raja and Professor Francisca de Haan provided encouragement, assistance and information that supported the research. Sally Bevan at the London Metropolitan Archives and Sarah Garrod at the George Padmore Institute provided invaluable assistance and advice. This research has been enriched by the data gathering of research assistant Deneille Griffith who accessed collections in Guyana during the difficult pandemic period. Many others read the research as it progressed and provided extremely helpful feedback and comments.

ABBREVIATIONS

BCA	Black Cultural Archives
BGFA	British Guiana Freedom Association
CARIG	Committee Against Repression in Guyana
CECWA	Caribbean Education Community Workers Association
CPGB	Communist Party of Great Britain
FHALMA	Friends of the Huntley Archives at the London Metropolitan Archives
GPI	George Padmore Institute
HC	Huntley Collection
ICSL	Institute of Commonwealth Studies Library
LMA	London Metropolitan Archives
PPP	People's Progressive Party
TNA	The National Archives
WIDF	Women's International Democratic Federation
WPA	Working People's Alliance
WPO	Women's Progressive Organization

Introduction

Jessica Goes Home

*(A tribute by Ngũgĩ wa Thiong'o
Translated from Gĩkũyũ)*

*After she completed her work on earth
Jessica went home.
At the gate, George Padmore and CLR James welcomed her.
At the door, Walter Rodney and John la Rose greeted her.
On entering, Maurice Bishop and Kwame Nkrumah hugged her.
Nyanjirũ MeKatilili Rosa Parks and Tubman
Ululated for a daughter come home to rest.*

*This is your seat.
You have joined the sacred council of spirits.
May you protect the lives of the black people the world over.
And all others tortured for seeking truth and justice.*[1]

Jessica Huntley (1927–2013) was a Guyanese-born British political activist and publisher of radical literature on topics relating to Black and Third World themes, the education of Black children, justice for women, international workers' rights and Pan-Africanism. She grew up under British coloniality in British Guiana (now Guyana) and became part of the new politics that emerged in the 1940s which articulated independence from colonial oppression. From an early life of deprivation in one of the roughest

---

[1] Ngugi wa Thiong'o, 'Jessica Goes Home, A Poetic Tribute' (2013), Personal Correspondence, 14 September 2020.

1930s tenement yards in the country, she rose to help establish the country's first political party which brought enfranchisement to women and all workers. She breached expectations about the limited role women could play in formal political life. Overcoming the restrictions of marriage and motherhood, she enmeshed herself in the decolonizing political work in British Guiana in the 1940s and 1950s.

After migration to Britain in 1958, she spent more than six decades as a leading figure in the struggle against racialized injustices on behalf of Black people in Britain and elsewhere. She also built a famous radical Black publishing company and bookshop which published and showcased the best British and international authors of their generation. She developed some of the leading authentic Black voices in radical politics and enabled Black themes, histories, messages and dialects to emerge and flourish. This was achieved against a backdrop of significant personal and political adversity.

She was at the forefront of shaping the racial decolonization discourse in Britain during the 1960s, 1970s and later, to bring justice to people of Black and African heritage. She decolonized herself after decades of life in a colonial nation and encouraged other Black people to have a love of Africa and being African. She actively worked to break down hostility and apathy in Black people and others and worked tirelessly to build a sense of pride in Blackness and Africa. She went beyond this and fought for her community, and anyone suffering injustice who came through the doors of the bookshop of Bogle L'Ouverture Publications.

Pan-Africanism is an important theme explored in Jessica Huntley's history as a movement aimed at connecting and unifying ideas that promote the uplift of Africa and Africans. It is considered to have emerged at the turn of the twentieth century. A central theme in the struggle against anti-Black racialization during the twentieth and twenty-first centuries was the debate on the importance of Pan-Africanism as an ideology for liberation of Black people. It is most helpfully defined by Hakim Adi as 'a variety of ideas, activities, organizations and movements that, sometimes in concert, resisted the exploitation and oppression of all those of African heritage, opposed and refuted the ideologies of anti-African racism and celebrated African achievement, history and the very notion of being African'.[2] Its roots could be detected in the West Indies and the United States, for example in church movements that were designated 'African'. Henry Sylvester Williams convened the first Pan-African Congress of 1900. A series of further Pan-African Congresses were held until the 1945 Conference hosted in Manchester, England, signifying an important stage in the movement.

---

[2]Hakim Adi, *Pan-Africanism* (London and New York: Bloomsbury, 2018), p.3.

The origins of Pan-Africanism as a movement are associated with Henry Sylvester Williams.[3]

Garveyism is a strand of Pan-Africanism and was embraced by many radical Black activists. Marcus Garvey (1887–1940), was born in Jamaica into a peasant, agricultural family and became politically active in anti-colonialism, particularly in Kingston.[4] In 1914, with his first wife Amy Ashwood Garvey, he founded the Universal Negro Improvement Association (UNIA) which was to become one of the largest international movements for the liberation of African people and those in the African diaspora.[5] The central argument of Garveyism is 'race first', the notion that Black people are globally oppressed on the basis of their race. He considered that before they faced other oppressions, such as on the basis of class, education or wealth status, the universal oppressive factor faced by all Black people was anti-Blackness based on their membership of the African identity or membership of the diaspora. His principal argument was that 'the world has made being black a crime, and I have felt it in common with men who suffer like me, and instead of making it a crime, I hope to make it a virtue'.[6] His stance therefore was to reverse this and urge the celebration of being African and being Black, and its history, culture and arts and the idea of uplifting Black people. He also felt that if white power and influence were not challenged it would ultimately lead to the destruction of Black people as a race. He started to view Africa as the African homeland and the place to secure the liberty and future of Black people. An important strand of this perspective therefore was that Black people should work to move to Africa and build up the Black race, its identity and economic future.[7]

Garveyism also placed emphasis on Black self-help and self-reliance as the primary tool for race uplift and survival for Black people. He argued that independence of white power was critical to reduce the of exploitation he saw white people as holding over Black people. He felt it was a difference in power, economic and political, that enabled white people to oppress Black people.[8] Self-help as a route to Black independence and agency is explored throughout this research and its importance as an idea to Jessica Huntley and central to how she operated Bogle L'Ouverture Publications and lived her daily life.

---

[3]Hakim Adi and Marika Sherwood, *Pan-African History, Political Figures from Africa and the Diaspora Since 1787* (London: Routledge, 2003), pp.190–4.

[4]Tony Martin, *Race First: The Ideological and Organizational Struggles of Marcus Garvey and the Universal Negro Improvement Association* (Baltimore: Black Classic Press, 2020), pp.3–21.

[5]Ibid.

[6]Marcus Garvey, 'Speech at the Ward Theatre, Kingston Jamaica', *Negro World*, 7 January, 1928, in *Race First*, ed. by Tony Martin (Baltimore: Black Classic Press, 2020), p.23.

[7]Martin, *Race First*, p.24.

[8]Ibid., pp.32–4.

Racial decolonization was at the centre of Jessica Huntley's work and life. Decolonization in the context of her work had two dimensions. Firstly, decolonization can be viewed as the act of formerly colonized nations achieving independence from colonial powers.[9] Secondly, decolonization is also concerned with the post-colonial period in which independent nations become sovereign countries and establish independent identities in the world.[10] Because of the centuries of colonialism imprinted on the newly independent nations, dependence on the former colonial powers was not easy to depart from. Some independent nations sought a continuation of connections with former colonial powers. This led to continuing relationships with colonial powers in which the former colonizers retained varying degrees of strategic, economic and political control of the new independent nations.[11] Many believed that some of these countries continued to serve the interests of the former colonial powers, over the interests of its populations, some new post-colonial nations employed strategies widely viewed as corrupt and authoritarian to subdue and quell its people, particularly dissidents.[12] These nations became client-states, not truly pursuing aims of independence but serving as client-states of their former colonial powers.[13]

Decolonialization is therefore well-conceived as the 'process by which imperial and colonial power is overturned'.[14] But perhaps the largest shift is the transformational changes affecting new societies and citizens with new statuses. One of the largest changes shepherded in by independence was the shift of status of former subjugated enslaved or colonial subjects. They were no longer at the bottom of formalized and legalized racial hierarchies, but were now equal citizens, either in their home or in the countries which previously enslaved and colonized them.[15] Jessica Huntley was one of those who fought for decolonization before independence in her own country. In the post-colonial era, she contested the many legacies of racialized colonialization.

In addition to Pan-Africanism, Jessica Huntley was interested in the ideas of communism. Her commitment to Pan-Africanist ideas were embedded

---

[9] Mohammad-Mahmoud Ould Mohamedou, *A Brief History of Decolonisation*, online video recording, YouTube, 26 October 2021, https://www.youtube.com/watch?v=R9DBIKqmtq8 (last accessed 28 February 2023).

[10] Ibid.

[11] Ibid.

[12] Ibid.

[13] Ibid.

[14] Meera Sabaratnam, *Decolonialism, The Making of the Modern World*, online video recording, YouTube, 11 December 2020, https://www.youtube.com/watch?v=optdS1SDzwo (last accessed 28 February 2023).

[15] Ibid.

during her childhood and she became exposed to the ideas of communism in her twenties as she embarked on formal political work. Since the turn of the twentieth century, Communism has played an important role in the fight for Black liberation. Strategy was guided by the priorities of Soviet Union rather than of Black liberation.[16] Many, including historian George Padmore, argued that whilst it was inevitable that 'racially oppressed peoples inevitably receive the attention of the Communists', Black revolutionaries were viewed as expendable adjuncts to the central fight of the white working masses.[17] Padmore outlined how the 'Father of Bolshevism', Nikolai Lenin, sought to garner allegiance from global racial minorities, as well as exploited workers, in overthrowing ruling elites.[18] Joseph Stalin, from the same perspective as Lenin, wrote *Marxism and the National and Colonial Question*, a strategy document on the Communist approach towards colonized and racial minorities.[19] This strategy recognized that revolutionary overthrow of Western capitalism could 'only be broken by stirring the coloured colonial and semi-colonial peoples of Asia and Africa to achieve their national independence'.[20] In the view of George Padmore, 'Pan-Africanism offers an ideological alternative to Communism'.[21] He contended that Pan-Africanism cut through 'the narrow confines of class, race, tribe and religion' providing a level playing field for all, and a framework that 'rejects both white racialism and black chauvinism'.[22] This perspective amplifies the foundation of what was to become and remain a choice between two major philosophical perspectives, both in the academy and on the battlefields of the fight against anti-Blackness.

Jessica Huntley's political thought and activism can be predominantly defined as Pan-Africanism, throughout her life span. The period in British Guiana when she was committed to communist-inspired Jaganism, from the late 1940s through to the late 1950s can be regarded as her quest to bring an end to colonialism, an end to racialized capitalism that was viewed as oppressing Black people and workers. There was a brief foray into the politics of the Communist Party of Great Britain (CPGB) in the late 1950s, and the activities of the informal group of West Indian communist settlers in Britain, searching for their new politics. Summarizing her later reflections on this early association with communism, Jessica Huntley argued that:

---

[16]George Padmore (1903–59), *Pan-Africanism or Communism? The Coming Struggle for Africa* [with plates, including a portrait] (London: Dennis Dobson, 1956), p.289.
[17]Ibid.
[18]Ibid., p.291.
[19]Ibid., p.290.
[20]Ibid., p.301.
[21]Ibid., p.379.
[22]Ibid.

We weren't communists, we were just progressive people. Because when you think about what communism means, we weren't that. But we were progressive people, and I don't feel guilty about that. I feel good because it put me in a position of strength. It made me conscious, aware, to know who I am, what my goals are and how to achieve them, not only for myself and my children, but for the rest of my community And I am always happy to serve whenever I can.[23]

Cementing this thought, one of her closest friends, Anne Johnson, said:

Communism to Jessica was a bit like when I was growing up, Catholicism for me, it was about doing good, things being right, things being just, things being fair. Then of course the climate changed, and we heard about things going on in some of the communist countries, she would never give support to any despot or anyone trying to be despotic.[24]

She believed, like many Black progressives, particularly Marxists, that revolutionary overturn of capitalism would be an important factor in the liberation of Black people from oppression. But she did not view communism as the only route to this liberation.

The biography is based on four years of historical research. Research was undertaken in several archival repositories. The Huntley Collection, currently on loan to the London Metropolitan Archives in London, was the source of most the primary documents used in the research. The Huntley Collection was established by Jessica Huntley, Eric Huntley and associates over many years before it formally opened in 2005. It is a collection of personal and business documents collected over many decades which recorded life in British Guiana before 1958 and, subsequently, life in Britain. Many of the records accessed for this research are not generally available to the public and the rules of data protection was a factor that shaped what information could be presented in this biography. Special access permission was granted by Eric Huntley and the London Metropolitan Archives. The other main archive that was important to this research is the George Padmore Institute (GPI), also based in London. It is a collection of documents associated with the activism and publication of New Beacon Books and the many projects John La Rose was involved in. As a close friend and collaborator with John La Rose, many of Jessica Huntley and Bogle L'Ouverture's records are also held at the GPI. The National Archives in London, the National Archives of Guyana and the Cheddi Jagan Research Centres were also key to obtaining primary source documents.

---

[23]Carol Sidney, '60:60, Jessica Huntley, a Lifetime of Publishing', *Sable*, Spring (2005), pp.90–9, esp. p.95.

[24]Anne Johnson, interview with Claudia Tomlinson, 20 August 2020.

Oral history interviews were conducted with Huntley family members and many associates and friends of Jessica Huntley. Approximately fifty original interviews were conducted by the author and selected extracts were used in this biography. Some of the interview data in this biography is from interviews conducted by other researchers. The most important of these is the interview by George Fowokan Kelly who interviewed Jessica in 2010. Harry Goulbourne's interviews of Jessica Huntley and Eric Huntley together are also drawn on for this research. Jessica Huntley was interviewed on multiple occasions by researchers and the media, and this data was also used in this research. More information about the interview participants who contributed to this biography is summarized in the Appendix. The British Newspaper Archive was the source for many of the media articles on Jessica and Bogle L'Ouverture as its activities were featured regularly in the print media. Therefore, there was an abundance of historical sources and this research.

This biography is the first major history of the life and work of a beloved and charismatic figure, an intellectual who turned her very adverse upbringing on its head and built a life that brought care, justice, beauty and love into the lives of many of her generation and subsequent generations. She carried around the vision of her life's mission in her head and it impinged on every aspect of her life. It was a serious mission, so she often appeared to carry its weight on her shoulders, and in her intense, focused expression. This was tempered by her personality breaking through, for she loved people, life, laughter and fun. Her energy was boundless, and she worked day and night on her vision and struggle.

The purpose of writing this book is to foreground the life of an important African descended figure who was devoted to the struggle for global racialized decolonization. Further, it is a reparatory history, a corrective to the invisibilization of the history of Africa, Africans and its diaspora. Additionally, the life of an African-descended woman illuminates gender-based barriers within the struggle for Black liberation and tells a fuller story of the fight. The life of Jessica Huntley is both a history of a Black woman's struggle, and of Black people's struggle. This biography is intended to reflect, as Ngugi wa Thiong'o wrote in his poem to mark her death, that Jessica Huntley has taken her seat in the realm of inspirational Pan-African ancestors. Jessica Huntley's life and work is much more extensive than can be captured in a single biography. It is this author's hope that future researchers and writers will bring forth more of the stories of this remarkable life.

Claudia Tomlinson, London 2024.

1

Growing Up, Rising Up

Jessica Huntley was born on 23 February 1927 on the eastern side of the Demerara River which surges through the main artery of her homeland. Then a colonized nation, British Guiana sits on the north-eastern coast of South America. It is a natural beauty, rich in resources – a green, lush terrain, overflowing with rare and vibrantly pretty plants, lyrical birds and captivating wildlife. It is capped by a high, blue tropical sky which sits above the searing heat, softened by Atlantic breezes.

In Bagotstown, the village of her birth, she lived comfortably with her mother Hectorine Carroll, and her father James Carroll. Bagotstown had grown out of one of the former plantations, bought by freed Africans. Jessica Huntley's ancestors, once freed, had wheeled barrows full of money, earned from their underpaid and exploited hard labour, to buy the plantations and turn them into the villages from which Guiana grew as a free land. But by around the age of four, Jessica Huntley found herself growing up in Guiana's more desperate capital city centre of Georgetown.

Mr and Mrs Carroll were the parents of four sons, one of whom died in early childhood, and one daughter, Jessica, the youngest child. The couple were two very different individuals, with different outlooks and expectations of life. Hectorine lived by every word written in the Bible, and James by a desire to build a wealthy family. By the early 1930s, Hectorine found herself living alone in Georgetown with her children, with virtually no income. Georgetown is merely a few miles away from Bagotstown, but the urban centre was overpopulated and insanitary, with poorly constructed homes, many of which were merely wooden and corrugated iron shacks. As with many Caribbean children, the name by which she is known today, Jessica Huntley, was not her 'given name', She was born Elleise Carroll, but somewhere along the line, the name Jessica was felt to be the name she should be called. However, among her friends and neighbours, as a young child she was always called 'Sica'. In later life, she became Jess, Jessie and 'J'.

Jessica Huntley was reared in a nation founded on a bedrock of racialization, oppression and exploitation of its people. Britain was enriched through the colonial subjugation of its British Guiana subjects. Over centuries, Spanish, Portuguese and Dutch colonizers had developed their homelands on the wealth extracted from the backs, the bodies and the earth of this nation. When it took the land, Britain imbued rank, power, wealth and privilege through British Guiana's society, on the basis of not just racial group, but skin colour, shade and tone. The degree of personal liberty afforded to individuals was mediated by systems of racialization. A spectrum of 'Blackness' to 'whiteness' determined the extent of people's rights, social standing and access to the basic dignities of life such as money, housing, education and employment.

Economic pressures caused by the 1930s global recession, and hardships caused by the Second World War, were severely felt in British Guiana. The impact on an artificially created plantation society such as British Guiana with the fate of its economy appendaged to Britain's was debated in the British Parliament. The debate acknowledged that being tethered to Britain's economy, for the colonies, meant that Britain 'interfered with their natural advancement, while as to those colonies in the western hemisphere, which we had so much prided ourselves on possessing, they had actually been reduced by us to a state of ruin and beggary'.[1] Colonies once promising so much for Britain were now a burdensome responsibility. The prevention of the 'natural advancement' of the country describes the effects of structured economic exploitation at the heart of colonized nations. The plantation economy depended on exporting profits abroad for its survival.[2] There was less attention on the production of food and goods for its own people. Now a global recession was rippling through the anglophone West Indies, British Guiana was also severely impacted. Sugar prices fell and as this was British Guiana's main export, there were major effects on its economy.

Such was the degree of suffering in the British West Indies during the 1930s, there were widespread uprisings and labour rebellions right across the region.[3] Leading intellectuals and radicals in the region, such as Trinidad's Cipriani and Grenada's Marryshow, called for full independence in the region. To investigate the uprisings and the claims in its colonies, Britain established The Moyne Commission to report on the

---

[1] House of Commons, *Hansard's Parliamentary Debates: The Official Report* (24 July 1849 vol. 107, cc920-) [Online].

[2] Anne Patricia Cook, 'Social Policy and the Colonial Economy' (unpublished doctoral thesis, The University of Surrey, 1985), p.9.

[3] Sahadeo Basdeo, 'The "Radical" Movement Towards Decolonization in the British Caribbean During the Thirties', *Canadian Journal of Latin American and Caribbean Studies*, 22, no. 44 (1997), pp.127–46.

causes of the disturbances and make recommendations.[4] The Commission found extremely dire social and economic standards in the region. Standards which were low before the Depression now severely impacted employment and living conditions in the region. It reported that 'the standard of the housing of most of the poorer people is deplorably low. The maintenance of housing is generally completely neglected'.[5] Anglophone coloniality in the Depression-era meant destitution, hunger and poverty for large sections of the working population. The Commission made many recommendations for social welfare relief across the region, greater protections for trade union activism and limited political reform.[6] The Moyne report was widely criticized for its failure to provide full political reform, however, it is recognized as laying the groundwork for social, political and economic improvements in West Indian societies.

Hectorine Carroll, Jessica's mother, was born around 1897 and died in 1997. Hectorine's parents were probably the children of African enslaved people born in British Guiana or under Dutch enslavement before the region was ceded to the British in 1814. The history of African people in British Guiana means Hectorine's family could alternatively have been brought to Guiana from the enslaved populations held across the West Indies. She was a tall, dark-complexioned Black woman, with a keen talent as a herbalist. She was part of the Esbrand family lineage, and had two brothers, James Maxton Esbrand and Thomas Esbrand. James Esbrand had a son, James Maxton Esbrand, Jr – Jessica's cousin, to whom she was close and who maintained correspondence and contact with her throughout her life. There is no information about Hectorine's upbringing, but she was clearly educated, literate and cultured. Her correspondence with her daughter and son-in-law, from the time of their departure from British Guiana, suggests an education modelled on the British education system. Ironically, the language and tone of her letters to her family are suggestive of a formal upper middle-class English gentility and dignity that belied the reality of a life spent mostly in poverty.

Hectorine told her youngest child that her father, James Carroll, had died when Jessica was three years old. James Carroll appears to have worked predominantly as a 'pork-knocker', the colloquial term given to mineral prospectors of gold, diamond and precious stones located in the interior region of the country. From the late nineteenth century, African-descended people started working in the inhospitable rainforest terrain of British

---

[4]Ibid., 137.

[5]Dennis Benn, 'Introduction', *Report of the West India Royal Commission: The Moyne Report* (Kingston: Ian Randle, 2011), p.436.

[6]Ibid., pp.422–55.

Guiana.⁷ The work was arduous and very dangerous. They did so in greater proportions than those of other ethnic backgrounds, and in particular they braved the deepest interior regions, trekking for hundreds of miles.⁸ Deaths of prospectors, due to disease and accidents, were common and this would rob families of crucial income.

James may have died in the interior. Jessica was not clear about what had happened to her father. She said of Hectorine: 'her husband left … I don't know if he died or what, I don't know my father, and what she said is that he died when I was three years old. There was nobody else around'.⁹ He was a reasonably successful prospector, and this meant that, at the time of Jessica's birth, the family had a home that met their needs. After he died, or left, there was a devastating downturn in the family's living situation. In later life, Jessica expressed her belief, due to evidence she had come across during her teenage years, that her parents had actually separated and were in the process of becoming divorced, and it was not the case that he died when she was very young.¹⁰ Whatever the actual circumstances, she grew up without a father in her life from the age of three or four.

Living in a Tenement Yard, Not From the Yard

The displaced family moved into a rented home at 35 Howes Street, Charlestown, bordering on La Penitence, Albouystown. It was about fifteen-minute walk from the loud and lively Stabroek market in the city centre, and a ten-minute walk from Camp Street prison. By her own account, Jessica Huntley's 1930s upbringing in the La Penitence tenement yard in British Guiana was extremely rough.¹¹ As a child, she would be woken from time to time by the scream of a woman shouting, 'murder! murder!' – the alarming sound piercing the warm Caribbean night air. It was a neighbour being so severely beaten by her man that she feared for her life. Violence and crime were everyday sights and sounds of the community that she lived in as a child.

---

⁷Barbara P. Josiah, *Migration, Mining, and the African Diaspora: Guyana in the Nineteenth and Twentieth Centuries* (New York: Palgrave Macmillan, 2011), p.9.

⁸Ibid.

⁹Jessica Huntley, interview with George Fowokan Kelly.

¹⁰GPI, CAM/6/32, The Caribbean Artists Movement, Papers of Anne Walmsley, 'Interview with Jessica Huntley of Bogle L'Ouverture Publications and the Walter Rodney Bookshop', 22 November 1985.

¹¹Jessica Huntley, interview with George Fowokan Kelly, 30 November 2010.

The tenement yards were large, unfenced dwellings. Visitors to Jessica's home would first encounter, and have to navigate, a large open gutter at the front of the home. There was no bridge across the gutter, instead shaky and rotting wooden planks were placed across it that inhabitants and visitors perilously walked upon to get into the tenements. When it rained, the gutter would flood and spill its contents, causing an insanitary and unhealthy environment for the tenement yard residents.

A room was occupied by a single family, and in Jessica Huntley's case, she lived and slept in one room with her three brothers and mother. The children slept on the only bed, and her mother slept on an old travelling trunk, its hardness softened with old rags and cloths. Along with the other families living in the yard, Hectorine and her children had a cooking area in a separate kitchen building. Aside from the family rooms everything was communal.

The open space at the front of the dwelling, the yard, was the sometimes cantankerous heart of the community. All life and activity that took place in the yard was for public observation, privacy was at a minimum. In the 1930s and 1940s, when Jessica was growing up in the tenement yard, many of the residents in the yard were migrants from the Eastern Caribbean, the Leeward islands of Antigua, St Kitts, Nevis, who had moved to Guiana following the 1928 Okeechobee Hurricane which resulted in heavy destruction of crops, and the loss of more than 1500 lives in the region. They lived alongside the native Guianese in the yard, and obtained work on the waterfront, for example in the sawmill and timber industries and as stevedores. The Guianese inhabitants living in the yard also did these jobs, but also worked as domestics and in labouring jobs.

At the centre of the yard was a standpipe. This single standpipe was the only source of water for all the families for all purposes; bathing, cooking and cleaning. There was no piped water going into individual homes. Water had to be collected there and taken into the rooms, kitchen, washrooms and anywhere it was needed. All the children had to be bathed at the standpipe before going to school each morning, and this happened in public view. Sometimes a mother would receive a word in her ear if she hadn't noticed that it was time for her growing child to start using the private enclosed washroom. This was also in the yard and was used by adults and older children.

The standpipe was also a meeting place as people, generally the women, gathered around it and waited to collect their water to cook or to bathe a small child, and where they would converse, laugh, share their woes and gain support from each other. The standpipe was the place where they would sometimes argue and fight over any simmering disputes. Eusi Kwayana, the former People's Progressive Party founder, government minister, founder of the Working People's Alliance (WPA), poet, author, researcher and historian, observed that the tenement yards 'gave rise to a lot of communal living, sometimes communal quarrelling and disputation – you know what human beings are, it could go either way. But at the same time, in my opinion, it helped to build up a solidarity among the poor, with regard to social issues like the economy, wages, housing'.[12]

Those who lived outside the tenement yards generally avoided close association with those who lived in the yards. Waveney Bushell, formerly a schoolteacher in British Guiana, observed that this separation between the communities was not always as strictly observed as sometimes thought:

> In the West Indies, we copied that from the people who had colonised us. People who lived in houses, and cottages and so on, never particularly wanted their children to be friendly with children who had come from the tenement. But lots of friendships were forged between those two groups of children. But it was very obvious, particularly boys smiling with girls who had come from the tenements.[13]

Residents of tenement yards suffered many deprivations and exploitations, and as such, the dwellings became a focus for activity by social justice reformers and activists. They recognized, as Eusi Kwayana observed, that:

> Several social issues arose, and sometimes social organizations and the activity of trade unions would be heavily concentrated on those, like Nathaniel Critchlow, and his great concern with rent. A tenement would be run by a landlord, and the rent had to be paid, at the time before the rent restrictions laws came in, which trade unions had to fight battles, you could be evicted, put on the road.[14]

The tenement yard was a place of social value to the residents, which could overcome the day-to-day deprivations and tensions to bring forth community cohesion and communal joy.

These slums have now largely been cleared away but their meaning for Black people has been immortalized in the well-known poem of resistance by Martin Carter (1927–97), Guyanese poet and political resistance fighter of the 1950s and 1960s, 'I Come From the Nigger Yard of Yesterday'.[15] Carter's poem amplifies the picture of the inextricable connection between the colonial oppression that Carter saw as overshadowing the existence of Black people in the tenement yard, the 'Nigger Yard'. There is a defiance

---

[12]Eusi Kwayana, interview with Claudia Tomlinson, 19 June, and 16 August 2020.

[13]Waveney Bushell, interview with Claudia Tomlinson, August 2020.

[14]Kwayana, interview with Claudia Tomlinson.

[15]Martin Wylde Carter, 'I Come From the Nigger Yard', *New World Journal*. Available at: https://newworldjournal.org/volumes/volume-1-1963/i-come-from-the-nigger-yard/.

expressed that despite the pain, injury and self-hatred, there is conviction that the future will bring empowering release from this existence in the yard.

Some referred to tenement yards as 'Nigger Yards', a term that evolved from its original use in describing the slave-quarters on the plantations before the emancipation of enslaved Africans in the colony. These dwellings, for the most impoverished, then came to be known as 'Nigger Yards'. They were viewed as a very undesirable and stigmatized dwelling places. Walter Rodney, the Guyanese historian, and political figure who is an important part of this history, wrote about how these dwellings were viewed: 'if you come from the niggeryard, you are very backward. You come from the lowest stratum, and not just the lowest in a sort of economic sense. Crude, violent, thievish behavior would be associated with a niggeryard. The niggeryard was the lowest form of culture, but it was the only culture that existed under slavery'.[16] Therefore, the term was a remnant from more than a hundred years prior, but with a new corrupted meaning to describe the worst dwelling conditions for the poorest in the city slums.

Working people in British Guiana have been recognized as being at the cornerstone of not only building the country, but also in at the forefront of decolonization activities. There were two locations that became the central flashpoints for worker and employer conflict: the waterfront in Georgetown, and among the agricultural workers on the sugar plantations. The struggle for the legalization of the right of workers to organize and to legally take industrial action had a long and violent journey in British Guiana. The success of colonialism and capitalism in the country rested on Britain's capacity to suppress the rise workers' rights.

The country's first trade union, the British Guiana Labour Union (BGLU), was founded in 1919 by Hubert Nathaniel Critchlow (1884–1958). It was the first Caribbean trade union to be legally registered in the country. Critchlow pioneered the movement for cooperation and participation between the unions and workers, and employers in the British West Indies during this period. Critchlow was a dockworker on the waterfront in 1905, part of the crew of men and boys responsible for loading cargo onto ships for export abroad, and for unloading cargo for Guiana. They were employed on very low wages, with a pay system structured to avoid paying them a full day's work and no additional pay for night work.

In the same year, Critchlow called a strike of dock workers to prevent the ships leaving Georgetown harbour laden with goods to enrich Britain and other parts of the world.[17] Strikers against low pay and long hours

---

[16] Walter Rodney, 'Plantation Society in Guyana', *Review*, 4 (1981), p.652.

[17] Hubert Critchlow, 'History of the Trade Union Movement in British Guiana', in *The Voice of Coloured Labour*, ed. by George Padmore (1945), https://www.marxists.org/archive/padmore/1945/labour-congress/ch12.htm.

were treated with unceremonious brutality by the colonial authorities. The strikers were joined by workers on the sugar estates who were also met with brutality. Critchlow, in one of his speeches to a conference in London in 1945, told of how the authorities 'were shooting the people coming down from the estate. At the news of the shooting, the women started a riot. The magistrate ordered the women's hair to be cut off. They "catted" the men and sent them to prison'.[18] The act of 'catting' involved beating individuals with the cat-o'-nine-tails, a whip for lashing criminal suspects, deviants, prisoners and other dissidents. The formation of the BGLU did not bring an immediate end to violent action taken by the state police against worker's protests. The activities of Critchlow, his associates and those workers who took action, which sometimes cost them their lives and their liberty, paved the way for the legalization and normalization of industrial rights.

Hectorine, Mother to the Community

Once Hectorine became a lone parent and lived in Georgetown, the new situation was one of which Jessica said: 'my mother fathered me ... there was no other male other than my brothers'.[19] Hectorine's parenting was mostly guided by her devout Christian beliefs which she used to steer every aspect of her life. Jessica described her mother's occupation: 'she went to work as a domestic and of course it was the Portuguese people who could afford to hire, and this woman, she said, used to leave her bracelets and earrings all around the house as a way of testing to see if she were honest'.[20] According to her daughter, Hectorine eventually became enraged by these constant tests of her integrity, and one day she verbally upbraided this employer, and walked out of the job, even though she had no other regular income to buy food for her children. A young, hungry Jessica learnt from her mother's explanation why she had left her job, that there were principles in life to be considered more important than personal comforts, including food. It is unlikely that Hectorine earned much as the family appeared to have not much more than a subsistence level of existence most of the time. In fact, Jessica commented that the family's survival was precarious, including the irregular provision of food in the home. Jessica said that: 'we lived by the Grace of God' which would be the main factor whether the children ate or not. Nonetheless, Hectorine was very generous

---

[18]Ibid.

[19]Jessica Huntley, interview with George Fowokan Kelly.

[20]Ibid.

in bestowing on her family, and those she cared about, and Jessica has spoken about her in very fond terms, being unequivocal that 'my mother was kind, she was loving, she was giving, she gave whatever little she had, and I brought up to that'.[21]

Hectorine was an outspoken woman who shared her opinion loudly and freely in the yard, whether it was wanted or not. She had a strong Christian evangelical belief, and she considered it her duty to intervene and do good where it was needed. Her interventions in the tenement yard were charitable, and she regularly donated much of what little provisions she had, almost as soon as she received them. She was also the moral voice of the tenement yard, she was called 'Aunt', and addressed as such by everyone, including her children and grandchildren. Aunt was a title of respect rather than a signifier of familial relationship. She saw it was her godly duty to correct all immorality and wrongdoing in the yard, and protect her children, especially her daughter from falling into any traps. Domestic violence, within couple relationships, was common in the yard, and Hectorine had a two-pronged approach in dealing with it. Hectorine cared deeply about the fate of these women and would counsel them to get out of their abusive relationships, pointing out the risk they faced of severe injury or death.

Hectorine's prime concern as a parent was to protect Jessica from negative influences in the neighbourhood, and this extended to limiting her social contact with other children in order that her daughter didn't become like them. Jessica often spoke about, not just the deprivation of this period, but also of the joy and happiness in her childhood, recognizing 'I don't think I had a lot of things, but whatever I had I was happy with it. I went to school, I grew up when I came down to Georgetown, I grew up in a tenement yard and my mother would say, all the time, that I am growing up in a tenement yard but that I'm not part of the tenement yard.'[22] This approach was successful, according to Jessica's recollection:

> In terms of the neighbourhood, I grew up in, the girls in the neighbourhood ... I must have stood out, I didn't behave like them, I wasn't swearing ... cussing, I wasn't doing those things. And their parents would say 'why can't you be like Sica!', that was how they called me, Sica. And so, there was a resentment, which was quite natural. And those girls were wise, they very wise. I didn't dare. And because Aunt told me I'm living here but not from there, later on I understood what she meant.[23]

---

[21]Ibid.
[22]Ibid.
[23]Ibid.

Jessica would also come to understand that her mother was protecting her from the fates that befell some of the girls from the yard:

> The American soldiers were there, prostitution was high, very high. My mother forbid me to stand up in the street and talk to anybody, I just could not speak to anybody on the street, no way, to any boy, or any girl for that matter, bring them home so she knows exactly who they are.[24]

This posed some problems for the highly outgoing and sociable Jessica who was hungry for social contact with other children but found herself having to avoid friendships with those on her doorstep. She interpreted her mother's dictum as inferring permission to socialize with others outside of the yard but this too posed a problem: 'I was not allowed to play with children in the neighbourhood, but I looked outside of the neighbourhood to see children who probably had a better life. They lived in a cottage, I lived in a room, the brothers had bicycles and the father had a car.'[25] The children she identified as likely to meet her mother's standards as playmates would possibly not want to associate with her. The result was a degree of isolation, the opportunity to form friendships with children outside the yard was curtailed because of the differences between their social standing/wealth, and Jessica's. She anticipated rejection due to how they would perceive her social status in the same way that she had been taught to reject those in the yard.

A big part of Jessica's life was about the community spirit, working and caring for others, to make their lives and daily experiences better. As a child, she played a role in overcoming and defeating the daily threat to existence, dirt and disease. Probably encouraged by Hectorine, as a child in the yard, she had a particular daily routine:

> I would wake up, I would sweep the whole yard. There was a standpipe that had a brush, I'd scrub that brush, scrub the standpipe with it, and then I would go to … they had a toilet, they had two toilets, one that was locked up with a key, and one was left open. And I would clean that, and I would clean the shower room. Well not shower, we had a bucket and we put water from the tap you know, and I would clean that.[26]

She learned about making a personal contribution for the greater good, giving to others, no matter how unpleasant the task, and she learned about

---

[24]Ibid.

[25]Jessica Huntley, interview with George Fowokan Kelly.

[26]Ibid.

rising above the grime of the city, bringing a new daily optimism, with a relentless commitment to defeating the threat with daily vigour and energy.

As Jessica's brothers grew up, Robert and Munroe, the eldest, shared the burden of helping the family's finances. Robert, probably more than eight years older than Jessica, was the eldest and he worked in the 'bush' as the interior region was called locally, as a logger. He married and sent money back to his wife to forward onto his mother, but the money didn't reach Hectorine and her family reliably. Robert was the most disciplinarian of the brothers, and young Jessica was particularly fearful if Robert saw her misbehaving, or out on the street conversing with anyone, as she loved to, but was forbidden to do by her mother, she would then have to hurry home as fast as possible.

The financial responsibility then fell to Munroe, the second eldest to provide for the family, and pay Jessica's school fees. Munroe, about four or five years older than Jessica, became an electrician and worked for a bauxite company, and he seems to have been the brother that Jessica was closest to. He was also a competitive body builder, and would flex his muscles to amuse his sister, prompting her to test their hardness by getting her to punch them. He was sociable, outgoing and fun-loving with a wide group of friends in the bodybuilding world. Hadden was the youngest brother, closest to her in age by a year or two, and he worked at Texaco Oil. Jessica was very close to and loved all her brothers, and as the youngest and only girl, they played a loving, protective and disciplinarian role towards their sister, the family baby. Born into this African family, headed by Aunt, survival meant resistance to the many onslaughts to the dignity of family and community life.

2

Raised to Resist

Jessica frequently spoke about how her mother raised her to believe that all of humanity was equal, and no part of humanity was superior. She said: 'my mother said God made all of us equal, and that is what I grew up to understand'.[1] This was the childhood lesson she used as the guiding principle throughout her life and work. She specifically saw her mother rebut ideas of Black racial inferiority in their daily lives and did the same throughout her own life.

During this period, the strong dislike of African features, a dark skin and an African nose, was widespread in the country. In the 1930s and 1940s, Eric Huntley described the situation where 'a lot of people growing up at that time used "Palmer's Skin Success" to whiten themselves, and they even used a clothes peg to straighten their nose'.[2] He added that 'Jessica's mother was very strong' in resisting these ideas in her home.[3] Palmer's produced a range of cosmetics for Black women, encouraging them to lighten their skin and this was popular in British Guiana at the time. Jessica Huntley often spoke with approval and contentment of the strength shown by Hectorine in ensuring that her daughter's self-concept and confidence as a Black girl and woman was very strong.

Jessica described Hectorine's strength on this issue when 'one day a man came in and said if my nose were straight, I would have been very good looking'.[4] Hectorine said to her daughter: 'your nose suits her face and nobody is better than you are!' Jessica believes this was at the root of the strength and determination she showed all her life: 'I grew up with

---

[1] Jessica Huntley, interviews with George Fowokan Kelly.
[2] Ibid.
[3] Eric Huntley, interview with Claudia Tomlinson, 2019–23.
[4] Jessica Huntley, interview with George Fowokan Kelly.

that kind of confidence.'[5] Jessica expressed lifelong gratitude for her mother, the woman who 'gave me confidence in myself that I was black and that the Chinese man or the Indian man, they were not better than I was. So, I grew up with very strong feelings of me, as Jessica'.[6] She learnt to reject any notion that others were better than her by virtue of their race. Hectorine showed her how it was done. Bluntly and forcefully. For Hectorine, part of the job of being a loving, caring Black parent was to protect your child from attacks on their racial identity.

Jessica said that she 'grew up a very happy child' in British Guiana, and experienced great joy in a very basic, frugal lifestyle. She loved school concerts and regularly enjoyed taking part in school plays. Her mother taught her how to enjoy the simple things in life and share them with others. They were poor but found many ways of giving to others. For example, when it was a friend's birthday, if they had no money to buy gifts, Jessica recalled how her mother would help her learn a verse to recite to the friend 'and we'd pick up a lily or something like that and we'd put a piece of cloth around it, and that's what I would present to my friend on her birthday'.[7] Jessica observed that her mother 'gave what she had and that was it'.[8]

Hectorine also brought Jessica into her church, the Brethren Church, at an early age. The Brethren Church was set up in British Guiana by a British missionary in the eighteenth century and focused on converting enslaved Africans to Christianity. In doing so, they often incurred the rancour of plantation owners, and they were frequently driven from the plantations. As a teenager, Jessica became a Sunday School teacher with a strong and proud knowledge of the Bible that was to last a lifetime.

Maintaining a high position in the community, and some sense of separation from the others living in the tenement yard was a priority for Hectorine. Female strength and self-reliance were of key importance. Solving the problems through the provision of items to those without was central to Hectorine in being a strong, respected woman in the neighbourhood. It was important for Hectorine, for reasons of faith and religious belief, to be in the position of benefactress. In the Charlestown yard, Hectorine was the 'go-to' person for people with problems and difficulties. Her daughter Jessica always perceived her as such, saying of Hectorine:

> She was so strong, and very independent thinking. In this very neighbourhood all of them went to her, if there is a crisis, whatever they want, they want onion, some sugar, some salt, they would go to 'Aunt!'

---

[5] Ibid.
[6] Ibid.
[7] Ibid.
[8] Ibid.

give her this Aunt! 'Give her this' and she would always be there to give them whatever they want, and I saw that.⁹

Basic supplies were limited, but Hectorine's second son Munroe had access, through his work with American pilots during the war, to the rare supplies that people in the yard wanted. When he went home to the yard, he would take large quantities of scarce supplies such as sugar, rice, flour, and oil to his mother. This precious stock was soon depleted as Hectorine was determined to share it with those in need in the yard, enlisting Jessica to participate in the process: 'my mother would get bottles and put some paper for everybody in the yard, and I would had to take them to them'. When Munroe returned wanting access to some of the supplies for a friend he was incensed to find it all depleted: 'One day my brother Munroe wanted some for a friend, and he was so angry with my mother: "Mum, you can't give out everything like that! You can give yes, but don't give out all!"' But for Hectorine, the act of giving was much more important and spiritually satisfying than possessing anything herself, and her daughter grew up with the same beliefs.

Jessica received formal general school education up to the age of sixteen. She attended Trinity, a Methodist primary school, and Washington High School until the age of sixteen. Primary education was free, but secondary or High School education was fee-paying for all children. Jessica left school before sitting the secondary school exams, the Junior Cambridge, which was equivalent to O levels at the time. Her brothers paid the school fees, but this came to an end due to a family disagreement. After leaving school, she attended commercial training at the high school where she studied shorthand, typewriting and bookkeeping.

Relief from life in the tenement yard came during the school holidays when Jessica would be sent to spend time in the village of Mocha, with her mother's best friend. This was an important aspect of growing up, an experience of which Jessica said, 'there's where I learnt our culture. Folk songs and so on, and I would come back down after the holidays, and I would tell her and did a dance to show her'. On her return she would show Hectorine the Kwe Kwe dances she had learnt. Kwe Kwe is an African ceremony with traditional dance and music, normally associated with marriage.

Hectorine was a member of Friendly and Burial Societies in British Guiana, and inducted her daughter into participating in these movements. These organizations were established to ensure the poor could afford to bury their dead with a fitting cultural dignity, through the collection of membership fees. The groups also funded and supported cultural activities Hectorine took Jessica with her to the annual meetings and the conventions

---

⁹Ibid.

where she made an active contribution. Jessica would read poetry, read psalms from bible, sing and perform at these meetings, providing her with a strong cultural base during her childhood.

A Sister for Life

When aged about eleven years old, Jessica met Cecily Haynes-Hart, who would become her lifelong best friend. They would regard each other as sisters. Cecily came from a large family of strong matriarchal women that also became part of Jessica's world during childhood.

Cecily was an African descended child, one of five children, and although she had sisters, her playmates were her brothers because of her age, and she felt the need of a female friend. Cecily was a brilliant, prodigious child, who attended a selective school on a scholarship, and was a model pupil at the top of her class in school, surpassing her peers in all subjects. She was an all-rounder, gifted in all areas she turned her attention to, including extracurricular activities such as dressmaking and playing musical instruments. Cecily became a teacher at her own school from the age of sixteen, and rose to become a head teacher in Guyana. She was passionately dedicated to education and regularly held classes for any children who wished to attend, outside school hours.

Together, Jessica and Cecily navigated parental rules that both their mothers set for them, and spent a lot of time together. The children had childhood together full of, as recalled by Jessica: 'moonlit nights … evenings on the sea-wall, playing hopscotch, telling stories and singing songs'.[10] They got involved in exploits such as attending a Cumfa ritual at the East Bank, which Jessica believed was a ceremony to 'celebrate one of the Gods in African cosmology'.[11] Whilst they appeared to escape discovery and sanction for that exploit, they were caught when, with male friends, and without permission, they made a fowl (chicken) curry using one of Cecily's mother's birds.[12] Cecily qualified as a teacher in Guyana, and eventually travelled to England to build her career and family life. The two women shared the lifelong milestones of marriage, parenthood and grandparenthood. Cecily became involved in the Black Supplementary Schools movement in Britain.

Jessica was brought up surrounded by African descended women who were advocates and agitators for the rights and dignity of women, Black

---

[10]LMA, HC, LMA/4463/F/03/005, 'Jessica Huntley Speech on the Occasion of Cecily Haynes Hart 70th Birthday Celebration', 15 September 1996, p.1.
[11]Ibid.
[12]Ibid.

people and poor people. These included her mother, Cecily Haynes-Hart and her family, and her godmother in the country village.

In addition to these women, Jessica was exposed to the pioneering work of Gertie Wood, and benefited directly from Wood's activism. Gertie Wood (1892–1976) was a social worker who particularly dedicated her life to programmes intended to improve the lives of poor women and children in Georgetown.[13] Outside this, she had a number of talents including as a concert artist, music teacher and politician. In 1933 Wood stood for election to a seat on the Georgetown Council, the first woman and Black person to seek political office in Guiana. Although she did not win the seat, she was commended for breaking barriers for both her race and her gender in her bid for office. She was a prominent figure in the 1930s and celebrated for her work with young people through the establishments of universal youth clubs and activities for all children. She was an advocate for women's empowerment and liberation, and challenged them with her question 'Why should women be always willing to sit down mute and let me talk for and against them?'. Wood became president of the Circle of Sunshine Workers in 1931.[14] She ran the breakfast club for poor children in Georgetown as part of the activities of the Circle of Sunshine Workers. The motto of the club was 'Feed my Lambs, Feed my Sheep', indicating the central importance of this aspect of the work of the organization.[15]

As Jessica was aged four or five when she moved into the tenement room in Georgetown, in the early 1930s, she may have been a recipient of Wood's charitable feeding programme at this time, she was certainly a beneficiary of Wood's social work by the 1940s, however. The Circle of Sunshine Workers operated youth clubs for children in Georgetown, leisure, sporting and games for children and young people. Along with Cecily, Jessica joined Wood's youth clubs and was a member of the Circle for several years from the early 1940s, in her mid-teens, through to her early twenties.

Jessica participated in Wood's youth clubs, which offered games, public speaking lessons, and brightened a childhood lacking in financial resources. She later reminisced about the Sunshine Workers Club as a 'youth club where we did all sorts of activities, mainly games and sports, singing and dancing, and you made friends there'.[16] Jessica and Cecily learned shorthand and typing, and attended the Sunshine Youth Club run by Gertie Wood, which Cecily said 'offered many opportunities to us', and they attended a

---

[13]Nigel Westmaas, 'Gertie Wood: Pioneer Women's Rights Activist', *Stabroek News*, 2018 https://www.stabroeknews.com/2018/01/14/news/guyana/gertie-wood-pioneer-womens-rights-activist/

[14]Ibid.

[15]Ibid.

[16]Jessica Huntley, interview with George Fowokan Kelly.

celebration in honour of Wood held at the AME Zion church in Georgetown. The Circle of Sunshine Workers was a charity and trade union established by Gertie Wood. According to Cecily, the ethos of the club was focused on 'telling you how to live life successfully and gracefully'.[17]

As part of her vision for improving the chances of women, Gertie Wood particularly railed against what she considered to be the exploitative practices of employers towards those employed as seamstresses and in garment factories. She said that 'Woman, and woman, only bears the lash of this damnable scourge ... in homes and in the shirt factories'.[18] Employment options for Black girls that Wood catered for were very limited and many found themselves working in the textile manufacturing sector or in domestic service to the wealthy families of Georgetown. However, she did offer girls and young women training in sewing and use of a sewing machine but stood against their exploitation. It was a short time after Jessica Huntley's participation in Wood's clubs that she too would find herself trapped in the very form of exploitation that Wood fought against.

---

[17]Cecily Haynes-Hart, interview with Margaret Andrews, August 2011.
[18]Westmaas, 'Gertie Wood', 2018.

3

The Emerging Activist

Jessica was twelve when the Second World War started and she grew out her childhood years during this time. This was a period of great hardship for colonial subjects due to continuing economic pressures compounded by Britain's neglect. Trade unionists and progressive activists in Guiana were advocating for racial equality and independence following the involvement of thousands of colonial subjects fighting alongside the Allied nations.[1] Hubert Critchlow, then President of the British Guiana Labour Council, went to London and addressed The World Trade Union Conference (TWTUC). He called on the international trade union movement to enshrine racial equality for all soldiers:

> The workers of my country feel that all soldiers and camp followers under the banners of the Allied nations should be given equal treatment in all respects. We feel very strongly about this, for too often even among comrades-in-arms, coloured men and women called upon to make the supreme sacrifice are discriminated against in the matter of pay, opportunities for promotion and other respects.[2]

Critchlow was also concerned that racial discrimination would seep into plans for post-war rebuilding and investment and he agitated against it:

> On the question of Post-War Reconstruction, it is our feeling and our just claim that the Colonial and subject peoples should be included within the terms of the Atlantic Charter, which should apply to them as much as to

---

[1] Michael S. Healey, 'Colour, Climate and Combat: The Caribbean Regiment in the Second World War', *The International History Review* (2000), pp.65–85, esp. pp.65–6.

[2] Hubert Critchlow, 'Greetings from British Guiana', *The Voice of Coloured Labour* (1945), ed. by George Padmore, https://www.marxists.org/archive/padmore/1945/labour-congress/ch07.htm.

the white-skinned nations of the world. We strongly resent any attempt to discriminate against us. For if we are good enough to fight for the freedom of others, we are good enough to enjoy it ourselves.[3]

This background of uprising against the exploitation of coloniality in the country was present when Jessica Huntley started her working life.

First Job, First Struggle

Jessica was very aware of Hectorine's constant financial struggles and was very pleased with herself when she got her first job at a garment factory close to her home. She had applied for clerical office work and passed the employer's tests in typing, shorthand, English and general knowledge so she was disappointed when she was offered a job on the factory floor. She was put to work making boxes as she disliked sewing and was told she would work in the factory until a vacancy opened in the office.

The racialized context of Guiana was present in every aspect of society. It did not escape the observation of a teenage Jessica that those with European heritage owned the factory and deployed white and creole staff in the office while 'we the blacks, did the hard work' on the factory floor. A standard factory, it operated on systems of conveyor belts where, Jessica recalled, 'you had one set of girls, young girls like myself, sewing different parts of the shirt, and the other section were those of us who made the boxes'.[4] She felt that exploitation was built into the working practices of the factory:

> What I saw they seemed to be so exploitative what they were doing with those girls. Say every Thursday is the cut off time, you know, some girls made the sleeves, some made the shoulders and so on, and they would wait until those girls have done most of the shirts and stop the belt and they didn't get their bonus.[5]

The garment factory was situated on Lombard Street, close to the waterfront in Georgetown. In the vicinity were a number of sawmill and logging companies which used the waterways to transport the lumber. The waterfront, as the major site of the colonial trading exports of Guianese labour, was a battleground of labour rights for workers, among the dockworkers, for example. The logging and timber industry was an important part of

---

[3]Ibid.
[4]Jessica Huntley, interview with George Fowokan Kelly.
[5]Ibid.

the employment sector for Black men and due to tensions with employers over pay and conditions the workers were unionized. There was a sawmill company close to garment factory, and one of Jessica's brothers, Munroe, worked there at the time she worked at the factory. Workers at the sawmill were very knowledgeable about employment rights and were experienced in fighting for this in their workplace. But they also looked out for the rights of other workers, kept them informed and educated about their own rights, and encouraged them to seek their own rights in the workplace. Such was the relationship between workers at the factory and the nearby sawmill who knew and associated with each other. It is likely that the sawmill workers knew something of the exploitation at the factory; certainly, Jessica would have discussed it at home with her brother, Munroe. She decided this had to be confronted and took action at the factory in relation to the exploitation she observed in the factory:

> I sat there looking at this, and I said to the girls one day 'why don't you all strike?' 'I don't know about strike' they said, 'Strike, yes, let's see the bosses them, and tell them you want more money, and tell them how they have been treating us you know' ... and we all agreed we would go down, we had to go down to Water Street where all the big directors, and so on, big shots, had their offices.[6]

She was chosen to lead the strikers in a delegation to confront the managers at the company headquarters in Water Street, nearby. In a non-unionized setting, the strike was high risk, and some of the workers were reluctant to take such action. Jessica started the walk to Water Street with a few of the factory workers, but by the time she was at the headquarters and making the demand, she found herself doing so alone as her colleagues had decided to drop out of the delegation and go back to the factory for fear of losing their jobs. She proceeded to press the case of the workers' exploitation on her own, at the company headquarters. This action had limited impact, and after Jessica was identified as one of the strike organizers, she found herself 'ostracised by the office staff' who also acted as the managers. She also faced some backlash from some of the factory workers who had been threatened with losing their jobs as a consequence of the strike.

News of Jessica's action attracted the attention of the union workers at a local Woodworkers Union, at the nearby sawmill works who had heard about the strike attempt. She was approached by the General Secretary of the Woodworkers Union to attend a meeting in their workplace and talk about her experience. She recalls that:

---

[6]Ibid.

I must have been eighteen or something like that, and of course it was pure men, and my second brother Munroe came with me to this meeting, and I was called up to speak, 'Jessica Carroll we now have Jessica Carroll representing ... '. I went up and I just told them exactly how I saw these girls were being exploited, so on and so forth. People were aghast. The men were so pleased.[7]

The union at the sawmill determined to work with the women at the factory to ensure it became unionized.[8]

Jessica, however, was eventually sacked for her role in the strike. It had cost her the first job and desperately needed income, but the experience paid her handsomely as an early lesson in activism, organizing and resistance against oppression, and that experience is what she took with her into her future. Still a teenager, she had her first experience of leading resistance against workplace exploitation.

Following this episode, Jessica grew into a teenager who showed increasing interest in developing a political education. She started to regularly attend public talks by influential activists and intellectuals held at different locations, including the public library. Some of these speakers probably included some of the eminent British Guiana literary and political figures as Cecily recalled that 'Martin Carter and Wilson Harris gave lectures and Jessica used to go to them after her involvement in politics.'[9] Cecily stated about Jessica, 'She would say, I want to go and hear them make speeches. She would go and hear them make speeches.'[10] Cecily was convinced that it was through attendance at the library speeches that 'that gave her the inspiration and the courage to get on a platform and make her speech'.[11] Still in her teens, aged about seventeen or eighteen, this was the start of Jessica's fiery and charismatic political public speaking whilst in British Guiana. It was in the public libraries of Georgetown that she overcame her dislike of public speaking by focusing on her growing intention to be influential and help change the lives of others.

Eric Huntley, the Boy on the Bicycle

In 1948, Jessica was walking home after evening classes in Georgetown, where she was studying typing, shorthand and art classes, when a young man on a bicycle rode up alongside her and jumped off his bike to speak

---

[7]Jessica Huntley, interview with George Fowokan Kelly, 2010.
[8]Jessica Huntley, interview with George Fowokan Kelly.
[9]Cecily Haynes-Hart, interview with Margaret Andrews.
[10]Ibid.
[11]Ibid.

to her. Mutually interested in each other, they walked together, passing the time of day. They were in Brickdam, a suburb of Georgetown, and a fifteen-minute walk to her home in Charlestown. Eric Huntley, two years younger at nineteen years of age, had no particular plans that evening on his way home from work as a messenger in Kitty Post Office in Georgetown. He was the son of a prison warder who had been living in New Amsterdam, a provincial town, and had recently returned to Georgetown following his father's posting back to the capital city. The family had settled back into their home, a cottage on Bent Street, Wortmanville. Jessica and Eric had grown up only about a fifteen-minute walk from each other yet did not know each other or meet until they were young adults.

She told him she lived in Kitty, Georgetown. This was a white lie, whilst she summed him up. Eventually, she permitted him to escort her home to the tenement room at 35 Howes Street, where she called her mother out of the room to meet him. Hectorine, formidable Georgetown matriarch, appears to have approved of him, and perhaps his warm and deliberate 'Goodnight, Aunt' greeting assured her of his respectfulness, and knowledge of her senior status in the community. There was a friendly acceptance from Aunt whose response indicated that Eric had passed his first test with her. On the walk to her home, Jessica had informed him of her mother's standing and status in the yard, so he could demonstrate this respectfulness. Looking at the sweet-faced, handsome and charming boy, standing with her strong-headed, confident, beautiful, popular daughter, Aunt saw a well-matched young couple. They formed a bond that day that lasted for the remainder of their lives.

Like Jessica, Eric Huntley was from a Methodist family, and his father was Frank Huntley. With his wife, Selina Thorne, Frank Huntley parented eleven children including Eric, of whom ten survived. Frank suffered extensive periods of unemployment and had the fate of many Black workers at this time, with no alternative but to seek work in the interior region, the 'bush', where he worked mining precious gems for a period of time.

When Frank Huntley obtained regular employment in the prison service, this stabilized family life for the Huntleys. The prison service in British Guiana was modelled on ideas developed in colonial Britain and across Europe, and included what was considered the particular requirements of punishing colonial prisoners.[12] It included all aspects of British prison design, the treatment of prisoners, and the punishments to be provided. The prison system adhered to British ideologies on race, intertwined with the political objectives for achieving domination in the region, and

---

[12]Clare Anderson and others, 'Guyana's Prisons: Colonial Histories of Post-Colonial Challenges', *The Howard Journal of Crime and Justice*, 59 (2020), pp.335–49, esp. p.338. https://doi.org/10.1111/hojo.12382

suppressing colonial populations. Flogging, hard labour, capital punishment and solitary confinement were examples of the punishments meted out in British Guiana's prisons during colonialism.[13] Prison played a central role in the life and experience of Jessica and Eric Huntley, and they formed part of the British colonial political weaponry against those involved in anti-colonial movements.

Georgetown prison, on Camp Street, and New Amsterdam prison were built by the Dutch who were succeeded by Britain in the colonization of British Guiana in 1814. The British administrators enlarged these prison facilities, and in 1843 built a prison in the Mazaruni region of the country.[14] A further thirteen prisons were built between 1837 and 1931, plus a number of other smaller points of detention. The use of prison sentences increased in British Guiana after the end of the Slave Trade, so that there was a quadrupling of the imprisoned population in 1869, compared to 1831.[15] Prior to this, punishment of Black enslaved people fell within the jurisdiction of the plantation owners and overseers. After emancipation, increasing numbers of Black people were incarcerated in prisons. After the introduction of indentureship, the prison population also swelled with Indian immigrants who had infringed the terms of their labour contracts.[16]

Frank Huntley was an imposing, dark-skinned, formal man who was a highly respected figure. His work as a prison warder brought him added authority. However, his work also carried a number of very stressful duties. He was responsible for prisoners who were at the time used for cleaning public buildings and spaces such as the botanical gardens.[17] If a prisoner escaped, the warder in charge of that prisoner was held responsible and heavily sanctioned. The duties that Frank Huntley carried out included administering the corporal punishment to those prisoners sentenced to be lashed with the cat-o'-nine-tails. He was also involved in the hanging of prisoners who were sentenced to death, including preparing the prisoners and the equipment, such as ensuring the trapdoor was working.[18]

As one coping strategy, prison warders, including Frank Huntley, turned to alcohol. His son Patrick recalled that they 'used to drink, and they drank often anyway'.[19] He was a father figure to the prisoners, and in addition to his authoritarian side, he was also very compassionate, and Patrick recalled

---

[13]Ibid.

[14]Ibid., p.340.

[15]Ibid.

[16]Ibid.

[17]Patrick Huntley, interview with Claudia Tomlinson, 18 December 2020.

[18]Ibid.

[19]Ibid.

that 'the prisoners used to call him "Daddy", so he was like a father figure. He would say to them "try and don't come back here again"'.[20] Frank would give some of his food to prisoners he considered in need of feeding. For Frank Huntley to then be involved in the hanging of those who had regarded him as a father figure would have been repeatedly traumatizing.

Frank was temporarily posted to the prison in New Amsterdam when Eric was thirteen or fourteen. The whole family moved there, and Eric finished his education in New Amsterdam. When Eric reached the end of his education, he seemed destined for a career in the church, as he delivered his first sermon aged seventeen or eighteen whilst in New Amsterdam as a fledgling preacher. When he moved back to Georgetown in 1948, however, all thoughts of the church left Eric's mind and his interests moved in other directions.

Eric's mother Selina was a housewife whose grandparents, including a white grandmother and a Barbadian father, had migrated from Barbados to Guiana. Light-skinned, she was 'classed as a creole' according to Patrick Huntley, which raised her status in the racialized society. Selina was in poor health and relied on her eldest daughter to care for the household. Even though the family lived in a cottage in Kitty, Eric grew up experiencing similar hardships to Jessica, possibly more as he was from a much larger family. For example, Jessica slept on the only bed in the family's tenement room, whereas Eric grew up sleeping on the floor of his home with his brothers.

Younger brother Patrick Huntley reflected on the Huntley family childhood, 'I don't know how we survived. In Georgetown we had no garden, so there wasn't anything we could really get from planting, so everything had to be bought, so hunger ... we had a puff belly, we suffered quite a lot'.[21] The 'puff belly', a sign of malnutrition, arose from prolonged periods without eating, or just with 'sugar water' to drink as the main meal for the day.[22] Jessica and Eric both grew up together with a number of shared experiences in Georgetown, including hunger.

After their first meeting, Eric visited Jessica regularly at her home as part of their courtship. British ideas of sexual respectability were ingrained into British Guiana's colonial society. Courtship had to be acceptable to the respective families, undertaken with family approval, particularly of the girl's family, so it was usual for the boy to visit the girl at her family home, rather than vice versa. Given the circumstances of Jessica's housing in Howes Street, courting was a difficult undertaking. As Jessica lived with her mother

---

[20]Ibid.
[21]Ibid.
[22]Ibid.

and two brothers at home, there was no private space for their courting to take place or for the new couple to talk privately.[23] Courtship had to partly take place under the family gaze. But with Eric's bicycle, the couple would ride together on it to go to places. Most of their early courtship was spent riding to visit Jessica's many friends from school, youth clubs, which included Cecily Haynes-Hart. As the relationship deepened, the couple would make more outings on their own to places frequented by traditional courting couples such as the Sea Wall, and the Botanical Gardens.[24]

Political Ferment in 1940s British Guiana

Their relationship grew against the backdrop of a nation in political ferment with an intensification of anti-colonial resistance movements, both at home and abroad. Resistance to state authority started to take a new direction in the 1940s. Since Critchlow's victory in securing the legal recognition of the first trade union, the trade union movement had grown in strength. Many of these were organized to empower workers in agricultural industries where they faced most exploitation, particularly in the sugar industries. Workers' resistance to oppression by the sugar plantation owners in Guiana and in the British colonies during this period was a significant part of the anti-colonial resistance. Greater trade union recognition, one of the recommendations of the Moyne Commission of the 1930s, was being implemented. After the British Guiana Labour Union (BGLU) was established, there were several other important unions founded, including the Guyana Industrial Workers Union (GIWU).[25] Despite this, the violent suppression of workers' uprisings continued to be part of life in British Guiana.

An example of this continuing state violence against workers involved in industrial action was clearly on display in 1948. The sugar industry was heavily challenged for its exploitative practices, and its domination of many aspects of life in British Guiana. The British sugar company, Bookers, was much despised for the oppression and harsh conditions faced by its workers. A protracted strike was called in 1948 by the GIWU, against conditions on the Enmore Sugar estate. During the demonstration, police opened fire. Five Indian striking workers were shot dead and several others injured.[26]

---

[23]Eric Huntley, interview with Claudia Tomlinson.

[24]Ibid.

[25]Samuel J. Goolsarran, *The System of Industrial Relations in Guyana* (Trinidad and Tobago: International Labour Office, 2003), p.2.

[26]Mel Carpen, 'In Memory of the Enmore Martyrs' (2008), *Guyana Journal*, http://www.guyanajournal.com/Enmore_Martyrs_melcarpen.html.

This incident was a throwback to earlier decades before the introduction of trade union legislation which protected the rights of workers to take industrial action. Industrial relations had improved since the establishment of the Department of Labour in 1942, and there was an expectation that violence of the past would no longer be witnessed. It had been about a decade since such a major incident had happened in Guiana and it greatly traumatized workers. But it also played a role in intensifying the politicization of the workers in the country. Importantly, outrage at the Enmore incident became part of rage against colonialism that was at the heart of the programme of the emerging People's Progressive Party (PPP), formed two years later, and in greater resistance of coloniality. Eusi Kwayana said that the killing of these workers 'was the event of our time that made a great impression on the working people'.[27]

In 1949, Eric Huntley was transferred from the Post Office at Kitty in Georgetown to work as a postman in Buxton village. Buxton is the historic settlement purchased by the former enslaved, and developed into a model of Black community building and organizing and early political education. Eric lived in temporary accommodation until he became established in his post. After settling into his post, he joined the Post Office Workers Union, eventually becoming Assistant General Secretary. From 1949 onwards, with Jessica, he started to participate more in the political and community life of the village.

The romance took a severe blow when Eric took Jessica to meet his parents, in late 1949 or early in 1950. The visit went disastrously wrong. The relationship between the couple was now serious and established and they were thinking about marriage. Although they were now meeting Jessica for the first time, it was clear that his parents had been aware of her relationship with their son, and they were decided against her. They did not approve of their son marrying someone from her background. The British class system and prejudices were so entrenched in Guiana that the Huntleys viewed themselves as socially superior to the Carrolls. The Huntleys lived in a cottage and Frank worked hard to provide for this family even during the hard economic times. As a prison warder, he was a man of some status and heralded respect. His wife came from a 'white background', and Eric's sisters were all employed, either working in shops in Georgetown or as seamstresses to the wealthy of Georgetown. Jessica was the daughter of a single woman, a struggling mother of several children – a cleaner from Charlestown, an area which was seen as far from respectable. She was not the sort of wife the conservative, religious father wanted for his son. When Eric introduced her to his parents, they made their feelings known directly to the young couple, with Eric recalling that his father was 'very horrible to her' that day.

---

[27]Eusi Kwayana, interview with Claudia Tomlinson.

Perhaps high in confidence as an independent young man, fighting for the political freedom of his country, who had met a woman he was in love with, whom he wanted to make his life partner, he was always on a collision course with Frank Huntley, the conservative, patriarchal, and deeply religious head of the family. Eric's brother, Patrick Huntley, was a witness to the events of that day and concluded that to their father, Frank Huntley, 'anybody who came from that area, she came from an area which wasn't a very salubrious area, so that was a mark against'.[28] The legacy of slavery and colonialism contributed to the stereotyping of Black working-class women as truculent with loose morals, and responsible for undermining the moral fabric of society.

A further reason for Jessica's rejection by Eric's father that day was possibly a perceived failure by Eric to adhere to the family standards and norms required for such an occasion. Patrick Huntley concluded that: 'My dad was a bit on the strict side, normally if you wanted something from your dad, you would talk to your mum first and get her on your side. So, I think he [Eric] was a bit too brash.'[29] It would have been considered a bold approach for a young man to just turn up with a young woman to present to his father, who may have felt blindsided by this action. Patrick Huntley remembered the outcome that day. He said: 'there was a quarrel at that time, there was a division'. Patrick Huntley also thought it was possible that alcohol might have played a part as 'dad used to drink, so whether he'd had a few drinks first, I don't know, so, there was no communication after that. My dad told them he wasn't happy'. Distraught and upset at his prospective wife being treated in this manner, Eric left his parent's house that day for good. He moved in with an aunt who lived on Carmichael Street in Georgetown and never returned home, not visiting the family home again until 1956 when he was preparing to leave the country to move to Britain.

The full reasons for Frank Huntley's displeasure in meeting Jessica that day cannot be truly known, however the changes in their son since his return to Georgetown could not have pleased Eric's parents. Before the family left New Amsterdam to return to Georgetown, he was emerging as a young Methodist preacher with the prospect of a career in the church which would have made his parents very proud. Since his return to Georgetown a year ago, he was now spending all of his spare time in a rough tenement yard with the daughter of an unemployed single mother. Eric was also increasingly being drawn into the new political consciousness sweeping Georgetown and the country which Eric's father was suspicious of, and ultimately opposed. He was not sympathetic to the PPP, seeing it as a blasphemous organization, according to Eric's brother, Patrick Huntley:

---

[28] Patrick Huntley, interview with Claudia Tomlinson.
[29] Ibid.

Cheddi Jagan and the group, they were very anti-religion, and anti-God. The PPP had a banner saying, 'Turn the Churches into Houses', so I think my dad was a very, very, religious person, I've seen him praying and reading the bible, he had a strong belief and so anybody who said: 'there's no God', he wouldn't have much appreciation of, so that anti-religious message which came through put off my dad, he had issues.[30]

Eric was unrecognizable from their son of a year ago, and the events of the day of Jessica's visit were likely caused by the bubbling over of a cauldron of anxiety that had built up about their son over the past year.

Marriage and Politics in the Village

Jessica and Eric's wedding day, on 9 December 1950, was a happy event. For Eric it was marred by his parents' refusal to attend. From his very large family, only his eldest brother attended as a guest. He also spotted two of his sisters, Stella, and Vera, in the crowd of onlookers, but apart from this was saddened to recall that for his wedding and marriage, 'I had no support from my family.'[31] After their marriage, they travelled to the village of Buxton, where Eric had been working as a postman for a few months, and had been given a small, unfurnished cottage as part of the job. They lived in the part of the village known as the 'Buxton Front' as it was near the Sea Wall.

As a working-class woman of African heritage in the late 1940s, Jessica's political participation was restricted. She was unable to vote in local or national elections, disqualified on the grounds of income and property ownership. Most working-class Black women were employed as domestics, in factories, or they were housewives. After her marriage, Jessica fell into this second category. Being a wife and the domestic sphere became her primary identity. In 1951, she gave birth to her first child, Ken Karl Huntley (1951–2011), always called Karl. Karl's birth was traumatic. He was delivered at home by their next-door neighbour, with Eric present, as the midwife was late, arriving after the birth.[32] Needing to recover from the medical complications she experienced as part of Karl's birth, as well as needing to take care of him, kept her mostly within the domestic realm. Their second son, Chauncey Huntley, was born in 1952. Jessica lived life as the stay-at-home wife of a postman, with childcare and housework

---

[30]Ibid.

[31]Eric Huntley, interview with Claudia Tomlinson.

[32]Ibid.

FIGURE 3.1 *Jessica and Eric Huntley's wedding in 1950. Courtesy of the Huntley Collection, London Metropolitan Archives.*

as her primary activities. The family home was her primary domain. It is unlikely that she was entirely satisfied with this role, and the evidence of this is that she took every opportunity to participate politically in village and community life. Although most Guianese women were unable to participate in formal political activity during this period, women were very involved in community politics which involves all aspects of building and developing a robust village identity.

In Buxton village, Jessica and Eric formed what would be some of the most politically important and enduring associates of this period. Some of these became long-term friends and comrades. Eric became associated with three village activists, whom together were known as the 'Three Small Boys', due to their youth. The most important of these was Eusi Kwayana; born Sidney King in 1925 in Lusignan, he had grown up in Buxton from the age of seven. In his mid-twenties at this time, he was renowned as a young agitator for the rights of working people. From the age of fifteen, he had been working as a teacher in Buxton. He was not particularly interested in party politics or the political infrastructure of the country, activities which he considered far removed from the daily struggles of the villagers. Kwayana has described Buxton at this time as a political hotspot, a hotbed of activity. Kwayana's main associate was Martin Stephenson, part of the group of small boys, and the main target of their agitation was resistance against the activities of plantation owners against the villagers.

Their leading activism in the village could be broadly described as an anti-plantation movement. Buxton was bordered by the Enmore estates which had a plantation on either side of Buxton. Enmore estates management managed other plantations in other regions of British Guiana. The anti-plantation movement involved activities directed at resisting the incursions by plantation owners into the rights, freedoms and enjoyment of village life. The villages, owned by proud liberated Africans, were an ideological anathema to the planters, who had previously owned these individuals and their labour, now thriving and building a new British Guiana on the doorsteps of the plantations. According to Kwayana, the villagers had to resist many incursions into the rights of the villagers. One example is that the plantation owners, such as Enmore estates, controlled the water supply to the villages. Villagers accused Enmore management of frequently flooding the villages to deliberately ruin agriculture and livelihood as a way of pressuring villagers to seek work on the estates which were short of labour. The planters also sought to dig a canal through a section of Buxton village to connect their plantations and enable transportation of sugar and molasses from the Enmore estates to Georgetown for export to Britain. Kwayana argued that 'if you were anti-plantation, you were anti-government'.

Jessica was therefore part of life in Buxton as it became the centre of the new politics in British Guiana. In 1947, Cheddi Jagan was elected as an Independent for the Central Demerara constituency which was in Buxton. At the Buxton cinema, Jagan and his group addressed the villagers, in the most important ward in the constituency. Cheddi Jagan (1918–97), the grandson of indentured workers, contracted from India to work on the sugar estates in British Guiana, as replacement for enslaved Africans following emancipation in British Guiana. He was educated in British Guiana and trained as a dentist in the USA before returning home in 1943. Cheddi Jagan met Janet Rosenberg Jagan (1920–2009), a white Marxist from Chicago in the United States, who became Secretary of the PPP when it was incorporated in 1950, and he married her in 1943. She was a dental nurse and rose to become the first female President of Guyana in 1997. During his period of study in the United States, Cheddi Jagan became firmly affiliated to Marxism, and on his return to British Guiana, began a programme of political activism based on this perspective.

Jagan provided new political messages that inspired many including Jessica Huntley and Eric Huntley. For Kwayana, 'Cheddi Jagan ... was very open and candid about race and the need for racial unity and exposing the plantocracy to the hilt, as they had never been exposed before'.[33] 'Here was a man speaking straight'; 'We moved throughout the coast and mobilised a lot of villages'.[34] Young activists were convinced of this new political direction espoused by Jagan and his associates. Kwayana concluded that: 'my age group, men, and women. I was very active among them, engaging them with this new politics that had arisen. The new politics he brought in at that time ... People were hearing messages of oppression and racial unity, that they had not heard before in that generation or in those terms'.[35]

The PPP aimed to achieve self-government for British Guiana, the development of the economy, and the establishment of a socialist state. It was anti-colonial and anti-imperialist, and on the side of the working class, thus bringing a new perspective, rejecting the view that the countries such as British Guiana were colonies to be ruled for the benefit of Britain. The PPP strategically twinned an Indo-Guyanese (Jagan), with an African Guyanese (Forbes Burnham) to coalesce the support of the fractured society divided along these racial lines, following the impact of both slavery and indenture. Forbes Burnham (1923–85) was an African-Guyanese barrister, qualified in Britain, and became Party Chairman.

Jessica Huntley was part of this emergence of a new, radical politics in her country. She was a member of a progressive political study group that met weekly in her home in Buxton in the 1950 and 1951. Part of the new politics was the expansion of political knowledge, and young activists attended political study groups and Discussion Circles in Buxton. Jessica was a member of the political study group held in her family home with Eric in Buxton, reading communist and progressive texts. Eric and Eusi Kwayana were part of the self-taught classes and the latter recalled that 'the first thing we studied was the history of CPSU-B. That was the history of the Communist Party of Soviet Union. That was the kind of orientation we had at that time. We were sitting there, looking through these pages. Everything finally determined. And praising the great leaders and so on. And I remember well the recitation of this line: "In order not to err in policy,

---

[33] Eusi Kwayana interview with Claudia Tomlinson.
[34] Ibid.
[35] Ibid.

one must be revolutionary and not reformist."'[36] This was a book that was recommended for beginners reading Marxism, but Kwayana observed: 'it was not really Marxism as we found later on when we encountered people like C.L.R James and others. But it was the prescription to hold the nation and the party together. And it worked as we know for decades'.[37] Jessica Huntley's experience of political participation at a village level in Buxton provided an important grounding for her growing political education.

---

[36] Ibid.
[37] Ibid.

4

National Freedom and Women's Emancipation

On 1 January 1950, Jessica and Eric attended the first meeting of the People's Progressive Party (PPP) at the Metropole cinema in Buxton to establish the new party. The Party was led by Cheddi Jagan and Janet Jagan who were in attendance, along with other founders including Eusi Kwayana. This iteration of the PPP was a multi-ethnic, anti-colonial political party, the first political party in the country. It introduced mass enfranchisement to the country for the first time. These co-founders were predominantly Marxist-Leninists, Leftist progressives with workers as its main constituency. Its main objective was to achieve 'national independence of British Guiana'.[1]

Jessica and Eric both wanted revolutionary change in the country with full enfranchisement, justice and rights for workers. Eric was more immersed in the trade union movement and may have risen to the top political ranks through this route. Jessica was also a trade union activist and an advocate for human rights and equality, particularly for women, children and young people. During this period, she navigated personal gendered barriers in her life to become influential in mainstream politics of the country.

In the period before the general election of April 1953, progressives such as Jessica were full of expectation for what the new political dawn would herald in their country. She lived for around three years in Buxton until 1952 and was part of the new anti-colonial politics spreading through the country. She was part of the new generation of young activists preparing for revolutionary change in the country. She formed collaborations with those leaders, such as Kwayana, Cheddi Jagan, Janet Jagan and others identified

---

[1] Kimani S.K. Nehusi, *A People's Political History of Guyana, 1838–1964* (Hertford: Hansib, 2018), p.201.

as being at the helm of this new politics. She was determined to be part of this new future for British Guiana.

After this time spent in Buxton, Eric was transferred to Rosignol, on the west bank of the Berbice River, and the terminus of the train line. When Jessica arrived in Rosignol with Eric, she was the mother of one-year-old Karl and Chauncey who was only a few months old. She wanted more than marriage and motherhood. She had a clear view about gender power relations within marriage which she reflected on in later years and said:

> Within the home confines, the man exercises a lot of power on that woman. A hell of a lot of power he exercises. And whether or not the woman allows that power, and to a certain extent I think she does, and the woman is the one, I think who, nearly always, makes the concession within that relationship, because the man seldom does make the concession. Because the man is always right. So, the woman very often is left very confused, and very, in a sense, humiliated by it all.[2]

Now at the age of twenty-seven, she still had the example of the striving, influential women in her life. Women who had beliefs and contributed to making a difference in life. By this time, she was a very confident political activist, speaker and committed to her political view that revolutionary change that had happened. She shrugged off hecklers in the audience who would shout out at her 'why you don't go home to your children?' when she was giving speeches. She was part of this political work of building momentum on the ground for the PPP. She worked to persuade people to take more control of their rights, to be involved and to be wise and learn about the world around them.

As a working-class Black woman, Jessica Huntley was herself disenfranchised from formal political participation of her own country until 1953 when women of her background could vote for the first time. Race, sex and class collided to determine the political participation of working-class Black women. African Guianese women were highly active as organizers and participants in activities to build community solidarity and identity. In village administration, certainly in relation to Buxton, there was no gender inequality, and women were eligible to vote in village the political councils and to stand for election in their villages.[3] In the example of Jessica Huntley's mother, Hectorine Carroll, and other women in the community, they had strong levels of participation in building community resistance to

---

[2]LMA, HC, LMA/4463/F/07/01/001/E, Eric and Jessica Huntley interviewed by Harry Goulbourne (Session Four), 3 June 1992.

[3]Nehusi, *A People's Political History*, p.176.

degrading aspects of life, building pride and a strong and dignified African and worker's identity. This form of involvement does not often feature in official records. There is limited scholarship or historical narrative of such activity.

Jessica Huntley's white, 'creole' and wealthier sisters had been able to vote since before she was born. At the time of Jessica's birth in 1927, the involvement of women in the formal political arena, particularly Black working-class women, was limited by law. Most women were disenfranchised, and only property owners, in possession of a house valued at $5,000 or more, and with a disposable income of $12,000 were able to vote in 1926.[4] This meant that less than 5 per cent of the population had the vote. In 1930, women were permitted to vote, but the income qualification was doubled to $24,000, and the property ownership qualification was maintained. Very rich, mostly white women could now vote in British Guiana. In 1947, the electorate was extended to include almost 15 per cent of the adult population, and those with an income of $120 per annum and who were literate in English became enfranchised.[5] Universal suffrage for all adults over the age of twenty-one was introduced at the April 1953 general election. Jessica was therefore only eligible to vote for the first time in the general election won by the political party she had helped to build and bring to power. In the 1953 elections, the PPP was the only party to field women candidates, as it fielded three women out of a possible twenty-four. Overall, 128 seats were available, so the fielding of three women only, who were all elected, is highly indicative of the position of women at this time.

Between 1945 and 1953, political participation by women grew to a significant scale. The politicization of women during this period has been attributed in part to the work of the Women's Political and Economic Organization (WPEO). The WPEO was founded by Janet Jagan and Winifred Gaskin (1916–77) in 1946 and operated a number of campaigns until 1949.[6] Gaskin was a woman of African Guianese origin, born in Buxton, and was a founding member of the Political Affairs Committee (PAC) and the PPP. She would achieve a successful career in Guyanese politics, becoming Minister of Education, and participate in race equality activism.[7] The WPEO aimed to encourage women to increase their participation in the social and economic life of the country and to take an interest in the international

---

[4]Ibid., p.709.

[5]Ibid., p.710.

[6]Roberta Walker-Kilkenney, 'Women in Social and Political Struggle in British Guiana 1946–1953', *History Gazette*, The University of Guyana 49 (1992), p.6.

[7]Clyde W. Thierens, 'Winifred Gaskin – An Early Guyanese Politician', *Stabroek News*, 10 December 2009, https://www.stabroeknews.com/2009/12/10/features/winifred-gaskin-an-early-guyanese-politician-2/.

position of women.[8] Other WPEO organizers were Gaskin's sister, Thelma, and Frances Stafford, a white European.[9] The raising of women workers' consciousness therefore appeared aligned to anti-capitalist ideology, seen as the root of the exploitation and disenfranchisement of Guianese workers, which women were increasingly being encouraged to unify with. A central element of the WPEO's objective was to support and assist as many eligible women as possible to register to vote.

The campaign by those heralding the new anti-colonial political movement was building momentum. The PPP had been building its grass-roots support over several years on the estates, in the villages, in the factories, and on the waterfront. It was the first political party in the country, and the first political movement to deliberately seek to empower working-class people and women. Its strategy was to be a broad coalition that provided a place for those in the business and public sector and the professions. But above all, it sold itself as the party of the people. The general election of 1953 was held on 27 April and the PPP won with a landslide victory of eighteen out of twenty-four seats. The PPP had correctly gauged the appetite of the country and the work of grass-roots activists such as Jessica Huntley paid off. Jubilant with Eric, party workers and supporters, she was in no doubt that it was the universal enfranchisement of women that contributed to this massive PPP victory. She took the earliest opportunity available to her to take her place at the helm of women's empowerment in British Guiana.

Co-Founding the Women's Progressive Organization

Jessica was at the forefront of the founding of a new women's organization to reflect the ambition for women in the new era. The WPEO had ceased operations in 1949 and there was a gap to be filled to increase women's participation. In the build up to the 1953 elections, Jessica was part of a small women's group which operated as a policy or strategy group for the PPP. It included Janet Jagan and was possibly the most influential group of women intellectuals in the country. It was also at the centre of setting the national strategic direction for women. She forged a close friendship and political allyship with Janet Jagan. Janet Jagan had worked closely with husband Cheddi to develop the strategic vision for the new Guiana. Janet

---

[8]Walker-Kilkenney, 'Women in Social and Political Struggle', pp.6–12.

[9]James G. Rose, 'British Colonial Policy and the Transfer of Power in British Guiana, 1945–1964' (unpublished doctoral thesis, King's College London, 1992), p.89.

became the General Secretary of the PPP when it was founded in 1950, with Cheddi. Like Jessica, she was also the mother of two small children. Janet Jagan became the editor of *Thunder*, the PPP's journal.

Following the 1953 elections, as part of this group, Jessica Huntley set about establishing a new women's political organization within the PPP. The Women's Progressive Organization (WPO) was brought to life in a meeting on 27 May 1953, held in the auditorium, at the top level of Washington High school where Jessica had been a pupil ten years previously. She was at the helm of the WPO and co-founded it with Janet Jagan, Jane Phillips Gay, and M.H.A. Aukland. Jessica acknowledged her role in the formation, clearly stating: 'I founded the WPO after 1953, when the party had won ... I was the person who initiated the women's group.'[10] Jessica saw the objectives of the WPO more broadly than a focus on female empowerment. At that meeting, the WPO elected a provisional committee with Jessica as its secretary. She wrote the mission statement of the WPO in the June 1953 issue of *Thunder,* the organ of the PPP, in the same year, in an article titled 'Women and Peace'. She argued that:

> It is in the face of those evils (war and destruction) that the WPO has taken its stand. It stands for a better educated woman who can bring up her children in surroundings for security; it stands for the raising of our living standards, and it stands for peace and friendship among the peoples of the world, and for the ultimate liberation of our women from colonialism and poverty.[11]

She consistently sought the empowerment of women and 'called on women to take an active role in the fight against rearmament'.[12] She explained in her arguments, made in *Thunder*, that the 'massive expenditure on arms' diverted money away from social needs. Further, she called on Guianese women to 'struggle against imperialist domination and exploitation'.[13] She brought an international perspective to women's liberation, educating and drawing their attention to the position and experience of women in Communist and Socialist nations, showing that women did not have to live oppressed lives. Her later writings in 1958 echo these themes:

---

[10]LMA, HC, LMA/4463/F/07/01/001/B, Eric and Jessica Huntley interview with Harry Goulbourne (Session One), 20 May 1992.

[11]Gail Teixeira, 'History of Struggle of Guyanese Women, The People's Progressive Party, Forward with the Women's Struggle. A Publication of the Women's Progressive Organisation in Honour of its 30th Anniversary', *WPO Publications* (1983), pp.9–16, esp. p.11.

[12]Walker-Kilkenney, 'Women in Social and Political Struggle', p.14.

[13]Ibid.

> The landslide victory of the People's Progressive Party on April 27th is to a great extent due to the progressive stand taken by the newly enfranchised women. Already three women are elected on the PPP to the House of Assembly. In other parts of the world, women are spearheading the attack against imperialists and oppression. They demand equal rights, equal pay for equal work, and equal opportunities for employment. In the Metropolitan and war-ridden countries they are the chief fighters for peace. Mothers are waging a ceaseless and successful war against the butchery that is being prepared by the capitalists (in America, England and France) whose profits depend on the manufacture of deadly weapons.[14]

Her voice and message, highly influential, spoke to the women of British Guiana through the articles she wrote for *Thunder*, as well as her speeches:

> Our women must learn that the whole problem that faces us at the moment is national liberation, and they must assert themselves with their men folk in the struggle to free us and our children from imperial domination. The solving of the housewives problems, the ability to rear well-fed, healthy and educated children capable of holding their own, in a war-free socialist world of tomorrow depends on the success for failure of this important struggle.[15]

The importance of this voice of a leading, working-class Black woman spokesperson for the PPP, in rousing support among women and Black people, disenfranchised for generations, and now having an influential voice in nation building, cannot be underestimated.

Some of the activities of the WPO involved direct action to correct perceived injustices against women. One evening, when returning from a meeting of the organization with her comrades she said that 'a family was being evicted by a private landlord … and a number of us went into that house and we put the woman back. It was a spontaneous reaction. We were coming from a meeting, the bailiff was there throwing the things out into the street, and the women just went and put her back in.'[16] This was a sight she would have witnessed many times growing up in the tenement yard

---

[14]Jessica Huntley, Cheddi Jagan Research Centre, 'Call to Our Women', *Thunder*, 9 February 1958.

[15]Ibid.

[16]Sidney, Carol, '60:60, Jessica Huntley, a Lifetime of Publishing', *Sable*, Spring (2005), pp.90–9, esp. p.94.

and a threat she and her family lived under. Here was her opportunity to correct a perceived injustice. The PPP ultimately paid a fine levied for this action.[17] Helping to bring justice for the women of the nation and educating them to recognize that their oppression was connected to colonialism and racial capitalism were important aspects of Jessica Huntley's work for the national independence for Guiana. This vision was needed for the personal and political peril she would face in the next few years.

---

[17]Ibid.

5

'Bound with the Chains of Colonialism and Imperialism'

In 1953, British Guiana was thrown into its greatest political crisis when the fledgling government of April 1953 was forcibly ended a mere six months after it formed. The British Government ordered the removal of the People's Progressive Party (PPP) administration. It sent its Royal Navy warship, the HMS *Superb,* to Georgetown on 8 October 1953 and mobilized troops throughout the country. The constitution was withdrawn, and the PPP leaders were dismissed from their duties. Many were to be imprisoned. Britain accused the PPP government of planning to turn Guiana into a communist state and of leading the country into ruin. This suspicion about the PPP's socialist programme was shared by Guianese conservatives as well as British authorities.[1] The suspension of the government in October 1953 was followed by the imposition of emergency regulations by Whitehall which resulted in the banning of many progressive organizations labelled by Britain as communist and dangerous to the development of a democracy.

British troops remained in British Guiana until after the 1957 General Election, enforcing the emergency regulations introduced by Parliament to quell the rise of socialism in a nation strategically and economically of high value. This was not a form of independence that Britain was prepared to sanction for one of its colonies. It wanted a more palatable independence to support its political and economic interests in the region in the post-independence period. The PPP was anti-colonial and was not expected to work with Britain in a way that served colonial interests in its future. Jessica Huntley continued her political work during this period. It was a time which also resulted in the biggest personal crisis experienced by her family.

---

[1] Kimani S.K. Nehusi, *A People's Political History of Guyana, 1838–1964* (Hertford: Hansib, 2018), pp.216–20.

Clandestine Work with the Women's Progressive Organization

The activities of the Women's Progressive Organization (WPO), and particularly its articles in *Thunder*, were cited by the British Government as part of its justification for the suspension of the PPP government. It was claimed as evidence that the PPP intended to turn Guiana into to a Communist State. Jessica Huntley wrote regularly on women's activism in *Thunder* until the government was suspended in October 1953. The first article, which was written by Jessica, was entitled 'Women and Peace'. The Robertson Commission report, the report to the British Parliament on the reasons for the removal of the PPP government stated that in *Thunder*: 'considerable space is devoted to adulation of the Soviet Union, other Soviet bloc countries and China. On the other hand, there is frequent vilification not only of "capitalist" countries such as the United Kingdom, the United States and France.'[2] Included in the list of examples of this alleged Communist stance was an extract from Jessica Huntley's article in *Thunder*:

> In the U.S.S.R., China, Hungary, in brief in the countries which are not bound with the chains of Colonialism and Imperialism the rights of women are guaranteed by their governments and written in the law. (*Thunder*, June 1953 article, 'Women and Peace' by Jessica Huntley).[3]

Britain branded ideas of anti-colonialism, anti-imperialism, workers' rights, and women's liberation as dangerous. By selecting Jessica Huntley's article as an example of such danger posed to its interests, she was highlighted as a significant intellectual and fighter for British Guiana's liberation and a threat to British capitalist interests.

After living for a period in Rosignol, Jessica, Eric and their two sons moved again to Stanleytown in New Amsterdam, where Eric was transferred after the suspension of the government in October 1953. Their time there was to be short-lived. The PPP and the WPO were not banned, but as the majority of its leaders were imprisoned and subject to severe personal and political restrictions a ban on the two organizations was effectively in operation.

Because of this situation, it was necessary for PPP activists and former officials to find new ways operate and women were particularly effective during this period. WPO activists employed subterfuge as part of the ongoing campaign against the colonial repression in the country:

---

[2]James Robertson and others, 'Report of the British Guiana Constitutional Commission 1954 (The Robertson Commission Report)', https://www.1953movement.com/.
[3]Ibid., p.80.

The women of the WPO undertook the clandestine distribution of Party Literature and messages. Using no disguise, save that of a Guianese woman going to market, these women carried hundreds of illegal pamphlets in their baskets. Messages were delivered as well, and funds raised. Though the colonial authorities were soon aware some resistance network was developing, the police and the soldiers generally paid little attention to the women that passed by.[4]

Further details of this work have been described in later evaluations of the work of the WPO, particularly during the four-year period the Emergency Regulations were in force. The WPO remained very active during this period:

> The women were able to achieve what few others were able to do. During this period of illegality, the women proved how useful they could be in doing clandestine work. They carried pamphlets in the bottom of their market baskets and found many devious methods in order to ensure that the PPP and the PYL [Pioneer Youth League], as well as the people, were informed as to the situation as it developed. This was one of the methods used by the party with the assistance and initiative of the WPO in order to ensure that Party members are well informed and organised.[5]

Women were evaluated as being of particular importance to the PPP's secret programme of resistance during this period of British military suppression. Women were 'perhaps the most important advantage was the militancy of the female population, young and old, who seemed above the suspicion of the military and the local security forces'.[6] Jessica therefore continued her political work with the PPP, undimmed, throughout this period of political suppression.

Eric Huntley also remained politically active and he was under greater surveillance. As a man and a former official of the PPP on its General Council, he was assumed to be a greater risk than Jessica. Additionally, as a Post Office worker he had access to the telegraph service used by the police and the security forces as well as the general population, and although Morse code was deployed, there was still concern that he might be able to access these communications. He was therefore suspended from working with these telecommunications.[7] The Huntley family home was raided by the British Army personnel on a number of occasions, sending their

---

[4]Roberta Walker-Kilkenney, 'Women in Social and Political Struggle in British Guiana 1946–1953', *History Gazette*, The University of Guyana 49 (1992), p.15.

[5]Ibid.

[6]Ibid.

[7]Eric Huntley, interview with Claudia Tomlinson.

children scurrying for cover under beds and tables. Security services seized the Gestetner typesetting and duplicating machine that had been purchased when they were living in Buxton for producing a newsletter for post office union members. Jessica had co-produced this newsletter, *The Post Office Journal*, with Eric.[8]

Family in Political Peril

Eric and his political associates continued to participate in demonstrations and protests against the suspension of the PPP government. He agitated for strike action by sugar workers who were members of the Guyana Industrial Workers Union (GIWU). Eric focused his efforts on persuading the workers on the Providence sugar estate to take part in a poorly supported strike. He addressed the workers in a demonstration whilst wearing his Post Office uniform which would have gained the severe disapproval of his employers as well as security services. Eventually security concerns about Eric were so great that he was transferred 50 miles from New Amsterdam, to Soesdyke, to a remote Post Office on the east coast of Berbice, near the Atkinson airbase. Eric was then served with a restriction order to remain in Soesdyke and it was unlawful for him to leave without official permission. Jessica did not have a formal position in the PPP, and as far as the security services were concerned, she did not meet the same level of threat as Eric. The family lived in the Post Office, with both commercial and residential sections in the building, and the home was linked to Eric's job.

Highly provoked by the British overthrow of the PPP government, Eric, like many PPP activists and supporters, maintained the resistance to colonial rule. The use of subterfuge was an essential part of the campaign of civil disobedience by those targeted by security services. Eric, rebellious and angered, continued his activism despite his restriction order. He broke the order by going to Georgetown, in disguise, still the centre of political activity. He was also restricted from participating in political protests and activities.

In Soesdyke, Eric organized a demonstration against the emergency regulations, and along with three or four others involved in the protest, he was arrested. At the end of the Atkinson airbase, which was also in operation as an airport, there was a gatehouse and this is where the arrested protesters were held overnight, there being no police station or detention facilities at that time. Atkinson Field Airbase had a section prepared as a detention centre, where some political detainees were subsequently held.

---

[8] Ibid.

The next morning the detained protesters were taken to court in Georgetown and Eric was charged, convicted, and sentenced to eight months in prison. As part of the campaign of civil disobedience being run by the PPP he did not co-operate with the legal process which he viewed as illegitimate and refused legal representation in court. From court Eric was taken directly to Georgetown prison. There he served an eight-month prison sentence in late 1954. The news agency Reuters reported on the frequent incidents of arrest and imprisonment of the PPP leaders and officials during this period of Britain's repression: 'Huntley, Georgetown, British Guiana, Dec 9. Reuter – Eric Huntley, a People's Progressive Party member and an official of the country's Youth Organization, was sentenced to six months imprisonment today for holding illegal meetings. Another member, Burchell Aaron, was sentenced to four months on a similar charge.[9] Passing sentence the Magistrate said: "It is clear the Youth Organization formed by Huntley and Aaron was indoctrinating ignorant masses in conscious propaganda to undermine and to create disaffection in the district", Huntley was also sentenced to two months for resisting arrest. The Magistrate ordered the sentences to run consecutively'.[10]

It will be recalled that Eric Huntley's father, Frank Huntley, was a prison warder working in Georgetown prison at the time of Eric's arrest. When Eric was imprisoned, he had already spent an extended period estranged from his father. Eric's decision to become a supporter of the PPP, and an official of the party, meant that he was effectively disowned by his parents. Eric, Jessica, and all reformers who supported the PPP were labelled as communists. Eric's parents very much viewed the PPP in this light and this was another reason to distance themselves from their son. The police had put Eric's parents' home under surveillance, during the period of emergency regulations, to identify if Eric was breaching his restriction order by visiting them which would justify an arrest. As well as being estranged from their son, Eric's parents felt they would be placing themselves at risk if they had contact with their son during this period. Eric Huntley's imprisonment in the same prison that Frank Huntley worked in was a great humiliation and a personal trauma for the proud man. During this period, the public and Frank Huntley largely held the perception that only criminals went to prison. Political imprisonment was not differentiated in Eric's father's mind.

Georgetown prison had a standard prison layout, with a main gate, buildings on each side, and an exercise area in the centre. There was a sentry box at the gate of the prison which afforded vigilance of the exercise area

---

[9]The National Archives, Colonial Office and Commonwealth Records, 'Security Issues in the West Indies', CO 968/1191, Reuters News Report 'Eric Huntley and Burchell Aaron Prosecution', 10 December 1954.

[10]Ibid.

and a good overview of the prison. Frank Huntley was located in the sentry box and it was impossible for him to avoid awareness of the presence of his son. However, as Eric stated: 'every morning when he arrived at work, he saw his son in prisoners clothes, and what he regarded as the most degrading situation for anybody to be in, he had to put up with that'.[11]

The father's experience was possibly more traumatic than the son's. Eric and his father saw each other on a daily basis in prison but couldn't interact. But his father did help to alleviate to hardship of his son's experience as best he could. For example, he sometimes put an extra piece of fish, or bread, or meat on his son's plate and he kept an eye on Eric's welfare. He couldn't protect his son, for example from three days in solitary confinement, with a bread and water only diet, for insubordination or not obeying a prison warder's command to put on his prison cap, therefore being deemed improperly attired.

Eric remained in prison for at least the full eight months he was sentenced to and possibly for a full year. His experience was alleviated when other PPP politicians were also detained in Georgetown prison at the same time as him, including Cheddi Jagan and Ram Karran, the PPP treasurer, and they were free to associate, including playing table tennis. After a period of a few months, the other political prisoners were transferred to Mazuruni prison and Eric served the majority of his sentence alone, without his comrades. The reason for transferring Jagan, Karran and the other PPP officials was the frequent demonstrations by PPP supporters outside the prison.[12]

In Soesdyke, on the day of Eric's arrest at the demonstration, Jessica was made aware of what had happened but was powerless to act. As he had been imprisoned, Eric was inevitably sacked from his job, and Jessica, with Karl and Chauncey, then aged two and three years old, were evicted from their home in the Post Office. She returned to Howes Street, Charlestown, her childhood home, to live with mother Hectorine, whilst Eric served his time in prison. Living with her mother again, after years of living independently as a married woman and mother of two children, compounded Jessica's experience of the political crisis, and Eric's imprisonment. Hectorine, however, has always supported her daughter's political activities, and stood behind her very solidly. Hectorine had to withstand the political ferment that her daughter was part of. She faced down the taunts from political opponents and supporters of opposition parties. She was mocked when she went to Stabroek market that her daughter was a communist, and that her son-in-law was a jailbird. She swiftly and roundly dealt with these taunts by

---

[11] Eric Huntley, interview with Claudia Tomlinson.

[12] Odeen Ishmael, 'The Guyana Story', https://www.landofsixpeoples.com/TheGyStory.html (last accessed 9 April 2024).

the use of suitable retorts befitting a loyal and proud Caribbean matriarch. She supported the PPP and had wanted to see them come to power.

History had repeated itself, and Jessica Huntley found herself traumatically removed from a comfortable home, back to the tenement yard. The events of Soesdyke meant that the lives of the family, as described by Eric Huntley: 'were completely torn asunder'. But Jessica's commitment to political change was dampened by the current political and personal crisis. There was no question of her feeling any shame at her husband's imprisonment, on the contrary, Eric said: 'she held her head high'. She visited Eric during his imprisonment and kept him abreast of what was happening and continued her political work with the PPP and the WPO during the military occupation of British Guiana.

6

Struggles in Male Ranks

Although the women of British Guiana had achieved universal suffrage in 1953 and the People's Progressive Party (PPP) was actively promoting women's liberation and equality, Jessica found that politics was still largely viewed as a masculine endeavour. The Legislative Council, the ruling administrative body led by the British colonial governor which had been dissolved following the PPP's victory in April 1953, was reinstated in October 1953. Jessica at this time was now more determined to participate in formal politics with the PPP, and not solely as a woman's activist. She found herself mostly working alongside male activists. She needed to penetrate these ranks and carve a space for her own participation.

One of the consequences of this prolonged period of emergency regulations was the weakening of the PPP. In 1955, the party split into two ideological factions, with Jagan and his followers occupying the socialist left ground, and Burnham moving to a Centrist-Socialist position. In 1956, the left under the broad leadership of Jagan fractured further with the emergence of a group of intellectuals and radicals known as the 'Ultra Left' PPP group, included young radical intellectual reformers such as Eric Huntley, Martin Carter, Brindley Benn, Sidney King, Lionel Jeffrey, Keith Carter and Richard 'Rory' Westmaas who were all of African or mixed African heritage.[1]

They emerged to the left of Cheddi Jagan following a further rancorous split in the party. The divide was due to Jagan's stance on a range of issues including positions that were seen as advantaging the Indian-descended population over the African-descended population.

The Ultra Left also differed from Jagan on the question of a West Indies Federation, the development of a political and economic unit of nations in the West Indies region following independence. This was supported by the Ultra Left but Jagan did not support it. Jagan's caution, the Ultra Left argued,

---

[1] Kimani S.K. Nehusi, *A People's Political History of Guyana, 1838–1964* (Hertford: Hansib, 2020), p.272.

was driven by a mutual fear of ethnic domination, with Indians fearing African domination in a Federation of the West Indies given their numerical advantage in the region, and Africans fearing Indian domination in Guiana in the post-independence period.

However, it was Jagan's criticism and disciplinary stance, formally presented at the PPP's 1956 Congress, that triggered the Ultra Left to exit the party and break with Jagan. His purported list of criticisms included accusations that the Ultra Left had subjected the PPP to criticism following the 1953 victory by a variety of activities. These included walking in the 1953 Mayday march in Georgetown with banners of Soviet Communist leaders held aloft, picketing the visit of Britain's Princess Alice, Countess of Athlone, to Guiana in 1952 with anti-colonial protest, and an alleged general failure to support the party leadership.[2]

As a woman PPP political activist, Jessica found that it difficult to find a space in this landscape amongst her political peers. Kimani Nehusi argues that the Ultra Left:

> Were chiefly men in the British Guiana Peace Committee and youth organizations, the militant Demerara Youth League and Pioneer Youth League: Richard 'Rory' Westmaas, Martin Carter, his elder brother, Keith Carter, Lionel Jeffrey, Sydney King [Eusi Kwayana] and Eric Huntley ... steeped in a comparatively advanced understanding of Marxism when compared to him. They were also all Afrikan or Mixed-Race Guianese.[3]

The prevailing assumption about Jessica's position in the formation of the Ultra Left breakaway group of the PPP was that she was a member because of Eric Huntley's adoption of that stance and membership of that group. She was later to dispute that she formally adopted any political stance in relation to the divisions in the PPP, or that she was a member of the Ultra Left group, stating that politically 'when the second split occurred in the PPP, I didn't take any particular position'.[4] But it was assumed by all, including the party leadership that she had done so because that was Eric's position. Jessica was clear that 'they ought not to have assumed that'.[5] This led to difficulties with the leadership as she then felt ostracized by the party leadership at this time because: 'I don't think that Cheddi and Janet wanted to talk with me because of this assumption that I had gone to the extreme

---

[2]Ibid., pp.283–4.

[3]Ibid., p.262.

[4]LMA, HC, LMA/4463/F/07/01/001/B, Eric and Jessica Huntley interview with Harry Goulbourne (Session One), 20 May 1992.

[5]Ibid.

Left'.[6] It was at this time that she first experienced the perils of factionalism within political party membership and its disruption of grassroots work to bring about change and improvements in people's lives which she was most interested in. She accepted party membership as the route to large-scale societal change. She started to become disaffected with party politics at this time but continued to work within it due to the promise of revolutionary change.

It was a difficult position for her as a woman politician who, at this time, would be tethered to the political views of her husband. She was clearly sympathetic to the Ultra Left and shared their view that Jaganism should not align itself to racialized politics and stood firm on this view. She detested that, in her view, 'Jagan failed to deal with the overt racists in the party.'[7] Whilst she did not actively join the Ultra Left group during the breakaway, their position was closely aligned with her beliefs, and she co-operated with them closely.

Perhaps it was her optimism that led her to adopt a more conciliatory position. When she was approached by Brindley Benn on behalf of the PPP leadership, she considered that reconciliation could be achieved. Benn was a PPP government minister in the ousted 1953 administration and remained a trusted ally of Cheddi and Janet Jagan. Guyanese historian Kimani Nehusi's analysis of gender politics in British Guyana presents an argument that despite women's equality and rights being high on the political agenda in the anti-colonial fight, they were largely excluded from obtaining positions of power and status within anti-colonial movements and the new political parties.[8] Despite the formation of the Women's Progressive Organization (WPO) and the important role of women's liberation movements, and key figures such as Janet Jagan, Jessica Huntley, Jessica Burnham and others, political party structures and policy overlooked the inclusion of a gender strategy. Patriarchy was embedded in the anti-colonial movement. Nehusi concludes:

> Through its organization of the WPO, there was formal support and recognition for the expression of the politicisation of gender within the PPP. But in their developing political trajectory the Ultra Left had not yet explicitly articulated a position on this question of gender, though that would later be championed by Kwayana, the only one who remained active in formal political life within the country after 1956. The Ultra

---

[6]Ibid.

[7]LMA, HC, LMA/4463/F/07/01/001/B, Eric and Jessica Huntley interview with Harry Goulbourne (Session One), 20 May 1992.

[8]Nehusi, *A People's Political History*, pp.287–8.

Left appeared to have had a gender-blind perspective. Certainly, they often adopted masculinist terminology, as did the vast majority of anti-colonial freedom fighters in Afrika and the Caribbean during this specific era when gender was not yet widely politicised as an important issue in liberation from colonial domination.[9]

Eric Huntley was released from prison in 1955 and found himself with limited political and employment options in Guiana. He was disillusioned with the new policies of Jaganism, an idea he had fought for, for several years, and gone to prison for. He found himself barred from Post Office jobs, and the only other offer available to him was manual work or plantation work. He and Jessica agreed that the best course of action would be for him to travel to England for a period to undertake study and to secure employment to support the family. He left in December 1956, arriving in January 1957.

Once Eric departed for Britain, it was clear that the couple did not hold a completely shared view of what their future lives together would look like. There was an agreement that Eric would save money to pay for Jessica's passage to England. Once he arrived in Britain and settled in, Eric wanted Jessica to make the journey to be with him as soon as possible. Her activities in Guiana, however, showed that she saw her immediate and long-term future at home. She was at this time considering the option of going to England or staying in Guiana.

Eric became aware, with some unease, that she had renewed her connections with the PPP, and instead of giving serious consideration to moving to Britain, she was building a political career, and deepening her political alliances in Guiana. She informed him in a letter after he arrived in England: 'I am now employed at the Party as Organiser.'[10] In this role she organized meetings with party members throughout the country to re-build support for the PPP. Now on her own with two small children, she found it a struggle to attend and lead these meetings, many of which were held in the evening. She informed Eric that 'darling, it's about 6.45pm and I have to meet a group at Prospect at about 8.10pm. it's a tough job for a woman'.[11] Importantly, the job was paid employment which she desperately needed to keep the family finances going.

---

[9]Ibid.

[10]LMA, HC, LMA/4463/F/01/02/012, Jessica Huntley Letter to Eric Huntley, 19 November 1957.

[11]LMA, HC, LMA/4463/F/01/02/012, Jessica Huntley Letter to Eric Huntley, 11 December 1957.

A close PPP alliance she formed during this period was with Moses Bhagwan, who recalls their association:

> At that time there was a folklore about political activists in the PPP who were called revolutionaries, Ultra Radicals, other names were given to them because they had become estranged with the leadership of the PPP, people like Rory Westmaas, Martin Carter, Sidney King as he was then, and Eric Huntley and there would have been others too. They weren't formally a group, but they all bonded together because they were all of the same kind of perspective, ideologically. It is in that context I would have met Jessica and of course she was the spouse of Eric Huntley, who was active in the PPP, and I don't know whether he resigned from the group, but when I went in Jessica was there. I was aware of the fact that she was connected to Eric Huntley, that made it more interesting. When you speak about what was happening to those persons I've named, their relationship with the PPP, I wondered how come Jessica is still active with the PPP when her husband had left, and she had stayed at the time.[12]

Bhagwan's analysis of this situation accords with the view that Jessica's position as an independent political thinker, and one who was married, was markedly different to what would have been expected of married women at this time.

Irrespective of expectations she continued her work and held a position of power and influence in the group. She worked closely with her allies in the PPP, and Bhagwan was one she grew close to during this period. Then a civil servant, Bhagwan found that other PPP activists in the Ultra Left group, which he joined, had reservations about his involvement, while Jessica intervened to support him.

> There was not hostility, but some reservations, and Jessica became my protector, and would stand up for me in these kinds of relationships with other members of the party. The party apparatus had suffered because it split in 1955, and was badly organised and that was because of the split, so myself and Jessica started to work to re-build the Party in the community. So, together, we would go to Party groups and had discussions, and advise them how to form, how to set up, so we had gone to back, to the East coast the West coast, and the interesting thing was we would go with a bicycle […] that is how it worked. She was very outspoken, very direct, and we would get together in informal gatherings, spent time having discussions.[13]

---

[12] Moses Bhagwan, interview with Claudia Tomlinson (2022).
[13] Ibid.

Bhagwan's assessment of the importance of their contribution during this period was 'the days we bicycled to meetings helping to resuscitate an organization for the PPP'. This critical period for the survival of the PPP was safeguarded by the efforts of leading party activists such as Jessica Huntley.

The Fork in the Road: British Guiana or Britain

Despite her deepening political work, the period of separation from Eric due to his migration was very taxing on Jessica, following so soon after his imprisonment, her eviction from their home, and his subsequent unemployment. After Eric left for London, her sense of isolation and depression at the distance between them deepened. Her emotional bond and commitment to Eric was unbroken. Things were made even more difficult between the couple because of the problems of communication as they now relied on letters going overseas.

There were periods when letters between parties in England and Guiana went missing, meaning lengthy periods without communication, giving rise to anxiety on both sides. Jessica was suspicious about the possible interception of their correspondence by the security services, saying to Eric in one of her early letters to him: 'things seem very shifty. I will let you have a full detail when I see you because I have a strong feeling your letters are being opened.'[14] As time passed, she obtained clear evidence of this and warned Eric further: 'seems as though they are opening your letters. When I received yours yesterday, it was actually opened'.[15] This indicates the possibility that security services may now have had a more focused interest in Jessica's political activities in Britain now that her husband had gone abroad, and she was an independent political actor in the bosom of the PPP. Nonetheless, they continued to correspond very regularly by letter, and Jessica would then also tell him about the emotional toll their separation was having on her:

> I also inquired whether you had already paid down for my passage, let me know because I have being [sic] building all my emotions in leaving B.G by March. If I don't, I'll be terribly frustrated, no kidding ... quite a

---

[14]LMA, HC, LMA/4463/F/01/02/012, Jessica Huntley Letter to Eric Huntley, 19 November 1957.

[15]LMA, HC, LMA/4463/F/01/02/009, Jessica Huntley Letter to Eric Huntley, 18 September 1957.

number of things is responsible for that of course, loneliness, work, etc. So, Mr. Huntley, let nothing come between you, me and where you are ... Some girls do without their husbands for a very long time, however J has already gone through that sort of thing, so she has had quite a lot of that.[16]

The couple, from the evidence of the letters, struggled to, but managed to keep a sense of unity of purpose as a couple, and as a family. But there was no doubt that their attachment and affection for each other remained strong. Jessica chivvied Eric: 'So, darling, I don't know what the future holds for us. Situation seems very precarious. Nevertheless, let's have faith.' She appeared conflicted at times about how, as a prominent woman activist, she should seek and achieve personal agency within her marriage, maintaining a bond with her husband.

From her letters to Eric, it seems she was at times interested in reinforcing traditional gender expectations within marriage, saying to Eric: 'What I do is, if you say to come, I'll come, and if you say stay, I'll stay ... Understand that is definite. I've told Benn that I'll give him, or rather, them, help during the campaigning of course, that was after he came and asked me to do so. Regardless of that, what you say still holds and would hold good. Clear'. She was clear at this point that he would make the decision: 'Eric – Jessica – Elections. What does the future hold, where does Jessica stand at all. What has my husband finally decided.'[17] She was indicating her internal conflict to Eric that she was interested in political participation in British Guiana, but she was aware of her marriage and, it appeared, she wanted Eric to 'command' her to come to England or whatever course of action he decided. She had already made an independent decision to participate in the upcoming campaign in the 1957 general election in Guiana but was very mindful of her marriage and informed her husband that male leadership was the model in their marriage.

This position did not last. This was how Jessica felt in the early months after Eric left, but as time went on, she was drawn back into local politics and re-joined her former colleagues. When she decided to stand in the general election of 1957, it went some way to settle the turmoil she was experiencing and she informed Eric Huntley of her decision: 'I was relieved when I made up my mind to run for elections. Speaking about that, you mentioned that the only way I can be my usual self is by coming to England well when I get there would I not have to work and if I remain here would

---

[16]LMA, HC, LMA/4463/F/01/02/012, Jessica Huntley Letter to Eric Huntley, 28 December 1957.

[17]LMA, HC, LMA/4463/F/01/02/006, Jessica Huntley Letter to Eric Huntley, 19 June 1957.

not things be easier for me.'[18] It would appear that she was anxious about what migrating to England would mean for her and was of the opinion that she was likely to be in a worse situation. In particular, she did not seem to be enticed by the idea of joining the British workforce. Indeed, Eric's assessment of her options were not very appealing, as he wrote in March 1957:

> As regards a job for you over here – the position is this. I mentioned before that the employment situation here is very acute. It is hoped that this will not continue like this for long. You can find a job in a factory, a five-day week. Office work will be difficult. The transport services employ coloured people as conductors etc (you have to be able to calculate in £. s.d).[19]

She was also fiercely anti-imperialist and regarded the West, and Britain was viewed as one of the key oppressive nations. The idea, therefore, of moving to Britain and integrating as a Black woman into this society would have produced a great deal of cognitive dissonance and internal turmoil. After Eric left, she continued to build her political and personal life in Guiana, and her activities indicated she was more likely to remain there rather than move abroad.

Politics remained part of their communication, and Jessica kept Eric updated about political life in British Guiana. In January 1957, soon after his arrival in England, she let him know that 'The political scene is in confusion … Benn is trying to get me to speak at political meetings, I suppose they want me back in for various reasons, I presume. Elections are in the footing now.'[20] Benn, then Chairman of the PPP, approached Jessica on behalf of the Party to invite her to become involved again, and ultimately to stand for election to a seat in the next PPP government by standing in New Amsterdam general elections. Very torn about this decision and aware that the electorate was in a state of confusion by the in-fighting within the PPP she informed Eric: 'the people who will inevitably become more and more confused as it were, with the split. What I do know is that with hard work, they can win a majority, easily, in August.'[21]

During this period, Jessica renewed her contact with the PPP, and her friendship with Janet Jagan and began working as a party activist again. She informed Eric 'my friend J.J. is talking to me and I am speaking to her

---

[18]LMA, HC, LMA/4463/F/01/02/004, Jessica Huntley Letter to Eric Huntley, 29 April 1957.
[19]LMA, HC, LMA/4463/F/01/01/004, Eric Huntley Letter to Jessica Huntley, 18 March 1957.
[20]LMA, HC, LMA/4463/F/01/02/001, Jessica Huntley Letter to Eric Huntley, 5 January 1957.
[21]LMA, HC, LMA/4463/F/01/02/011, Jessica Huntley Letter to Eric Huntley, 19 November 1957.

when she does'. She was employed by the Party as its Organizing Secretary for about a year in 1956, to late 1957, and agrees this was a period 'when I travelled a lot in the country, organising Party groups'. She told Eric in a letter soon after he arrived in Britain, 'I have told Benn I'll give him, or rather, them, a help during the campaigning, of course that was after he came and asked me to do so.' She also said, 'it is the people who will inevitably become more and more confused as it were with the split. I am not on any side, but strictly saying right and wrong.'[22]

To supplement her pay, she also worked in a laundry, next door to the PPP office. She also continued to live at 35 Howes Street while Eric was abroad. The country was facing a racial divide and would be making a choice in the 1957 election, between an Indian or a Black party leadership, the PPP–Jagan or the PPP–Burnham. Jagan's party needed a strong Black campaign, and Jessica was selected to run for the New Amsterdam seat for the 1957 election. If she accepted the offer and won, her future for the next few years would be in Guiana and Eric would need to face years in England alone or make the decision to return. Returning to Guiana at this point would have been difficult for Eric politically and in terms of employment. He was keen for Jessica to join him in England. Once Jessica made up her mind to contest a seat in the 1957 general election, although initially opposed to the idea, Eric accepted it, and supported her in organizing her campaign, albeit from London.

Jessica was fielded by the PPP as a woman activist with its election flyer featuring her image and describing her as: 'Officer of the Women's Section of the PPP. Actively campaigned for the Party in the 1953 elections. One of the founders of the Women's Political Organization: an ardent fighter for peace and freedom in British Guiana, for the rights of women and children.'[23] Jessica was fully committed to her campaign in 1957, and although Eric was in Britain at this time, she had supporters in the PPP as well as in her family and friends.

Jessica was an appealing candidate for the PPP and its supporters but many expressed concerns that she had not been given a safer seat. Her friend Cecily Haynes-Hart said that on the campaign trail, she 'was able to hold her own, she had the crowds with her, people always wanted to hear what she would say next, she was a real rabble rouser'. She was fielded against W.O.R. Worrall, a well-established New Amsterdam, and the incumbent in the seat. He had been resident in the area for many years. She polled 18 per cent of the votes (561 votes) against Kendall's victorious result of 46 per cent or 1,420 votes. Burnham's candidate, fielded under his faction

---

[22]LMA, HC, LMA/4463/F/01/02/011, Jessica Huntley Letter to Eric Huntley, 4 February 1957.
[23]Election Flyer, People's Progressive Party, 1957, Georgetown.

of the PPP in New Amsterdam obtained 22 per cent of the vote, representing the faction that had broken away in 1955 which was the professional middle classes. Many of her supporters felt that if she had been given a safer seat, she would have been victorious, and questions were raised about the seat she was fielded in.

Eric sent word of commiseration on her election defeat: 'I can only guess how tired and disappointed you are now that it is all over. One thing is uppermost in my mind, and I would like you to put it at rest. Will you be joining your husband, and must I go ahead making plans?'[24] He was therefore very keen to persuade Jessica to join him in England.

Undimmed by her defeat, Jessica continued to work for the PPP, her position as one of the leading women's rights activists in the party grew stronger than ever. Editions of *Thunder*, published in 1958 position her as a key figure, reporting: 'Party Organiser Jessica Huntley, and Legislator A. Judah Singh visited Bartica over the last weekend and there held discussions with the Party group. They ... held meetings, and important discussions with the people on their return from Bartica. On Tuesday last, comrades Huntley and Singh visited the Essequibo Coast, and along with Pandit Ramovatar, held several group meetings'. *Thunder* also reported on solo campaign organizing undertaken by Jessica: 'Mrs Jessica Huntley paid visits to Party Groups at Anna Catharina, and Blankenburg, West Coast Demerara, during the past week.' The report of the Women's Section of the People's Progressive Party, reported in *Thunder* that: 'Mrs Jessica Huntley, Secretary of the Section, read her report for 1957. She stated that the section had a fine record during the year, but much more could have been done. She stressed that there was need for a greater contribution by women in the political field.'

It is likely that Jessica wanted to remain in British Guiana where she had a bright political future with the PPP, and once they returned to victory in 1957, she continued to work for them. It is also probable that her decision to walk away from a political career in Guiana at this time was because she was married, and her husband was abroad, and a re-unification between the couple was also a priority. Best friend Cecily Haynes-Hart concludes that Jessica's commitment to her marriage was the reason she chose to walk away from a political career in Guiana: 'because Eric wanted her here [England], Eric had already left and they had put her up for a parliamentary candidate in the election, and she wanted to do that, and Eric wanted her not to do that, and to come to join him in England'.[25]

---

[24]LMA, HC, LMA/4463/F/01/01/006, Eric Huntley Letter to Jessica Huntley, 18 May 1957.

[25]Cecily Haynes-Hart, interview with Andrews.

Jessica had a very large network of not only party workers, and family members, but also a large group of friends who lamented her planned departure for Britain. Her long-standing childhood friend, Cecily Haynes-Hart, wrote to her in April 1958 of another female friend's upset at Jessica's departure and her thoughts on Jessica's prospects in Britain: 'said she was hoping to see you, did not know you were leaving so early, and a lot of sentimental stuff about you ... The darn thing is, all they're saying is true. You're really a swell girl and that is why I know you'll make good in England. As I told Aunt last night, we'll be looking forward to meeting Dr Eric Huntley and Dr Jessica Huntley'. Torn by what she was leaving behind, including her two young sons and her beloved mother, Jessica finally made the decision to leave, and started her preparations to leave British Guiana for Britain.

7

An Old Fight in a New Place

Jessica left British Guiana on 11 April 1958 and made the journey to Trinidad and Tobago by 'Bookers' boat, the shipping arm of the giant sugar corporation. This was the first leg of her journey to Britain. She then sailed from Trinidad on 15 April 1958, on the *Antilles* which docked at Plymouth on 28 April 1958.[1] She was passenger 141 of 179 passengers, and she was listed as a 31-year-old housewife. Her passport stamped her planned stay in England as 'indefinite'. Her address was given as 82 Great Cambridge Road, Tottenham, in Haringey, north London, where Eric was living at this time.

She had a very slight frame from a lifetime of frugal meals and looked not much older than twenty years of age. She was dressed in European clothes, prepared for her first experience of winter. Her hair was 'pressed', by passing an iron comb that had been heated on open flames through her curly African hair to straighten it. The straightened hair would then be put in curlers, or strips of rolled up newspaper if the budget was limited, then styled to resemble European hairstyles of the period. This was a common practice at the time among West Indian girls and women who would always press and curl their hair when attending special or formal events and occasions. It was less common for men to press their hair, but they would sometimes also do so for very special events such as weddings. Black American performing artists such as Chubby Checker, Chuck Berry and Jackie Wilson led the way in this trend. It was then an accepted practice among Black people around the world. It would be some years before pressing and curling Black hair would be politically contested and rejected as a form of anti-African expression. This would form a major part of the self-decolonization and decolonization work that Jessica herself would later become involved in. Her chiselled bone structure, in a small face, emphasized her eyes. Her expression was sombre, quiet and thoughtful in repose. But her smile lit up and warmed those upon

---

[1]'All UK and Ireland, Incoming Passenger Lists, 1878–1960', Ancestry Collections, https://www.ancestry.co.uk/search/collections/1518/.

whom she bestowed it, travelling as it always did up to her eyes. Those hearing her infectious laugh found it impossible not to be uplifted and join in the brightened mood. She was very serious, but warm and outgoing, and naturally attracted people to her.

When she broke her journey in Trinidad, she exchanged letters with her friends and family. It was also in Trinidad that she met John and Irma La Rose for the first time, as she visited them while waiting for her ship to England. The La Roses, a young married couple, also Caribbean intellectuals, and progressive anti-colonial political activists, would form a lifelong personal and political relationship with Jessica, and Eric Huntley in Britain. Eric had made the same stopover with the La Roses on his journey to England a year earlier. He had been introduced to the La Roses by the People's Progressive Party (PPP) which supported its travelling comrades by connecting them to the network of sympathizers in other countries.

Jessica dealt with the pain of separation from her children, mother, brothers, friends and her homeland with great fortitude. Many mourned her departure from British Guiana. Her close ally and friend of many years, Janet Jagan, pledged to send her copies of *Thunder* to England, and counted Jessica among the good comrades that the PPP had now lost, expressing the sentiment: 'I hope you will not stay away too long.'[2] Her PPP comrade and friend, Moses Bhagwan, sent her a letter which she received in Trinidad saying that he had anticipated he would miss her and her departure would be a loss. He told her: 'now you are gone, the loss is even more difficult to bear'.[3] He also wrote, 'I shall always have two thoughts of you, the first as a comrade in our struggle, and in the second place, as a personal friend. I can hardly say in which role you helped and taught me more.'[4]

Cecily Haynes-Hart wept uncontrollably at her friend's departure and informed Jessica of this fact: 'call me Baby, or what the devil you like, I cried, and that's that'.[5] She went on: 'well you can imagine my state of mind on Mon night – couldn't eat, couldn't talk, all nerves'.[6] This was due to the thought of her friend making this major journey that potentially risked severing a lifelong friendship. Cecily also wrote to Jessica about how much her many other friends would miss her, but all knew she would do well. In fact, with much foresight, Cecily said 'I told Aunt last night, we'll soon be meeting Dr. Eric Huntley and Dr. Jessica Huntley. If they are Doctors of Medicine, we will arrange to get sick for spite.'[7] Decades later, Jessica would go on to be

---

[2] LMA, HC, LMA/4463/F/01/06/008, Janet Jagan Letter to Jessica Huntley, 16 May 1958.
[3] LMA, HC, LMA/4463/F/01/06/004, Moses Bhagwan Letter to Jessica Huntley, 29 April 1958.
[4] Ibid.
[5] LMA, HC, LMA/4463/F/01/06/07, Cecily Haynes-Hart Letter to Jessica Huntley, 14 April 1958.
[6] Ibid.
[7] Ibid.

awarded an honorary doctorate in London, and Eric would also become the recipient of multiple awards and tributes for his work in fighting racialized injustices Britain.

A Taste of Freedom in Eastern Europe

When she arrived in Britain in April 1958, Jessica only spent a few weeks there before she departed in June 1958 for Eastern Europe. The time for her to fully settle down to life with Eric in London was postponed by this trip. She spent time in Eastern Europe in June 1958, in Austria and Hungary, for the Fourth Congress of the Women's International Democratic Federation (WIDF), held in June. She represented British Guiana as its delegate, and more specifically the delegate of the PPP where she had just left her job as Organizing Secretary for the Party. This was pioneering as she would have been among the first Black women from British Guiana to represent her country at an international conference and may have been the first to represent the government of her country. Attendance at this conference was the final direct duty she carried out on behalf of the PPP and government of British Guiana.

FIGURE 7.1 *Jessica Huntley seated at the WIDF Conference in Hungary, 1958. Courtesy of the Huntley Collection, London Metropolitan Archives.*

The WIDF was an important organization for women activists from colonized countries because it was one of the few organizations that provided a platform for these women to contribute ideas on an international stage at this time.[8] It was founded in 1945 and stated that its principal objectives were to contribute to halting the spread of global conflict in the form of major wars, to campaign for the rights of women, and to provide better lives for children. It was based in East Berlin between 1951 and 1991, and was strongly associated with Eastern European communist philosophies, due to its anti-war stance, its commitments to the advancement of women in the Third World and its anti-colonialism. The PPP's association with the WIDF formed part of the British government's narrative in its justification for overthrowing the 1953 democratically elected government in British Guiana. Britain criticized an action by Janet Jagan when she sought to build international support for the independence movement in British Guiana:

> In May 1953, a body known as the Women's Progressive Organization was formed at a meeting held in Georgetown by Mrs Jagan, and a decision taken to apply for affiliation to the Communist controlled Women's International Democratic Federation (headquarters Soviet sector of Berlin). Immediately afterwards Mrs Jagan left for Copenhagen to attend the Third World Congress of Women organised by the WIDF. Mrs Jagan was elected to the Congress Presidium. In a speech she said "We need guidance and help ... We in the colonial world are tied economically and politically like the slaves of old ... Our people turn their eyes to the great socialist countries which have been moving forward with great rapidity and success ... Help us to win freedom for all the oppressed colonial peoples of the world.[9]

This demand by Janet Jagan for anti-colonialism in Guiana was re-cast as dangerous communism. It was from a progressive politician, and about countries seeking freedom from capitalist oppression and British coloniality. This was not evidence that the WIDF was a communist-controlled organization or that the PPP and the Women's Progressive Organization (WPO) were seeking to transform Guiana into a Communist state, but a plea for freedom from racialized capitalism. As co-founder of the PPP and

---

[8] Yulia Gradskova, 'Women's International Democratic Federation, the "Third World" and the Global Cold War From the Late-1950s to the Mid-1960s', *Women's History Review*, 29 (2019), pp.270–88, esp. p.274.

[9] Labour History Archive, Papers by Workers Party of Jamaica, and People's Progressive Party, CP/CENT/INT/31/04 (14), British Guiana: Suspension of the Constitution, 20 October 1953.

the WPO, and a close comrade of Janet Jagan, Jessica would have been fully briefed about the WIDF and its role on the world stage. That she was selected by Janet Jagan as the most suitable Guianese woman delegate to represent the PPP, and the country, on this important platform points to the importance in which Jessica Huntley was held.

The objectives of the conference were the liberation of women from domesticity, freedom to work and nuclear disarmament. For Jessica and the other delegates from colonized regimes these objectives were unlikely to have been regarded as the most important concerns. For example, a hundred years prior to this conference, slavery had not long been fully abolished. Colonized Black women were not fighting for the right to work, their fight was for access to all jobs, not only those menial jobs that exploited them and kept them in servitude and penury. However, there were elements of the Congress Manifesto more likely to resonate with women living under colonial rule. For example, the Manifesto pledged its commitment to: 'a world free from hatred and racism where all children will be able to know to understand, and to love one another'.[10] It also agreed that 'We support all women who are struggling for national independence and who are victims of repression. We demand that the governments respect the principles of national independence and human rights as embodied in the Charter of the United Nations.'[11]

Jessica was not a seasoned traveller. She wrote to her husband that she found the conference 'very fatiguing and has taken quite a strain on me'.[12] The conference day was very long and she shared with Eric, by letter, that 'the Congress is now in its last session, it is now 10 o'clock in the night and will certainly go a long way'.[13] She also confessed to Eric that 'today I feel homesick wanted to come home'.[14] After a week in Austria, she travelled to Budapest, where she had been invited for an extended period, by the National Council Hungarian Women, for further conference activities. The second letter sent to Eric was from Jessica's hotel in Budapest, Hungary. Her fatigue and the congested programme continued, as she informed Eric in London: 'darling, I can hardly afford to write you because I am so tired. I arrived in Hungary at 11:30pm and got to my hotel at 12pm, 1 o'clock. Since then, I am having a very heavy programme and there seems little rest for me'.[15]

---

[10] Ibid., p.160.
[11] Ibid.
[12] LMA, HC, LMA/4463/F/01/02/015, Jessica Huntley Letter to Eric Huntley, 5 June 1958.
[13] Ibid.
[14] Ibid.
[15] Ibid.

Her few weeks in Eastern Europe gave her a greater sense of inclusion compared with life in Guiana, and expressed that 'the people of Hungary are at their best in welcoming me and I sincerely feel not as a stranger but as part of the human race'.[16] Taking a more light-hearted view with her husband, she told him 'you never told me I have nice eyes and smiling teeth and a fascinating figure, well I've been told all that here in Austria'.[17] This was a happy experience for Jessica.

The distance from Guiana strengthened her view of oppression in her homeland. She stated angrily in her communication to Eric that 'the people in British Guiana want some shaking to let them realize their responsibilities as a people who should strive very hard against the system of those bastards'.[18] She felt that many at home were sustaining colonial structures through their political inactivity and acceptance of their oppression. She wanted to see them railing up against all that was injuring the progress of Guianese people. She dedicated her entire career to educating others and alerting them to the possibilities for change and national liberation.

At the conference, Jessica made a speech about the condition of British Guiana that clearly chimed with the themes of the conference, but also highlighted her past and ongoing struggles:

> On behalf of the Women's Section of the People's Progressive Party, I bring to this Fourth Congress of the WIDF, our warmest greeting. We hope that this great meeting of women will grow from strength to strength and that all of its deliberations will be taken to the respective countries. You no doubt would like to know something of our country.
>
> British Guiana is the only British possession in South America and first attracted the attention of the navigators in the fifteenth century by the rumours that the streets of its city of Eldorado were paved with gold. Its population is over half a million and made up of six peoples – Africans, East Indians, Portuguese, Chinese, Aboriginal Indians or Arawaks and Whites.
>
> Our history is one of great struggles against poverty and misery and a will to rule ourselves. In 1953, a change came about in our country, a People's Movement was born and it has consistently championed the cause of all of its peoples. In this period, women saw a new awakening and the Women's Progressive Organization was formed. Women won the right to vote at the age of 21. Then came a period of repression, our

---

[16] Ibid.
[17] Ibid.
[18] Ibid.

country was in a state of emergency, British troops landed, homes were searched, leading members of the Freedom movement were detained without trial, and many were imprisoned. They threatened to halt our Women's Movement which was spearheading, among other demands for women, Social Security for mother and child, Natal and Pre-Natal Care, the right to be jurors etc.

In the field of labour, women are employed in nearly every field, but daily, as a result of modern equipment, women and girls are being replaced by men. Only two months ago, domestic servants were drafted into the Compensation Ordinance.

Juvenile delinquency is a burning question at the moment. Data from 1956 showed that 620 children and young people were found guilty of offences, an increase of 89 over 1955. The rate of delinquency was 5.57 per 1,000 in 1955, and 5.85 per thousand in 1956. Fully up to date data for 1957 is not yet to hand. Our women feel strongly on the matter. The growing number of delinquents is caused by the dumping of comics, bad films and the growing number of unemployed young people.[19]

This address was for an international audience and on behalf of British Guiana's government rather than a personal address. It had to address a number of conference conventions including the issuing of comradely greetings, scene setting and the geopolitical context. Her individual voice and views could be detected most clearly when she spoke about the rise of the women's movement which she had co-founded within the Party. The Compensation Ordinance refers to the Workmen's Compensation Ordinance, a scheme underpinned by legislation in Britain to provide compensation for injuries incurred during the course of work. The conference theme included children and youth which would have, in part, prompted the inclusion of her remarks on juvenile delinquency.

As someone involved in youth club activities and teaching young people in church, she would have been acutely aware of the issues. Also, growing up in the tenement yard, she was aware of young people who drifted into delinquency. British Guiana had a network of cinemas since the 1930s. Most of the films were imported from the United States, but also from England and from India. Westerns were popular and it can be imagined that these were the films Jessica was referring to in her speech.

---

[19]IVth Congress of the Women's International Democratic Federation: Plenary Session, 'British Guiana, Mrs Jessica Huntley, Delegate of the Women's Section of the People's Progressive Party' 1958, p.38.

A New Reality of Blackness – Life in Britain

After the tour of Eastern Europe, Jessica returned to London to settle into her new life. She had mixed emotions about starting a new unknown journey in Britain. She was now removed from the highs of running for a seat in a national election in her beloved home nation. She had also just experienced weeks of immersion in intense intellectual work at her first international conference where she met like-minded socialist women comrades from the Soviet nations she admired for their progressive stance towards women and workers. There she had been treated with respect and equality and she had listened to messages of support for the liberation of colonized people.

Jessica was now faced with leaving all of that behind to become an ordinary Black immigrant worker and having to find work, perhaps in a factory or hospital. To do so in a country whose colonial policies she had spent years working to dismantle was a depressing prospect. Whilst very happy to be reunited with her husband, eighteen months had passed since they last lived together. This new married life was one that was unfamiliar to both of them. They were away from their friends, family and community networks, they had to forge a new way of being together, almost as a new couple. She had to learn who she was in this new setting, to learn who her husband had become and what sort of life they would be building together in Britain. She would also have had to embrace the primary identity of 'wife', something which she had not faced for some time. Previously, her main identity had been as a party-political activist and parliamentary candidate while her husband had been abroad.

Jessica was unhappy with her new life and immediately disliked Britain on arrival. Like many arrivals from the West Indies, she was determined that it would not be her permanent home, saying: 'I came to England, never to stay, not even for the "five years" that was talked about then. Eric came a year before I did, and even though I came to join him, I didn't like it here. I didn't like it here at all ... So many things I didn't like.'[20] She recalled the plan agreed between the couple was that 'Eric was supposed to study, and we go back.'[21] She found this early period in Britain almost intolerable, particularly how she was treated by Britons. She recalled: 'the unfriendliness of people, that surprised me,' cos it's like a shockwave you know. I couldn't believe the lack of humanity. And I don't even want to use the word "prejudice" because it's a new word you know, the unfriendliness, the coldness and the mask ... like is given for a smile. And that deep down there was this hatred they had of you.'[22]

---

[20] Carol Sidney, '60:60, Jessica Huntley, a Lifetime of Publishing', *Sable*, Spring (2005), p.95.

[21] Ibid., p.99.

[22] Mike Phillips and Trevor Philips, *Windrush: The Irresistible Rise of Multi-Racial Britain* (London: HarperCollins, 1998), p.127.

Back home, she had known of successful people from the Caribbean, particularly writers, who had made their mark in England, and the prospect of meeting them was something that lifted her mood. Her friends, Lionel and Pansy Jeffrey, who had already lived in England since the late 1940s, told Jessica and Eric about the Caribbean writers who were making their mark in Britain. She later wrote in an article that 'the Jeffreys so stirred our interest that I looked forward to meeting and reading these writers. At that time, I had no idea that I would find myself sailing for England soon to live among the very writers I so admired.'[23] Therefore, the idea of finding a familiar Caribbean community in Britain was a hopeful prospect for Jessica. She was later to become a friend and associate of Sam Selvon, the Trinidadian writer, and she made it a priority to become familiar with his work soon after arrival:

> On my arrival (in England), one of the first purchases I made was a copy of *The Lonely Londoners*. I was fascinated by its humour and descriptions of living in London and wondered whether the writer had experienced some of what he was so ably describing. The copy of *Lonely Londoners* was passed round from friend to friend, read aloud to each other, and took the place of a community newspaper.[24]

Jessica's interest in literature and the value of books was an embedded part of her consciousness years before she entered the world of publishing.

Renewing relationships with her old friends from back home who were now in Britain also helped Jessica to settle into her new life. Her friend Waveney Bushell (1928–) had travelled to London in 1956 to train as a teacher. In British Guiana, they knew each other through Jessica's best friend Cecily Haynes-Hart but were not particularly close. This changed when Jessica arrived in London two years later and she bumped into Waveney who recalls they:

> … met in North London, and we stood up and talked for a while, she happened to be living not far from where I lived, and we met, not by design, but we would meet up often like on Saturdays while we were going shopping, and we became friends. She invited me to her home, and I invited her to my home. And her children had come up to live with her and Eric, and I suppose because I was teaching, we had similar interests.[25]

---

[23] Jessica Huntley, 'Nostalgic Moments', *Kunapipi*, 17 (1995), pp.56–7, esp. p.56. https://ro.uow.edu.au/kunapipi/vol17/iss1/1/ (last accessed 17 June 2022).

[24] Ibid.

[25] Waveney Bushell, interview with Claudia Tomlinson.

Waveney had been aware of Jessica's profile back home, as 'she was very well known ... I think I sort of looked at her with awe, as there was this young woman, competing with men to be a Member of Parliament'. Bushell has described how Jessica was very active in politics in Guiana:

> This was a particularly significant time in Guyana's history as we hadn't too long had our Constitution suspended because of this very political party of which she was a member. British soldiers had been sent to Guyana because of this assumption by the British Government that Guyana was on the brink of rioting. So, soldiers had come to Guyana as a result of that political party, and Jessica was a member.[26]

Struggling to settle in England, Jessica was now able to witness for herself the heavy working lives Black immigrants experienced in Britain at this time. Since his arrival in London in January 1957, Eric had been engaged in a series of arduous jobs including working long hours at the Mount Pleasant Sorting Post Office. He frequently worked back-to-back shifts, day and night. He found solace in the company of the many West Indian immigrant workers who were doing the same long shifts, and like him, saving to send money back home to help their families survive. Eric had planned to study for a degree in Economics at Croydon College but found that he needed to study for A level exams first. He became ill during this period and was unable to work or study and was not able to pursue the degree course. He spent a period of time out of work, and later also did casual work such as in factories.

Jessica was eventually successful in obtaining employment in clerical and secretarial work throughout her period as an employed worker in England. This was a significant achievement given that the roles open to women without professional qualifications, such as teaching and nursing, were menial in nature, including cleaning and factory work. She worked for a shipping company and for the Ministry of Pensions based in Haringey, London. She was also employed by a magazine publisher in Fleet Street, at Collett's bookshop, and at a firm of solicitors in Ealing. While this success was cause for celebration, it was tempered by the fact that like most arrivals from the Caribbean, she experienced her share of overt, lawful racial discrimination.

One example of the racial discrimination she faced was when she went to the Labour Exchange in Manor House, London, and was sent for an interview to the Ministry of Pensions nearby. After her interview with the manager, she was offered a position and given a starting date. Satisfied, she went to her home nearby, a few minutes' walk from the Labour Exchange,

---

[26]Ibid.

and the Ministry of Pensions. A short while after settling down at home there was a knock at the door and Jessica was surprised to see the company manager from the Ministry of Pensions who had just interviewed her, on her doorstep. She let him in and listened as he tried to persuade her not to accept the job, telling her that the company was not somewhere she would want to work, and that she would not enjoy the job. Jessica insisted that whatever the conditions or hardships the job presented she would face it. She told him she would accept the job offered and start on the day agreed, no matter what. The manager left the house unsuccessful in persuading a confused but resolute Jessica to withdraw from the job offer.

She was later to learn that after she had left the interview earlier, the staff team had been made aware that a Black staff member was going to join their all-white team. They complained about it bitterly to the manager, prompting his hurried visit to Jessica's home. She appeared to be the first Black worker in that company and managed to survive what was probably a hostile and unfriendly environment, and she worked there for many years. Given her background and political perspective, she didn't fit in with the culture and interests of the company and its attitudes, and therefore it is a considerable achievement that she worked there for so long. It had a strong, organized union which meant that Jessica would know she had certain workplace protections. She was active in this workplace union and became its Assistant Treasurer.[27]

Finding and keeping suitable accommodation was also a difficult experience for the couple, and after arrival in London, Jessica lived with Eric in a series of rented boarding rooms. This was the story for most West Indian immigrants during this period resulting in an unstable housing situation. With no legislative protections and a strong anti-immigrant climate, landlords had the upper hand. Eric recalled: 'when I was living here as a bachelor, and with Jessica on our own, accommodation was a very serious problem. We lived in north London about five or six years, and we moved about ten times.'[28] While the couple were living in Hornsey, London, Eric said: 'the landlords had the heavy stake over the tenant, tenants did not have rights at all. So, if you slammed the door, or if you had a party, or if you cooked and it was curry and the scent was too much for the noses of the landlords, you'd get a notice to remove.'[29] He also described notices in the toilet warning tenants to beware 'how you slammed the front door, how you rang the bell, what time you came in, and the friends who came to visit and so on'.[30] The frequent movement of both homes and jobs was also

---

[27] Phillips and Phillips, *Windrush*, p.127.

[28] Eric Huntley, interview with Claudia Tomlinson.

[29] Ibid.

[30] Ibid.

a way of maintaining a level of control in the face of oppression at work and in their rented homes. Jessica remarked: 'jobs and accommodation of sorts were available, and so many of us took no nonsense from employers or landlords alike but looked for new jobs as well as accommodation at the slightest hint of prejudice or discrimination. I believe this attitude was typical of many like myself. Of course, it worked both ways for there was no security of either employment or accommodation.'[31] Despite these challenges, Jessica and Eric eventually found a new and comfortable life together in Britain, helped by friendships and networks, but with the ever-present thoughts of home and the family they left behind.

Reuniting the Family in Britain

Jessica and Eric's concerns about their children back home in Guiana grew because Karl and Chauncey were still very young. The children had been without their father for an extended period after he left in December 1956, and now their mother had left also. This had followed the period of family turbulence of their father's imprisonment, the family's eviction from their home in the Post Office and their return to live with their grandmother. Jessica and Eric now relied on correspondence from home to keep them informed. Cecily Haynes-Hart as well as Hectorine were the main informants.

Cecily played a major role in looking after Karl, Chauncey and Hectorine after Jessica moved to England. She let Jessica and Eric know that the eldest son Karl had 'outgrown most of his shyness and enters more freely into conversation. He would not start it, but once it is started and you are tactful enough, you can get him to talk quite a lot.'[32] Jessica was informed that Chauncey was also developing well, in a different, more confident, direction to his brother, and according to Cecily, 'he is very intelligent, and if he does not change, we should expect a lot from him. He has a very firm will and unless you can show him very good reason for changing his beliefs, then you are wasting your time.'[33] While Cecily's correspondence provided reliable information, Jessica questioned her mother, Hectorine, closely to ensure all was well.

---

[31]LMA, HC, LMA/4463/D/05/01/002, Draft Notes of a Speech for the Conference on Afro-Caribbean Youth: Succeeding by Overcoming Racism Posed by Society, 1983–1984.

[32]Cecily Haynes-Hart Letter to Jessica Huntley, 17 January 1960, Huntley Collection, London Metropolitan Archives, LMA/4463/F/01/06/007.

[33]Ibid.

Hectorine wrote to inform Jessica and Eric about their children's progress and about her ability to look after them. She informed the parents that 'Ken is in hospital, he was admitted on the 28th December 1958, his operation was successful thank God'.[34] In this same letter to Jessica, her mother remarked that 'Chauncey is disappointed in your sticking to the bargain in coming back home. He said you told him you will be back next Christmas, and two Christmases have gone and not yet returned (smile). So, you see you have committed yourself.'[35] Undoubtedly, this desire for her daughter to return home was also felt by Hectorine, as well as Jessica and Eric's children, particularly Chauncey. By May 1959, it was clear that Hectorine, getting older, was finding it more difficult to manage her young grandsons on many levels. She informed her daughter and son-in-law about Chauncey, 'at one time he will come and hug and squeeze and kiss me, but he is very wild and you can't tell him anything'.[36] But she informed Jessica, through mild jest, of her advancing years, 'the old lady's bones will ache at times, but thank God, not the worse for it. He is retaining my strength for you and your children's sake, I think.'[37]

Hectorine was wholly dependent on income from family members as she was now ageing and not working. She struggled to meet the basic necessities of living for herself and her grandsons. But with both Jessica and Eric working in England, they were able to send sufficient money and goods to ensure the family in Guiana were comfortable, and this appeared to be the case in February 1960 when Hectorine wrote to her daughter that: 'the cash which comes from you both is received without any trouble. The boxes (two) came safely. The boys' toys came, and the other box had pants, overcoat, bath towels, pyjamas, slacks, shirts, the cowboy suits, also hat, nightdresses.'[38] In this same letter, Hectorine assured Jessica and Eric in the that 'there is [sic] no debts whatsoever. It sounds ridiculous to think that way. No, my dear children, things are going fair. I am just asking the Lord to strengthen [sic] to care for your children.' Hectorine and the boys were not the only beneficiaries of Jessica and Eric's new income in England. They also sent money and supplies to an array of other relatives and friends who were supported in Guiana by the income Jessica and Eric earned in England during this period.

---

[34]LMA, HC, LMA/4463/F/01/05/003, Hectorine Carroll Letter to Jessica Huntley, 3 January 1959.

[35]Ibid.

[36]LMA, HC, LMA/4463/F/01/05/003, Hectorine Carroll Letter to Jessica Huntley, 1 May 1959.

[37]LMA, HC, LMA/4463/F/01/05/003, Hectorine Carroll Letter to Jessica Huntley, 20 August 1960.

[38]LMA, HC, LMA/4463/F/01/05/003, Hectorine Carroll Letter to Jessica Huntley, 6 February 1960.

Despite being able to provide for her mother, Jessica was concerned that the money she was sending would not completely ameliorate the risk of hunger for her mother and her sons. Hectorine had battled hunger with her own children thirty years earlier. She was being provided with money by her daughter, but she had no earnings herself and the debts started to grow again. Jessica was careful to keep track of this risk when she was in England, and this irritated Hectorine. In response to an apparent query from Jessica about this, Hectorine remonstrated with her daughter:

> My dear girl you are not to worry about our diet at all. I do not think you want me to outline our daily meals, do you? I am assuring you that the main thing to procure such foods is being provided by that Great God who gives you both the strength to do what you are doing, so why worry dear? We are very happy to enjoy all that He provides for us.[39]

Jessica respected her mother's Christian views, but by this time she had herself moved away from being a practising Christian. Word of this reached Hectorine and it caused her much grief in Guiana. In fact, Hectorine broached the subject with Cecily who promptly wrote to Jessica seeking a compromise between mother and daughter on the subject:

> On the question of prayer, Aunt has told me you no longer believe in God. You can't imagine how worried she is about it. Every time I see her, that is the main theme of her conversation. She says all the good you are doing for her is marred by that one big thing. Please try to humour her. Even if you have to tell her it was all a joke. Of course, you know my old policy of not interfering with a person's religious beliefs. So far, I still believe in God. If you have found a new and better religion, who am I to interfere? But anyway, please don't grieve Aunt further. Most of us poor colonials still hold onto our old religious beliefs and customs.[40]

Cecily was trying to alleviate the distress and anxiety in Hectorine that she was not only losing her daughter to another country, but perhaps a bigger loss in her eyes, losing her from the Christian faith. This was not the first time that Hectorine had to confront this fear. Although a PPP supporter, and a backer of her daughter's political work, Hectorine had to contend with taunts in Georgetown market that communists don't believe in God and her daughter had aligned herself with that ideological belief. Considering

---

[39] LMA, HC, LMA/4463/F/01/05/003, Hectorine Carroll Letter to Jessica Huntley, 30 July 1960.

[40] LMA, HC, LMA/4463/F/01/06/007, Cecily Haynes-Hart Letter to Jessica Huntley, 17 January 1960.

that Hectorine had devoted many years to carefully bringing Jessica up as a Christian, it was a difficult situation to accept. Additionally, Hectorine was so devout that she feared this new lack of faith would have adverse consequences for Jessica.

Jessica's bigger fears were for the very survival of her mother and children who she knew were going hungry in Guiana. These fears came true when only a few months later, Hectorine was forced to admit that this was now the situation in one of her letters to Jessica and Eric, she admitted there were occasions when she was not able to feed the children:

> My dear girl, I am very sorry I have to write you in this strain, but better cannot be done. Things are not what it should be with the financial side, funds are very low, and when I ask Munroe for help, he does not behave very nicely in his manner. The poor boys have sometimes to go without their regular meals. It grieves me to send to tell you this. When the money comes, I have to try to fulfil all the debts I make so nothing remains in my hand.[41]

Jessica and Eric then received further worrying news from Guiana that Hectorine had been served notice to leave Howes Street, the tenement yard that had been her home since the 1930s. She was expected to move out soon: 'a notice has been served to me for the house to be delivered at month end'.[42] It appears that the tenement rooms were undergoing repairs. Hectorine had not found other accommodation and in July 1960 she was still in Howes Street, informing her daughter: 'I mentioned about the notice we all received, but my dears that getting of a house will indeed be a big problem. I am very much concerned on getting out the yard, but it is not so easy to get a place, even if you are prepared to pay the $50 or $40 per month, so to get out means waiting a long time.'[43] It was December 1960 when the family moved from Howes Street to their new home at No. 9 Durban Street, Georgetown.

By the end of 1960 however, Jessica and Eric decided that the time had come to send for their children and their grandmother to come to England. They had been saving funds for their passages. Hectorine was relaxed about the suggestion of moving to England and wrote to her daughter: 'my dear what about that fancy joke you sent about coming over there. Are you serious? Where is this money coming from for the three of us? I guess it

---

[41] LMA, HC, LMA/4463/F/01/05/003, Hectorine Carroll Letter to Jessica Huntley, 10 December 1960.
[42] Ibid.
[43] LMA, HC, LMA/4463/F/01/05/003, Hectorine Carroll Letter to Jessica Huntley, 9 July 1960.

will cost you a big bite. Anyway, whatever will be will be.'⁴⁴ Doris Alleyne, a local teacher in Guiana and family friend, reinforced Jessica's view that the time had come for the family in Guiana to get more support from those that had migrated to Britain, and she wrote: 'I must add to your thoughts of sending for mother and boys as an appropriate thing. I helped to strengthen her willingness to accept the offer ... I think the boys do need stronger handling as they grow, which she would not be able to give of her best, a few years from now.'⁴⁵

Jessica and Eric were relieved to receive letters from their children showing how their education had progressed, as well as news of their activities and happiness. They were reassured by Chauncey who informed them that he was 'going to school and getting on with my work, dad, I'm having all the toys you and mum sent me'. He informed his parents that he had been to the school fair, Sunday school, and had flown his kite at the Sea Wall. He also informed his parents that he and his brother Ken (Karl) looked sharp in the suits their parents had sent for them from England. It would undoubtedly have gladdened Jessica to receive word from Chauncey at home: 'My dear Mother, I have passed my examinations, and am very glad, and Grannie was glad too. I know you and Daddy would be glad too.'⁴⁶

By 1961, plans to bring over Hectorine, Chauncey and Karl were very advanced, and the couple received a letter of recommendation sent by St Philips Anglican school to enable them to obtain a school place for the children in England:

> ... this is to certify that both Karl and Chauncey Huntley were both pupils at the above named elementary school, up to their time of departure from British Guiana. Their conduct has been very good and their attendance regular and punctual. They have been making good progress at school, always showing a keen interest in its activities. I hope they would be considered favourably for admission in a school in the United Kingdom. They deserve such consideration, and I take pleasure in recommending them.⁴⁷

With the plan to bring Hectorine and the children over now at an advanced stage, Jessica and Eric also needed a flat or a house as they would be a family of five and could not share a room in London. The couple saved

---

⁴⁴LMA, HC, LMA/4463/F/01/05/003, Hectorine Carroll Letter to Jessica Huntley, 4 June 1960.

⁴⁵LMA, HC, LMA/4463/F/01/06/002, Doris Alleyne Letter to Jessica Huntley, 30 August 1960.

⁴⁶LMA, HC, LMA/4463/F/01/04/001, Chauncey Huntley Letter to Jessica and Eric Huntley, undated, circa 1960.

⁴⁷LMA, HC, LMA/4463/F/01/04/001, Letter from Headteacher, St Philips Anglican School, Georgetown, British Guiana, 19 July 1961.

FIGURE 7.2 *Hectorine Carroll in Guyana with grandsons Karl Huntley, Chauncey Huntley and son Munroe Carroll preparing to travel to England, 1961. Courtesy of the Huntley Collection, London Metropolitan Archives.*

enough to buy a house in Walthamstow, East London, at 21 Haroldstone Road, with a significant saved deposit of around £300. However, they did not move in before Hectorine and the children arrived, so they stayed in their flat in Wood Green before moving to Haroldstone Road.

Jessica had been away from her children for more than three years when they arrived, in 1961, and Eric had not seen them for almost five years. They were almost like strangers to each other and had to build a new family life in a different country. Given the instability of their housing and work experience since arrival in Britain, Jessica felt the couple made the right decision to delay sending for their children. Her reasoning was, 'my first three years of living in London was spent both moving house and jobs. Fortunately, my two children did not join us until 1961 when we were able to move to our own home, and so spared hassles of having our children here and being tenants.'[48]

---

[48]LMA, HC, LMA/4463/D/05/01/002, Draft Notes of a Speech for the Conference on Afro-Caribbean Youth: Succeeding by Overcoming Racism Posed by Society, 1983–1984.

The initial experience faced by the boys on arrival, when the family lived in East London, was relatively favourable. Jessica's recollection of this time was that:

> My two sons, having arrived during the summer of 1961 we moved from rented accommodation to Walthamstow in East London. My two sons also had pleasurable beginnings of sorts, children from around the area from where we lived came to the house and welcomed them. They became acquainted with each other before school re-opened after the summer recess. I believe the headmaster must have told them they were expecting two new arrivals from overseas and that such a welcome would be good. Looking back to the period, although we lived in East London, which is a reputedly a hotbed of the racists and fascists, they appeared on the TV screens campaigning that we should be sent back home, the economic situation had not yet taken a turn for the worse and so relationships where we lived were good. The children in the street shared with our son's birthday party and the unhappiness when one of my sons was knocked down by a passing car and taken to hospital.[49]

The grandmother, Hectorine, adapted very quickly to life in England. Her first winter was very severe and despite her age she withstood it very well. She dedicated time to looking after the family and the home. It was a great reassurance to Jessica and Eric to have her at their home. Hectorine was only to stay a short time in England however because of tragedy in the family. While she was in England, her second son Munroe, the charismatic body builder, died in Guiana following an accident. Hectorine was brokenhearted, and although Jessica and Eric were very keen for her to settle permanently with them in Britain, Hectorine returned to Guiana around 1962 where she lived for the remainder of her life.

---

[49]Ibid.

8

Finding a Foothold in Activism in Britain

Despite the burdens and anxieties about the family back home, Jessica immediately embarked on her political work in Britain, devoting the first years to establishing alliances and co-operating with a number of organizations and campaigns. The first three political organizations she became involved in mirrored her political career in British Guiana. The first of these was the British Guiana Freedom Association (BGFA), the second was the Communist Party of Great Britain (CPGB) and the third was the West Indian Communist Party, an informal group of associates from the Caribbean. She would meet, and co-operate with prominent Black activists, all sympathetic to the communist lens on Black liberation.

The BGFA was the first organization Jessica joined in Britain after she was invited to do so by her Guianese comrades already in Britain. Within her first few weeks of arrival, she was photographed in Downing Street with her BGFA comrades at a British Guiana independence demonstration, bearing a placard on which was written 'An Inalienable Right', calling for the self-determination of British Guiana. The BGFA was established in Britain in the late 1950s, as an anti-colonial organization, campaigning for national independence in British Guiana.[1] It aimed to deliver its objectives by maintaining close contact with political developments and organizations in British Guiana. It did not align with any political party but co-operated with other organizations and individuals sympathetic to their objectives.

The CPGB was viewed as the natural organization for Jessica to campaign for in 1958, and she did so jointly with Eric and others. In the late 1950s

---

[1] Institute of Commonwealth Studies Library, British Guiana Freedom Association/ CS158/22/1 circa 1957–1970s, 'British Guiana Freedom Association, Annual General Meeting and Conference', 25 June 1962.

the Communist Party made strategic policy decisions, at the 25th Special Congress of the Communist Party of Great Britain held in 1957, which alienated thousands of members and supporters, many from its Black support base. It is not known whether Jessica became a member of the CPGB on arrival in Britain, but she campaigned, with Eric Huntley, on behalf of its candidate for Hornsey in the 1959. Her campaigning took the form of door-to-door canvassing, public speeches, for example in Finsbury Park, and Town Hall debates facing head on the Conservative opponents.[2] Her commitment to the CPGB was unquestioned at this stage as she recognized that: 'coming from the PPP [People's Progressive Party] where most of us believed we were communist because of all the things we campaigned and propagandised at home, it was natural for us to come and join the Communist Party. For ourselves, there wasn't any other Party, because it was the CP.'[3] With Eric, she attended a meeting of the West Indies Committee of the Communist Party (WIC). This was a formally constituted section of the CPGB for West Indian members. Jessica and Eric did not arrive in England as members of the Communist Party as there was no branch in British Guiana and they would have attended this meeting on an informal basis. Nevertheless, they continued for their first few years in Britain to consider the CPGB as an organization likely to deliver their political objectives. The end of British colonialism and the granting of independence to Guiana and all colonized nations was Jessica's political priority. This was now the mid-1960s and Jessica and Eric found that the political shadow from Guiana had followed them, and, at this meeting, they were forced to confront an issue they held a definitive position on.

The official position of the CPGB in relation to Cheddi Jagan was to provide him with unwavering support and at this meeting Jessica and Eric were asked to pledge their support for Jagan. During an emotive meeting, neither felt they could give this assurance, and following the meeting, they didn't attend any further meetings of the CPGB.[4] Both Jessica and Eric felt concerned about the direction of PPP policy as the country advanced towards independence.

By the late 1950s, there were West Indians in Britain with a connection to the Communist Party either through direct affiliation or through acceptance of its ideological principles of advocating anti-colonialism and rights for workers. Many were effectively exiles in London, from the Caribbean, because of their association with Communism, some had previous orders banning them from entering various Caribbean countries, including British

---

[2]LMA, HC, LMA/4463/F/07/01/001/C, Eric and Jessica Huntley interview with Harry Goulbourne (Session Two), 27 May 1992.
[3]Ibid.
[4]Eric Huntley, interview with Claudia Tomlinson.

Guiana, Jamaica, Barbados and Trinidad, whose governments viewed them as threats to national security.

The WICP was created to be an informal meeting and debating group.[5] It was not a political party and it was not constituted by the CPGB nor affiliated to it. Its goals were to identify ways the comrades could find a new direction for their political experience now they were based in Britain. A secondary but very important goal of the WICP was comradeship, philosophical affinity, friendships and bonds based on West Indian nationality and culture. They had a shared desire and need to combat isolation in Britain, and to enjoy Caribbean culture together in Britain.

The WICP included John La Rose and Irma, Eric Huntley, Lionel Jeffrey, Pansy Jeffrey, Peter Blackman, Cleston Taylor – the Jamaican trade unionist and Black liberationist and Martin Carter – the Guyanese poet and political reformer. These were Caribbean comrades and were present and former members and affiliates of the Communist Party. Peter Blackman (1909–93) was born in Barbados and was a theology student in Britain in the 1920s. He uncovered and challenged racial discrimination when working in the Gambia as a missionary.[6] His activism for the advancement of Black people and workers was shaped by leading roles in the League of Coloured People, the CPGB. He left the Communist Party in the late 1950s.[7]

Black activists and anti-imperialists objected to the central proposal in the CPGB's *The British Road to Socialism* about post-independent relations between Britain and its former colonies. The CPGB's proposal was that the new relationship between former colonies and Britain would be close, fraternal with a continuing economic relationship for the benefit of Britain.[8] For many anti-imperialists, this was further evidence that the Communist Party viewed Black and Third World people's priorities as subordinate to white workers and members. This was part of the rationale for many Black activists, including Jessica and many of her comrades, to move away from the Communist Party. The WICP functioned as mainly a debating group on issues affecting the Caribbean region. These individuals should more accurately be regarded as exiles from anglophone political oppression in the West Indies. The group comprised two factions, firstly one which retained membership or allegiance of the CPBG's ideals and programme,

---

[5]LMA, HC, LMA/4463/F/07/01/001/C, Eric and Jessica Huntley interview with Harry Goulbourne (Session Two), 27 May 1992.

[6]Marika Sherwood, 'Peter Blackman, 1909–1993', *History Workshop Journal*, 37, no. 1 (1994), pp.266–7.

[7]Evan Smith, 'National Liberation for Whom? The Postcolonial Question, the Communist Party of Great Britain, and the Party's African and Caribbean Membership', *International Review of Social History*, 61, no. 2 (2016), pp.283–315, esp. p.284.

[8]Ibid.

and the other side, there were those who were more distant, some hostile, to some aspects of the Communist Party's perspective in the West Indies and Caribbean region.

This latter faction included Jessica Huntley, John and Irma La Rose, and Eric Huntley. They viewed the CPGB as less concerned with political unity in the West Indies region, or to engage with an examination of race as an important factor in liberation in the region. Lionel Jeffrey was the 'Comrade-Secretary' of the 'Party', and as a long-standing member of the CPGB it was inevitable that he would seek to steer the fledgling group into organizing as an off-shoot of the Communist Party. The faction that Jessica belonged to was committed to action in Britain and globally to influence the direction of independence in the region. Once this group fragmented, the section Jessica was part of focused on delivering some of its main objectives in Britain.

The first of these was the decision to organize a Guyana Symposium, to examine and debate the road to Guyanese independence currently being pursued by Cheddi Jagan.[9] The permission of the Communist Party was not sought to hold this Symposium, and it is highly unlikely that it would have been granted due to the scrutiny it brought to Jagan's approach. Meetings to organize the Symposium were held at the home of John and Irma La Rose in Haringey. The Symposium was held on 23 and 24 October 1965, at the West Indian Students Centre in London, with students becoming members of the Organizing Committee for the Symposium. The committee invited a young student, Walter Rodney, to present a paper, and Eric Huntley and others also presented.

Walter Rodney (1942–80) was born in British Guiana. He came from a working background, with a father who was politically active in anti-colonial politics and was a member of the PPP. He was educated at Queens College in British Guiana, an elite school modelled on the British grammar school system. He then attended the University of the West Indies where he graduated with a first-class honours degree in history in 1963. This was followed by three years in London, where, in 1966 aged twenty-four, he completed a PhD at the School of African and Oriental Studies (SOAS). He worked as a renowned university lecturer at the University of Tanzania, the University of the West Indies and was appointed to teach at the University of the Guyana but that latter offer was revoked in connection with the political work he became involved in. His time in London meant he became a familiar figure in some arenas of Black activism and resistance in Britain during this period. By 1968, Rodney was emerging as an internationally recognized and respected scholar in Tanzania, Britain, British Guiana and Jamaica. In addition to this, he was recognized for his political thought

---

[9]LMA, HC, LMA/4463/F/07/01/001/C, Eric and Jessica Huntley interviewed by Harry Goulbourne (Session Two), 27 May 1992.

and action, particularly in his grass-roots talks and lectures on African history with marginalized and working people in Tanzania and Jamaica.

The Symposium was well attended and attracted the interest of parties from across the Caribbean region. Its focus was how to bring stability to British Guiana, which at the time was experiencing multiple uprisings. It was also focused on the terms and conditions that Jagan was negotiating for an independent Guyana. Jagan was accused of bringing an insufficient challenge to Britain's offer of independence on the basis of proportional representation rather than one-person, one-vote model. The latter was seen as preferable for empowering the country and achieving an authentic independence. The WICP only survived for a few years after its formation, having served its initial purpose of providing identity and comradeship for those arriving in Britain during the late 1950s and early 1960s. As Jessica engaged with the new terrain in Britain, they explored new political approaches, such as the emerging Civil Rights and Black Power movements. The CPGB held less significance as she had engaged with the problematic racialized landscape in Britain before.

A New Home in Windermere Road

The family lived in their own house in Walthamstow for a short period, between 1962 and 1963, before they were forced to sell it because of the high costs. While living in their own homes, Jessica and Eric, John and Irma La Rose and Lionel and Pansy Jeffrey took a decision to take turns to organize social events in their own homes, to keep the relationships going, and to broaden their social contacts through inviting others. When hosting the events in their Walthamstow home, Jessica and Eric entertained with calypso music, with the popular Sparrow anthem *Hot, Hot, Hot!*, kwe kwe music and offered their guests Guianese cake and rum sent by Hectorine from Guiana. Apart from these events, the friends would meet at 'bottle parties', where guests took a bottle of wine to the house of those hosting parties. Western music, though not played at parties, was gradually being enjoyed by Jessica and Eric. They enjoyed Sarah Vaughn, Ella Fitzgerald, and Jessica particularly liked Joan Baez, Joni Mitchell and those advocating disarmament and world peace.

Around 1963, after losing their Walthamstow home, Jessica and Eric accepted an offer to live with John and Irma at 51 Uplands Road in North London whose home was large and financial situation secure. John and Jessica had been close friends and comrades since 1958, and it would have been like moving into the home of a family member. Despite some political differences, the relationship between the families was warm and close over many decades. Steven Lewis said of the friendship between John and Jessica:

> It was like a brother and sister, I guess. John was a loving man anyway, John was like that, again, similar to Jessica, very trustworthy, a very warm man. He and Jessica had an excellent relationship. I think they were both intellectuals to be honest, so they were actually on the same wavelength, and they all came from a background, the Caribbean background of struggle, protest and resistance. So, they basically carried that into the UK, they were brother and sister, they were kin-spirits really. They had different views as to be expected.[10]

John was married to Irma La Rose, née Hilaire, in Maracaibo, Venezuela, in 1930 after her parents had migrated there from Trinidad. After marriage, and the birth of their two sons, Michael and Keith, the couple moved permanently to London. Irma and John were politically active in Trinidad and Venezuela for social justice, workers' rights and in the struggle for racial justice, before and during their marriage. Irma worked in education in London and alongside Caribbean radicals and women such as Pansy Jeffrey and Jessica Huntley. Some of the campaigns she was involved in included establishing the George Padmore Supplementary School, campaigning in the Black Parents Movement, the International Book Fair of Radical Black, and Third World Books, and the Campaign Against Repression in Guyana (CARIG), alongside Jessica. The end of Irma's marriage to John La Rose was very difficult, particularly when he started a new relationship with Sarah White, a young, white middle-class English woman.

Irma remained committed to the political struggle and a cherished friend to Jessica.[11] John and Irma's home attracted intellectuals, workers, students and unemployed Caribbean people and others, who spent all day and all night talking. Gus John was then a theology student in Oxford and recalled spending his Saturdays in the living room which was where the fledgling New Beacon Books book service was located. Gus John described how the company at the La Rose household meant 'hours and hours talking about our joint experiences in the Caribbean, and particularly issues facing the black community in Britain, what was going on in the United States of America, the riots in Watts in Chicago, New Jersey and so on, and particularly what was going on in Southern Africa with Ian Smith declaring unilateral independence in what was then Rhodesia'.[12]

---

[10]Steven Lewis, interview with Claudia Tomlinson, 4 December 2022.
[11]Michael La Rose and Keith La Rose, 'Eulogy for Irma La Rose' (2019), email, 21 February 2023.
[12]Interview with Gus John, 14 August 2020.

It was again their Caribbean connections that provided Jessica and her family with their next home, as Rory Westmaas, their PPP friend and comrade from British Guiana, was leaving his three-bedroomed house in Ealing. Jessica and Eric took this over as a rented home and moved into 110 Windermere Road in 1965. Their eldest children, Karl and Chauncey, were fourteen and thirteen years, respectively, at the time of the move to Ealing.

They had only been in England for a few years, and were still adjusting to life in Britain, and being with their parents. This was also the fourth home they had lived in with their parents during approximately four years in England. They were Black boys in the British education system which had been exposed as being engaged in oppressive practices against Black children. They were at school in Haringey when living at Uplands Road with John and Irma La Rose. The boys didn't want to change school when the family moved to Ealing, so they continued to go to school in Haringey where they completed their secondary education.[13]

FIGURE 8.1 *Eric and Jessica with Karl and Chauncey outside 110 Windermere Road, Ealing, circa 1965. Courtesy of the Huntley Collection, London Metropolitan Archives.*

---

[13]Chauncey Huntley, interview with Claudia Tomlinson.

Two years after moving to Ealing, Jessica gave birth to her third and last child, a daughter. Accabre was named after the female leader of a slave uprising in 1763 in the Berbice region of Guyana. This choice of name indicated Jessica and Eric's growing commitment to Pan-Africanism. This can be compared with the choice of the name Karl for their eldest son born in 1950 at the height of her commitment to communist Black liberationist ideas.

Ealing is known as the 'Queen of the Suburbs', meaning it enjoyed a position of supremacy in the London suburbs, possessing the coveted features of London suburban life. This usually means the population enjoyed an affluent lifestyle, with lots of green, rural spaces and semi-rural,

FIGURE 8.2 *Jessica Huntley with baby daughter Accabre, circa 1968. Image courtesy of Accabre Rutlin, the baby in the picture.*

almost provincial lifestyles. This was often viewed as being accompanied by reactionary political and social ideas, resistance to change and a love of British history and culture as traditionally narrated and celebrated. In the late 1960s when the family moved there, the area was experiencing evidence of cultural change, and regions such as Southall were starting to attract people of South Asian background to settle there. But the majority of the population overwhelmingly comprised the traditional white population.

The Huntley sons faced considerable racial hostility in Britain, and Chauncey Huntley has described how it affected him psychologically: 'even as a young black man in England, I remember I would pinch my nose to try to get it straight you know, then when James Brown came "Say it Loud, I'm Black and I'm Proud", we just had to embrace everything about ourselves'.[14] This revelation from Chauncey echoes the ridiculing of own his mother's African facial features more than twenty years earlier in British Guiana, that his grandmother Hectorine had railed against. In 1968, James Brown's record was one of the biggest anthems of the civil rights and Black Power movements that was providing emotional, psychological and political strength for Black people experiencing oppression on a worldwide basis. The boys needed this strength, and more, to survive on the streets of Ealing.

Some white youth of Ealing at that time, in the late 1960s, adopted the popular youth cultures of the period, and styled themselves as either skinheads or rockers. The Huntley brothers styled themselves as 'rude boys'. It was a youth style, but the boys did not adopt all aspects of rude-boy life. Chauncey Huntley has described this situation: 'I don't think we were rude ... compared to our classmates because some of the things they were going on with we wouldn't dare, we couldn't dare you know, through how we were brought up with our parents.'[15] There was a distinction between this upbringing, typically Caribbean, and the behaviour of their white peers which they regarded as disrespectful. However, politeness and respect were not a strategy for survival for Black youths when it came to life on the streets of Ealing, the Huntley boys found that:

> ... on the streets you had the racists, the skinheads, which we often had conflicts with, until they learnt to respect us in Ealing. In Ealing you used to get chased a bit, you had to be on your Ps and Qs, but there was a growing Caribbean community there, and we banded together, and we cleaned up the streets. And there was no more problems in Ealing like that.[16]

---

[14]Ibid.
[15]Ibid.
[16]Ibid.

In other words, Black youths had to confront violence and intimidation on the streets until 'attacks and things stopped you know. Cos, we had to retaliate and show them, you know, well this isn't like in slavery days, we're not taking that. So, we just dealt with them until they began to respect us.'[17]

By the middle of the 1960s, Jessica was working full time, living in her own home, with her husband and children. Having lived through severe personal and political instability, this was the first time in ten years that she was able to live in a settled family situation in her own home, and the family would remain at 110 Windermere Road for the next ten years. Their circle of friends were all political associates and they continued to build this network. Entertainment was mostly home-based.

An important figure for the social and emotional welfare of the newly arrived West Indian during this period was Virgil Duncan. A Guianese woman who arrived in Britain in 1958, a mother to three children, but who arrived as the only parent, was a central Caribbean mother and grandmother figure to the community in north London. Known by all as 'Mums', she was highly enterprising and had a house in Kentish Town where she rented out rooms. She was a supremely talented cook of Caribbean cuisine, a skilled seamstress, who everyone went to for their outfits for birthdays and weddings, and she provided childminding service at a time when there were few such services available. Above all, she was a warm, loving, friendly and cheerful Caribbean matriarchal figure who wrapped her expansive arms around the many lost and lonely arrivals from the West Indies. She died in 1988 and was mourned by a community of many. Mums also held parties at her home, where she provided an open heart, Caribbean music, and wonderful West Indian food and drink that reminded people of home. She personified the warmth, love, culture, family and community friendship that many were missing from home. She also served the community in whatever ways they needed her to and was also an organizer and supporter of a number of activities, including the Radical Black and Third World Book Fairs which took place in the 1980s. Walter Rodney and his family, after marriage, regularly stayed at Mums, and like many others, depended on her for day-to-day help with aspects of life.

By the beginning of 1968 Jessica was settled in Britain and building a family, work and political life. This was nested in the heart of the West Indian community in London and was a springboard for her to intensify and build her vision.

---

[17]Ibid.

9

Becoming West Indian in Britain

There were two main factors which can be identified as being important for the birth of Bogle L'Ouverture Publications founded by Jessica Huntley and associates in 1968. They are, firstly, 'West Indianism', and, secondly, Black resistance movements in the USA. By 1965, Jessica was part of the growth of 'West Indianism' in Britain, the new identity that first emerged in the Caribbean region. It was an idea that been growing in the region since at least the 1930s, but it was only after travelling to Britain that she became part of this identity. It is an idea that relies on travel and the merging of national identities. It was termed 'West Indian regionalism', by Gordon K. Lewis, who defined it as 'a growth of West Indian regional feeling'.[1] It was not simply an identity held by citizens of West Indian nations, but a political idea about rejecting former loyalties to colonial powers and forging a new sense of belonging to a substantial region beyond national boundaries. West Indian regionalism has also been described as West Indian Nationalism, a drive for self-government in the region and independence from Britain, and other colonial powers.[2] The West Indianism Jessica came to be most closely identified with was focused on the emergence of a new identity of liberation and sovereignty.

There were several factors that led to the emergence of 'West Indianism'. The first was the labour rebellions in the Caribbean in the 1930s, which drew attention to economic exploitation of workers in the region, worsened by the recession of the period.[3] These industrial rebellions saw workers from

---

[1]Gordon K. Lewis, *The Growth of the Modern West Indies* (Kingston: Ian Randle Publishers, 2004), p.370.

[2]Renee A. Nelson, 'The West Indian Press and Public: Concepts of Regionalism and Federation, 1944–1946', *Journal of Caribbean History*, 54 (2020), pp.82–105, esp. pp.84–8.

[3]C.J. Hogsbjerg, '"A Thorn in the Side of Great Britain": C.L.R. James and the Caribbean Labour Rebellions of the 1930s', *Small Axe: A Caribbean Journal of Criticism*, 15 (2011), pp.24–42, esp. pp. 24–5.

the West Indies region organize together in uprisings against the oppression and exploitation of their experience under British colonial rule. This resulted in the Moyne reforms and strengthened West Indian identity, ambition and prospects across the region.

Secondly, the emergence of 'West Indianism' was also driven by the formation of University of the West Indies in 1948, bringing together for the first time large numbers of young people drawn from the Caribbean region. They were immersed in a new consciousness, a new sense of unity and joint intellectual concern for the political and economic fate of the region and its place in the world.[4] As described by Woodville Marshall, a student at the University of the West Indies in the 1950s, a postgraduate student at the University of Cambridge in 1958 and a member of the West Indian Students Centre, and West Indian Students' Union: 'you might say the University College of the West Indies at Mona was in fact at the forefront of all that activity. We were West Indians, because we were mixing, this was the mixing of all of these young people, so that even before other people began to call themselves "West Indians" we thought were living it.'[5]

The two world wars also influenced the emergence of a West Indian identity as thousands of citizens from different West Indian nations enlisted. The British West Indies Battalion operated from 1915 to 1927 and whilst most of the soldiers were from Jamaica, most of the Caribbean region were represented. At the outbreak of the Second World War in 1939, many thousands of West Indians enlisted in the British Army from across the region. These members of the armed forces, often meeting other West Indians for the first time, formed bonds as a consequence of their joint mission in another land on behalf of the Mother Country.

West Indian identity was also driven by the journey of the anglophone colonies to independence from Britain after the Second World War. Independence in the West Indies was originally pursued on the basis of the formation of a West Indian Federation, a political and economic unit of West Indian nations working together.[6] There was extensive strategic discussion and planning, but the plan was not pursued beyond 1962 due to failure to agree a unified plan.

The West Indian Students Centre and with the West Indian Student Union (WISU) were organizations that were important expressions of West Indianism in London.[7] Jessica became a prominent Caribbean activist and

---

[4]Anthony Payne, 'One University, Many Governments: Regional Integration, Politics and the University of the West Indies', *Minerva*, 18 (1980), pp.474–98, esp. p.476.

[5]Sir Woodville Marshall, interview with Claudia Tomlinson, 6 November 2020.

[6]Nelson, 'The West Indian Press and Public', pp.82–105.

[7]David Clover, 'Dispersed or Destroyed: Archives, the West Indian Students' Union and Public Memory', *The Society for Caribbean Studies*, 6 (2005), pp.1–14, esp. p.8.

intellectual figure at both organizations, contributing reforming progressive ideas and activism. WISU had formed in 1945 but did not have a permanent home until the West Indian Students Centre opened ten years later. WISU promoted unity and fellowship between West Indian students in the UK. It also encouraged interest in the economic and political development of the West Indies. It co-operated with similar organizations in the UK.[8] Students who had political ambitions to play a part in the new independent West Indian nations often contested and won official roles on the management committees of the West Indian Students Centre and WISU.[9]

The West Indian Students Centre opened in Earl's Court in London when there were approximately 2,000 West Indian students at universities in Britain. It was opened as a leisure, social and welfare club for students, many of whom were the recipients of scholarships, or whose families were independently financing their studies. Most were the children of the professional middle classes of the Caribbean who expected to return to the Caribbean, or to travel to other countries, to become established as academics and professionals. By the late 1960s, the West Indian Students Centre and WISU broadened their interest and appeal beyond West Indian students from abroad. The wider West Indian community of settlers in Britain, their welfare and interests were of concern to the students. West Indian migrants, mostly workers, were also very interested in the activities of the West Indian Students Centre, particularly the social and leisure opportunities that were inaccessible to them in Britain.

The involvement of women in the Student Centre and Union was very limited in the 1950s. For Jessica, however, the importance of WISU and the Students Centre in resistance and reform for West Indian people in Britain meant that this setting was important site of contribution for her. The West Indian Students Centre and WISU both reflected the androcentrism of the colonized societies which had shaped the West Indian nations. There were women students, fewer than males, but they played a minor role in the organization of both the Students Centre and WISU.

Jessica leveraged her experience as a seasoned and respected West Indian activist to gain agency to participate and influence at WISU and the Student Centre. She also used her expertise in typing and stenography. Typing was a female occupation during this period, it was a highly sought after and very technical skill that many companies, businesses, organizations and institutions such as universities, political groups, students and clubs, relied on. At this time, without typing or secretarial services, organizations and individuals found it difficult to achieve professional, commercial business

---

[8] Ibid., p.6.
[9] Ibid.

viability. Individuals with good typing, stenography and shorthand skills were admired, valued and in high demand. Over time, with technological advancements, and as men developed typing skills and willingness to do it, typing lost the cachet of being a highly skilled technical profession, particularly when using the cumbersome manual typewriters and gestetners that were in use at the time. With this skill however, Jessica found many opportunities, and she was never out of work in her time in Britain before becoming a full-time publisher. These skills were also in high demand in political activism.

Women students were not well represented on the Board of Governors or the House Committee of the West Indian Students Centre. The Annual Report of 1969 shows that of twenty-one members of the Board of Governors, positions appointed by the governments of the West Indies countries, only one was a woman.[10] The House Committee membership, which was elected or co-opted by WISU, had four positions, and were all occupied by men during the 1968–9 period. John La Rose was deservedly co-opted to one of the positions and it is likely that Jessica would have welcomed the opportunity to influence at this level. The language, outlook, interests and culture were predominantly male, and women were frequently over-represented in the domestic elements of events such as acting as 'hostesses' at social events.

Jessica, therefore, was an important figure who despite not being a student, forged a path into the intellectual life of the Students Centre. She helped with the typing of the student's newsletters, for the Centre and for WISU. But she also played a role in mentoring some of the students and influencing the activities and intellectual direction of the Centre. She organized and chaired some talks, but the lack of a full record means it is unclear how frequently she did this.

The speakers at the West Indian Students Centre were predominantly male, and their events were well attended, particularly if they were well known. The warden's report for September 1969 on the Centre's activities stated that a talk on a recent Black Power conference in Bermuda, chaired by C.L.R. James was well attended. It also noted that 'another meeting during the month was – "Our Black Women Speak", speakers Jessica Huntley and June Doiley. This meeting only had a small attendance'.[11] The topic of the talk was 'The Role of Black Women in the Black Revolution'. In the description of the event in the newsletter, it was described as:

---

[10] GPI, Personal Papers of John La Rose, LRA/01/0823, West Indian Students Centre, Fifteenth Annual Report by the Board of Governors, 1 October 1968 to 30 September 1969.

[11] GPI, Personal Papers of John La Rose, LRA/01/0823, West Indian Students Centre; Warden's Report for the Month of August 1969, West Indian Students Centre, 1969–1970.

A unique programme in that it was the first programme in which the speakers were entirely Black Sisters and was also chaired by one of the Sisters. The speakers made the point that there was no special role for women, separate and apart from their Black Brothers. The discussion covered many aspects of the Black Brothers – Black Sisters relationship; the attitude traditionally of the Black male of assuming a subservient role for his Black Sister: the Black man/White relationship etc. Naturally the discussion was passionate.[12]

Given Jessica's knowledge of political experience and activities ten years earlier with the People's Progressive Party (PPP), and the Women's Progressive Organization (WPO), this debate is in keeping with her stance of the role women can play in revolutionary change. This would have been a very frustrating situation to find herself, once again, playing a secondary role to men, and excluded from full participation by virtue of regressive ideas about women's roles. But she cut through this and later the same month, August 1969, the student newsletter noted in the programme 'Saturday 16: Negritude And Black Awareness; the speakers were Merle Hodge and Andrew Salkey. In the Chair was Jessica Huntley.'[13]

Ansel Wong, former West Indian Student Union activist and representative, in the 1960s, observed how Jessica operated with students at this time and raised issues with them. He recalled that 'all of us were basically men and Jessica sometimes at meetings, she was the sole woman in the meeting'.[14] This situation was taken for granted at the Students Centre at this time, in the early to mid-1960s, however this was not the intended extent of Jessica's participation, and she pushed her role and influence. She brought challenge to the way things were run at the Centre and pushed for the involvement of the women in the committees. Wong recalled that at the committee meetings of men, Jessica would be 'taking notes, she's doing things. But then post meeting as you talk, walk, waiting for the bus or walking, whatever it is. That's where her intervention became evident, you know, questioning the approach where are the women?'[15] She questioned, pushed, queried about the male domination of WISU and the Students Centre. Wong recalls that 'she was very, very quiet individual, but for very much subtly influencing thoughts and thinking through the interaction'.[16]

With no formal role and operating in a male-environment she used the opportunities within her sphere of influence to achieve what she wanted

---

[12]Ibid.
[13]Ibid.
[14]Ansel Wong, interview with Claudia Tomlinson, 17 June 2020.
[15]Ibid.
[16]Ibid.

to. Ansel Wong has described how important Jessica's skills and influence were in the Student Centre and in WISU, and that 'without that support as students, we would have gotten nowhere. I mean, she not only brought the physical technical skills of typing and shorthand and stenography, just what was important in hindsight at the time, we didn't aware of it'.[17]

A clear example of her influence and impact is that she was a co-founder of the C.L.R. James School for Black Youth, an initiative of the Students Centre, aimed at providing educational opportunities for Black children and young people whose educational needs were not being met in Britain.[18] This school can be seen as one of the forerunners of Black Supplementary Schools. An article in the 1969 edition of *Bumbo*, the newsletter of WISU describing the launch of the school acknowledged:

> the progressive act of sister Jessica Huntley. It was her brainchild of getting together a group of youngsters from the Ealing area, and bringing them to the Centre, where prior to the official formation of the School, they engaged in a dialogue with Brothers Andrew Salkey, John La Rose, Eddie Braithwaite, and Aubrey Williams. This school owes its origin to this act. Once again, our Black women have been a light onto us.[19]

It is commendable that the contribution of Jessica specifically, and Black women generally, to the life of the West Indian Students Centre was acknowledged in this way. However, there is an unmissable tone of patriarchy with reference to the 'Brothers' who are positioned at the forefront of this ground-breaking movement at the Centre, with a woman bringing her ideas to present to them for approval. This is a retrospective observation however, and the spirit in which women engaged with leading male figures cannot be adequately assessed by contemporary standards, and it is known that Jessica was a highly respected figure at the time.

During this period, she formed new alliances and strengthened existing relationships with associates, many of whom would be lifelong comrades and supporters. It seems that this is where she met and befriended Maurice Bishop, Andrew Salkey, Cris Le Maitre, Errol Lloyd, Gus John, Ansel Wong, Bernard Coard, Richard Small and many others. These were all students, workers destined for political roles in the West Indies or the professions, and who were active in the fight against racialized injustice in Britain, around the Caribbean and in the United States generally alongside their mainstream careers. Jessica eventually became a Trustee of the West Indian Students Centre, in its later and final years of operation.

---

[17] Ibid.

[18] Black Cultural Archives, WONG/1, 'Education, the C.L.R. James School', *Bumbo, the Newsletter of the West Indian Student's Centre*, circa 1969–70, p.9.

[19] Ibid.

During this period, Jessica and her associates were concerned that the governments of West Indian countries approaching independence were committed to maintaining the colonial infrastructures after independence. The fear was that they would continue to serve European interests in the West Indies. Radicals such as Jessica Huntley opined that some of the new West Indian governments repelled movements and individuals who agitated for real change and an authentic break with colonialism.

For example, in August 1968, the West Indian Standing Conference, the Caribbean Artists Movement, the Campaign Against Racial Discrimination (CARD), the Movement for Colonial Freedom and other Black and African organizations co-operated with each other to condemn the Jamaican government's stance against the ideas of Stokely Carmichael, Malcolm X and Elijah Muhammed, who were all banned from entering Jamaica.[20] In a petition, they accused Jamaica, which had become independent from Britain in 1962, of adopting a course action in which it 'joins hands with white racist America', and that it demonstrated that 'Jamaica associates herself with the American policy of enslaving black people who oppose oppression'.[21]

The organizations also lambasted the Jamaican government's position on Marcus Garvey, that 'despite being our National Hero, Garvey's writings, philosophies and his opinions are not deeply part of how we think and act'.[22] It accused the Jamaican Government of trying to 'silence the voice of freedom and dignity which means so much to the black people of Jamaica as it does to our brothers in the United States and the rest of the Third World'.[23] Jessica was actively involved with this discussion with these organizations, many of whom met at the West Indian Students Centre, and it can be reasonably assumed that she was a supporter of this petition.

When, just two months after the submission of this petition, Walter Rodney received a banning order preventing him from re-entering Jamaica, it was clear that this narrative of resistance was well founded. Jessica and her associates in the West Indian organizations and movements during this period fought the neo-colonialism being pursued by the new governments. This fight was viewed as part of the broader fight for Black liberation and was increasingly taken up at this time in the shape of Black resistance movements growing in the United States.

---

[20]LMA, HC, LMA/4462/A/02/011, Petition handed to the Jamaica High Commissioner on Thursday 15 August 1968.
[21]Ibid.
[22]Ibid.
[23]Ibid.

Fuelling Black Power in Britain

The second impetus, in addition to West Indianism, that can be viewed as the context that spurred the birth of Bogle L'Ouverture Publications was the intensification of Black activism in the United States in the form of the Civil Rights Movement. This was followed by the emergence of Black Power, which also played a part in igniting the conditions for the birth of Bogle L'Ouverture Publications. When Black Power emerged in Britain in the 1960s, many embraced it as one weapon in the fight against the emergence of neo-colonialism being developed in the West Indies. Jessica played an important role in disseminating its ideas by making Black Power literature widely available, in enabling some of the figureheads from the United States to be heard by wider audiences, and hosting visits by leading Black Power figures to Britain.

Black Power is closely identified with Malcolm X (1925–65). Following his departure from the Nation of Islam, he founded the Organization of Afro-American Unity (OAAU) in 1964 and spread the vision of unity between Africans on the continent and in the diaspora as being important for the advancement of Black people. Other key figures associated with the growth of Black Power later in the 1960s and in the 1970s included Eldridge and Kathleen Cleaver, Stokely Carmichael and Angela Davis. As the 1960s advanced, Black Power spread globally through the Caribbean and to Europe.

Some of Malcolm X's visits to Britain have been well documented, including his visit in 1964 to speak at the Oxford Union.[24] In 1965, he visited Smethwick in the West Midlands to back the fight for justice for racialized people in the context of a general election being fought by the Conservatives on a platform widely seen as promoting of racial division.[25] His meetings with Black radicals in Britain to provide inspiration and to strengthen their struggles have been less well documented. One such documented visit, in which Jessica met with him, was possibly arranged through his connections with Michael de Freitas, who adopted the name Michael X, and appeared to have coordinated this visit.[26] It is likely that this visit to London was part of his visit to Britain to speak at Oxford or his visit to the West Midlands.

---

[24] Stephen Tuck, 'Malcolm X's Visit to Oxford University: U.S. Civil Rights, Black Britain and the Special Relationship on Race', *The American Historical Review*, 118 (2013), pp.76–103.

[25] Michael Higgs, 'Malcolm X's Visit to Britain', *Institute of Race Relations* (27 February 2014), https://irr.org.uk/article/malcolm-x-oxford-union/ (accessed 10 April 2024).

[26] Robin Bunce and Paul Field, 'Michael X and the British War on Black Power', *History Extra* (14 October 2017), https://www.historyextra.com/period/modern/michael-x-and-the-british-war-on-black-power/.

Jessica was included in a party of leading Black activists in the call that was put out to join the delegation to meet Malcolm X. She was contacted, probably by Michael X and she described the activity she was then involved in: 'I was given a phone call: "Sister Jessica, try and get A, B, C ... people together, pass the word around ... that Malcolm was coming"'.[27] The delegation she was asked to help organize appears to be a small, named group of individuals. She was then part of a small group of people to meet and escort Malcolm X to venues across London. Others identified by Jessica Huntley as being in the group that met Malcolm X on this visit included John La Rose, Andrew Salkey, Farrukh Dhondy, Darcus Howe and Michael X.[28] Given the nature of surveillance surrounding the movements of these key figures by security services, there are no records about what was discussed. Although Jessica has discussed her role in this visit on many occasions, the detail of the discussions or proceedings during the visit have not been documented.

Jessica heard Stokely Carmichael speak on several occasions during this period. He was a new, radical and exciting voice for Black liberation in the 1960s. She played a role in the interpretation of Carmichael's brand of Black Power in Britain. She heard him speak in July 1967, at the Camden Roundhouse when he gave a speech at the Dialectics of Liberation Congress.[29] The role of Black Power in igniting Black organizing in Britain was described as incendiary by Jessica: 'America was on fire, and here was this fire coming, and we go to meet the fire. We were all there. I remember it was very exciting, we came back feeling exhilarated.'[30] She observed the impact of Carmichael in shaping Black activism in Britain and noticed one immediate consequence. She noted that activists started to exclude white people from spaces that could be defined as having a Black purpose. Jessica said of Carmichael on this: 'he was anti-white, he didn't want no white people'.[31]

At his Camden Roundhouse talk, she felt this was implicit in Carmichael's words and actions. She recalled that 'when we went to the Roundhouse, and there were these hundreds of people, and Stokely said that he only wanted black people to be in front, and the others to be at the back. And

---

[27]LMA, HC, LMA/4463/F/07/01/001/D Eric and Jessica Huntley interview with Harry Goulbourne (Session Three), 28 May 1992.

[28]Ibid.

[29]Stokely Carmichael speaking at the Dialectics of Liberation, 1967, British Library, Black Power – Address to Black Community, https://www.bl.uk/collection-items/stokely-carmichael-speaking-at-the-dialectics-of-liberation-1967

[30]LMA, HC, LMA/4463/F/07/01/001/D Eric and Jessica Huntley interview with Harry Goulbourne (Session Three), 28 May 1992.

[31]Ibid.

there were all of us blacks moving forward.'[32] A visit by Carmichael to speak to a London audience was also organized by Oscar Abrahms at the Keskidee Centre in London, which Jessica attended.[33] She was in no doubt of the effect of Carmichael's stance on white people, stating: 'After that, it was sheer hell broke loose in London.'[34] According to her, 'After Stokely's visit, two things emerged, one was, at the Students Centre, black and white, and there were mainly white women who had black partners or whatever, and we weeded them out of the Centre, they just couldn't come, might share what we said.'[35]

Jessica made an important contribution in helping Black networks in London absorb the meaning of Black Power, and to move forward with positive elements it could offer, and steer people away from unhelpful interpretations. She was aware that Carmichael's visit to London generated further hostility towards Western education and intellectualism. She said there 'was also a class thing because some of the Panthers used to talk about middle-class people, and they didn't want anybody who they thought were from that middle class.'[36] She did not accept this position and recalled that she 'intervened a lot in all those things. My own son Chauncey was influenced by that, "no white man education".'[37]

She felt that in Carmichael, perhaps for the first time in the UK, 'was the catalyst that pushed blackness on the agenda'. The intervention she refers to is action she took to bring the two sides together, those who were anti-intellectual, and those who had received traditional education. Her position advocated collaboration between those who had benefitted from a traditional academic education, using it as a resource to be shared and something that could be useful in the fight for Black liberation. Indeed, she viewed intellectual prowess in Western education as a vital tool in Black liberation, and utilized academics throughout her political work. Bogle L'Ouverture Publications was founded on her ability to harness the power of Western intellectual and academic labour:

> I know that at the Students Centre I had to confront a lot of the brothers and sisters there. I said why should you be opposed to somebody who is intellectual, why should you oppose those who are academically inclined? Because those same very people, you would want them to fill in your

---

[32]Ibid.

[33]Norma Ashe-Watt, interview with Claudia Tomlinson, 1 March 2021.

[34]LMA, HC, LMA/4463/F/07/01/001/D Eric and Jessica Huntley, interview with Harry Goulbourne (Session Three), 28 May 1992.

[35]Ibid.

[36]Ibid.

[37]Ibid.

form, you need them, and so on and so forth. I think I got a hearing and people eased off of that pressure. I think that because of my work, I must say that people had a certain amount of respect, because I came from that whole thing, of struggle, and so I want to think that persons listened.[38]

This extract reflects her interaction and influence on those in the West Indian community, the workers and members of the political and community groups that met at the West Indian Students Centre. As she had become a well-established and influential figure there, this extract further indicates the standing she established for herself, with all who attended the Students Centre.

Jessica was also selected to host the London visit by Kathleen Cleaver, the leading Black Panther activist, married to Eldridge Cleaver, leader of the Black Panther Party. The Black Liberation Front (BLF) had organized her visit to London, around 1970, which included a large rally for her. The BLF also included the Huntley home as part of Cleaver's visit to London, with Jessica recalling that 'they brought her here, in this very house, the same room, and we had a very long discussion about politics, about women's role, and so on'. Jessica described Cleaver as 'most articulate, very, very articulate, and I think she was estranged from Eldridge at that time, I think. But she had a tremendous amount of support.'[39] Despite being a highly significant encounter, this research has not uncovered any other narrative accounts to expand knowledge further of this meeting. Kathleen Cleaver would have been a person of interest to international security services, and the absence of formal recording or photography of this meeting can be understood in that context.

Some years after hosting Cleaver's visit, Jessica was also invited to organize the visit of Angela Davis to London. The Anti-Apartheid Movement of Britain arranged Angela Davis's first visit to Britain following her release from prison, and Jessica recalls that 'they had asked me to assist in organising a rally for her, because what had happened is that she was coming to speak at this massive rally at Friends House and all the tickets were sold out'.[40] Jessica had been one of the prominent Black figures in Britain at this time who had joined the international campaign in calling for the release of Angela Davis, and others from prison.

This talk at the Keskidee Centre appears to have been added as an additional opportunity for Davis to address the Black community in Britain who had been campaigning for her release, and the release of other Black Power figures such as George Jackson. Jessica met Angela Davis on several

---

[38]Ibid.
[39]Ibid.
[40]Ibid.

FIGURE 9.1 *Jessica Huntley with Angela Davis at the Keskidee Centre in London, 1974. Photograph credited to Amit Francis. Courtesy of the Huntley Collection, London Metropolitan Archives.*

occasions following this talk at the Keskidee Centre, until late into the 1980s during her visits to Britain. Several photographs of Jessica seated alongside Angela Davis at this event have survived, not all of reproducible quality, and can be viewed at the London Metropolitan Archives.

The 1960s was a heightened moment of political militancy for Left movements, and Black Power, and all Black liberation movements gathered momentum as part of this. This coincided with young people, Black students and workers developing a greater international perspective on class and race oppression and willingness to resist and fight. This fight was taken to the shores of the Caribbean nations, from its nationals at home and abroad. The fight was also part of the momentous political ferment that fuelled the birth of Bogle L'Ouverture Publications.

10

'A Political Act', Bogle L'Ouverture Publications' Early Work

After ten years of life in London and now in her early forties, Jessica no longer had a raw sense of loss of the beautiful life and political possibilities she had left behind at home. She had moved past the sense that her future life was destined to be that of traditional domesticated housewife and Black immigrant worker in Britain. By the middle and late 1960s she had built the friendships and formed the associations that would journey with her in decades ahead. She was determined to prevail in her mission. She was on the precipice of achieving this through her work with Bogle L'Ouverture Publications.

The decision to form Bogle L'Ouverture Publications is often described as being triggered by the banning of Walter Rodney from his academic post at the University of the West Indies, and from Jamaica, in October 1968. Indeed, this is the explanation generally given by Jessica Huntley, the students and radical activists who were part of the founding of the company. She said 'Bogle L'Ouverture Publications was born as a direct result of the political act by the Jamaican government in the banning of Brother Walter Rodney from re-entering Jamaica in 1968.'[1] She stated that the founding of the publishing company was triggered by the necessity of informing the world, and particularly Black people of the reasons for Rodney's expulsion from Jamaica.

Bogle L'Ouverture Publications was born in a cramped bedroom of the Huntley family home at 110 Windermere Road, in Ealing in London, in

---

[1] 'Creation for Liberation', Bogle L'Ouverture Publications Tenth Anniversary Celebrations, Cultural Media Collective (1979), https://www.youtube.com/watch?v=6H5oILEJir8. In

1968. Jessica, describing the conditions in which the co-founders of Bogle L'Ouverture Publications started out, said, 'our bedroom was the office, the dressing table was the desk, the bed and the floor were the chairs. We met there and planned what we were going to.'[2]

A bedroom, packed with perhaps ten or fifteen students, and workers, one or two babies including Jessica and Eric's baby daughter, played on the floor, or bounced on knees and passed from hand to hand. In the rest of the house, family life continued with the two teenage sons, Karl and Chauncey, playing

FIGURE 10.1 *Founding members of Bogle L'Ouverture Publications at Windermere Road, with Jessica Huntley and baby Accabre Huntley, circa 1969. Courtesy of the Huntley Collection, London Metropolitan Archives.*

---

[2]Philippa Ireland, 'Material Factors Affecting the Publication of Black British Fiction' (unpublished doctoral thesis, The Open University, 2012), p.240.

records or the radio, watching the family's black and white television, doing schoolwork, waiting to eat the food whistling in the pressure cooker on the hob in the kitchen.

By this time, hardly anyone had pressed hair. Many were wearing their natural hair formed into an afro and that was the style everyone at the meeting had, including Jessica. They also wore flared trousers and psychedelically patterned fashions of the period. This was the core of the network that would go on to become the famous Black British publishing house, recalled by then law student, Errol Lloyd:

> There was a group of us, I remember Loxley Comrie, Earl Greenwood, Elaine Neuville, Richard Small, Fitzroy Griffiths, and quite a few other people and it was a lot of banter, a whole lot of good-humoured banter. Eric and Jessica were a little better off than us, they had a house, whereas most of us were living in bedsits, or small flats. So, some of the social activities took place at Jessica and Eric's. They were very gregarious, and so in the context of meeting, and having food and drink and all that. It was very, very pleasant, and a lot of joking and messing around.[3]

Those assembled did not have this as their objective at the time. The Windermere Road home was, said Jessica, 'where most things happened' at the time. It was a gathering place for workers and students to talk, eat and organize. For Jessica, with Eric, to be at the centre of this gathered grouping was different to how the generations might work together in the Caribbean, as recalled by then student, Errol Lloyd:

> In the Caribbean, normally there is this kind of generational gap, and there you were deferential to people who were even a decade older than you. So if we were in the Caribbean, it would have been Mr Huntley and Mrs Huntley, but they had this really amazing ability to communicate with young people. If I say to you that a lot of the time spent with Jessica and Eric was sheer fun, people would find it hard to believe.[4]

Even for Jessica, the idea of where this meeting would take her in the next few decades was not contemplated at this meeting. Yet, it led to the formation of a company that would publish and distribute some of the most celebrated, widely read and most influential Black political literature, and to the launching of the careers of some of the most successful Black writers and performers in the world. The growth of the West Indian identity, and the rise of Black Power were at the heart of the birth of Bogle L'Ouverture Publications.

---

[3]Errol Lloyd, interview with Claudia Tomlinson, 20 July 2020.
[4]Ibid.

'Not With My Blood. It Won't Fail'; Becoming an Africanist Publisher

Jessica made the personal decision to become a full-time publisher. It was not planned as a corporate profit-making business venture. It was born out of a passionate resistance, an anger about racialized injustices faced by Black people globally, and a sense that she wanted to take a major stand. She said that when starting this political work, 'we didn't think of it as long-term. It was a political act. We were making politics'.[5] She resisted attempts to dominate this early period of excitement by subsuming it under corporate, business activities:

> A friend said to me that I'm doing it all the wrong way, that I should first of all set about the rules, and have a feasibility study, and you must have your directors, and you must have policy statements, and all the things that a big commercial venture would have, that is how they wanted us to start and I said 'no', we don't need all that ... people goin' to buy your books once the book has some meaning to you. He said I'd never do it my way, its bound to fail. I said 'not with my blood it won't fail you know. I will make certain it doesn't fail'.[6]

At its inception, Bogle L'Ouverture was established to have a concern for Black history to ensure it had an accurate and visible presence. This was expressed as a 'pledge to re-write our own history from our viewpoint'.[7] Jessica also wanted to establish an organization would have wider importance than being a local publishing house:

> I am of the opinion that what we are engaged in is of concern and relevance to Black People all over the world. BLP is unique in more sense that one. It would be presumptuous of me to say that it is the only one of its kind in the world. We who are associated with BLP regard ourselves as trustees of Black People everywhere.[8]

She identified one of the early objectives of Bogle L'Ouverture as 'building a new relationship not only between ourselves and our readers but also

---

[5]Ireland, 'Material Factors', p. 241.

[6]'Creation for Liberation', Bogle L'Ouverture Publications Tenth Anniversary Celebrations, Cultural Media Collective (1979), https://www.youtube.com/watch?v=6H5oILEJir8.

[7]GPI, Personal Papers of John La Rose, LRA/01/0127/01, 'Constitution of the Bogle L'Ouverture Publications', December 1969–May 1991.

[8]LMA, HC, LMA/4462/A/02/011, Jessica Huntley, 'Draft Notes of Speech on the History and Future of BLP', 1968–1975.

ourselves and our authors'.⁹ Bogle L'Ouverture was a Black organization, and from the outset she wanted Black people to be deeply involved, arguing that 'in each Black man and woman lies our institution, they either organise sales in their areas, give us Ms, and help in any other way. Accounting, record keeping, just offering their skills, just enquiring, just showing interest'.¹⁰ She wanted the company to be owned by, supported for and by Black people and dedicated many decades to building this vision.

Bogle L'Ouverture's Earliest Publications

Although the decision was taken in late 1968 to form Bogle L'Ouverture Publications, and to publish Walter Rodney's *The Groundings with My Brothers*, a year would pass before that publication appeared. It is often thought that, because of its major success, that *Groundings* was the first publication by Bogle L'Ouverture. Less attention has been paid to the company's publications that preceded Rodney's book.

The earliest known publications by Bogle L'Ouverture Publications were, firstly, messages by Amy Jaques Garvey, Pan-African activist, and second wife of Marcus Garvey. Secondly, a poster featuring the work of Jamaican artist Ras Daniel Heartman was published. Next, there were two re-prints of important speeches by C.L.R. James, first published by independent Trinidadian publisher Frank John, then based in London. Although the messages from Jaques Garvey do not appear to have survived, a note by Jessica to her friend Andrew Salkey referred to her connection with 'Mrs Garvey' whom she sent Bogle L'Ouverture greetings cards and possibly other materials to, on a complimentary basis. It appears from this correspondence that Amy Jaques Garvey had insisted on paying for the cards, and complimented Bogle L'Ouverture by using them, and noting that they 'were so special'.¹¹ Doctoral research by Sandra Courtman also suggests that one of the reasons for setting up Bogle L'Ouverture initially was 'to print messages from Amy Garvey, and to respond to the expulsion of Walter Rodney from Jamaica by publishing his banned speeches'.¹² Anne Walmsley's research on the Caribbean Artists Movement (CAM), also acknowledged that Bogle L'Ouverture published a message sent by Mrs

---

⁹Ibid.

¹⁰Ibid.

¹¹LMA, HC, LMA/4462/A/02/011, Jessica Huntley Letter to Andrew Salkey, 21 December 1971.

¹²Sandra Courtman, 'Lost Years: West Indian Women Writing and Publishing in Britain 1960–1979' (unpublished doctoral thesis, University of Bristol, 1998), p. 86.

Garvey to a CAM conference. Walmsley wrote that at the conference, 'a message from Mrs Amy Garvey, Marcus Garvey's widow, was read out: it was later published, as a pamphlet, with the help of Jessica and Eric Huntley, who were soon to start Bogle L'Ouverture Publications'.[13]

Jessica was an associate of C.L.R. James since the 1960s, and in 1968 she re- published two of his speeches as pamphlets. C.L.R. James (1901–89), the Trinidadian Marxist political theorist and historical writer, was approaching seventy years of age when he was based in London for a period of time. He spent several extensive periods in Britain, where he was a major focus of interest for the Black intellectual and political communities of students and activists in Britain, particularly in London. It is not clear when or where he met Jessica, but as a prominent Caribbean leader and important leader since her arrival in Britain in 1958, she was inevitably part of the circles that would be of interest to him. The West Indian Students Centre is a likely meeting place as James was also associated with the Centre, and student activism.

The first of James' publications re-published by Bogle L'Ouverture Publications was *The Making of the Caribbean Peoples*, published on 4 October 1968.[14] It was published from the Windermere Road address in London, as well as a P.O. box address in Kingston, Jamaica. This publication was the speech given by James at the Second Conference on West Indian Affairs held in Montreal, Canada, in the summer of 1966. In the speech, James covered the history of Caribbean people between 1600 and 1800, dispelling beliefs falsely distributed by European colonizers. In particular, he criticized the Moyne report, the 1938 Royal Commission of Inquiry into conditions across the British West Indies. In this publication James wrote of his observation that the Commission members 'were not hostile to the West Indies. They were merely profoundly ignorant of what they were dealing with.'[15] James developed this publication into a historical and political Black Power treatise to counter the beliefs held by about Africans. The overarching message of this publication from James was the demand that uplifting histories of African-descended people were published. He argued that when readers are provided with examples of great Black achievement this connects to the future possibilities for Black leadership.

The second C.L.R. James pamphlet published by Bogle L'Ouverture on 2 December 1968 was titled *Black Power, its Past, Today, and the Way*

---

[13]Anne Walmsley, *The Caribbean Artists Movement, 1966–1972; A Literary and Cultural History* (London and Port of Spain: New Beacon Books, 1992), p.156.

[14]LMA, HC, LMA/4462/E/01/017, C.L.R. James, *The Making of the Caribbean Peoples* (London: Bogle L'Ouverture, 1968).

[15]Ibid.

Ahead.[16] It was also a speech given by James in London, in August 1967, but the occasion or audience is not made clear. It was however given a month after Stokely Carmichael's speech on the same topic at the Dialectics of Liberation conference at the London Roundhouse. In this speech, James took care to outline his intellectual contact with Stokely Carmichael who he heard speak in Canada in March that year, and James took the opportunity to write to him advising that in his opinion, US Black Power lacked historical analysis and context. James advised Carmichael this was essential for establishing he future direction for Black Power. In his own later speech, James told the audience that he received a favourable response from Carmichael. James said he observed that Carmichael's later speeches were transformed in that:

> He now speaks with a scope and a depth and range of political understanding that astonishes me. That the Stokely whom I heard in March and whose conspicuous political ability and character I recognised (that is why I wrote to him), in less than a year should have developed into the political leader we are seeing and hearing.[17]

James went on to point out that the transformed Carmichael had developed to such an extent that the speech James was giving, as re-published by Bogle L'Ouverture Publications, was influenced by the radical new intellectual approach taken by Carmichael. Both cover designs of these works were by Errol Lloyd, who acknowledged that these were some of his earliest designs.

It was Richard Small, the Jamaican law student, and co-founder of Bogle L'Ouverture, who made an important discovery in late 1968, of a news story featuring two illustrations on the Rastafarians by Ras Daniel Heartman. Ras Daniel Heartman was a Jamaican born Rastafarian, actor, artist, and activist for uplift of African people and cultures. He played Pedro in the acclaimed Jamaican film *The Harder They Come*. Two images of his artwork were published as posters by Bogle L'Ouverture and greetings cards, before Heartman's profile rose even higher, and 1968 therefore was very early for these types of images of Black people to be made available to ordinary Black people in Britain. Bogle L'Ouverture lays credible claim to be the first organization to have published these images in Britain, of Black Rastafarians, for commercial use. The first was Proud Defiant Rastafarianism, an image of a strong and determined Black African man with dreadlocks.[18] Errol Lloyd remembers: 'I have a strong recollection of me and Jessica going to this printer somewhere in Victoria with this original painting, and they were

---

[16]LMA, HC, LMA/4462/E/01/016,C.L.R. James, *Black Power, its Past, Today, and The Way Ahead* (London: Bogle L'Ouverture, 1968).

[17]Ibid., p.3.

[18]LMA, HC, 'Proud Defiant Rastafarian' poster, LMA/4462/E/03/004, circa 1968.

able make copies of it ... That poster, a lot of people would have found it quite shocking.'[19]

The second of the poster series by Ras Daniel Heartman published in 1968 was 'Mother and Child', with this poster likely to have been published just prior to or following the publication of *Groundings*.[20] This powerfully depicts a Black African woman breastfeeding her own Black child.

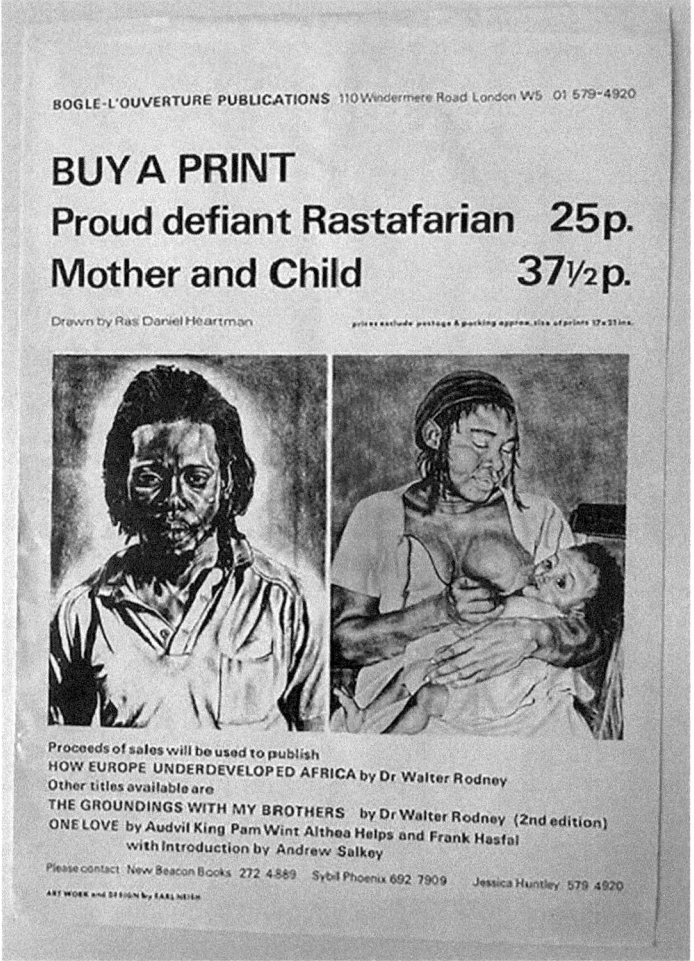

FIGURE 10.2 *Poster by Bogle L'Ouverture Publications advertising prints with original artwork by Ras Daniel Heartman, circa 1971. Courtesy of the Huntley Collection, London Metropolitan Archives.*

---

[19]Errol Lloyd, interviewed.

[20]LMA, HC, LMA/4462/E/03/001, 'Mother and Child' poster, circa 1970.

These early publications, along with twenty years of political thought and action, provided the foundation for the formation of Bogle L'Ouverture by Jessica, and the publication of the company's first major book. They brought in early income which helped to establish the company. Errol Lloyd has commented on the significance of these posters:

> Up until that time, the image of Rastafari was not generally greeted with approval in much Jamaica and elsewhere. The strength of that drawing, and the fact that it was a poster, tends to give a work of art a bit of a stamp of approval. There were later posters of other elements of his work, 'mother and child', those began to sell quite well. It fitted in with the mood at the time, of a re-appraisal of identity.[21]

The Banning of Walter Rodney from Jamaica

The sequence of events leading to Bogle L'Ouverture's publication of *The Groundings with My Brothers* started in 1968 when Walter Rodney left his academic post at the University of West Indies, Mona, in Jamaica and travelled to Montreal, Canada, to attend the Congress of Black Writers. This conference has been widely regarded by observers as 'the most important Black Power, Black left, Black radical political event – conference/congress of the post Second World War period that brought together many of the leading political figures of that moment'.[22] This was a key moment in transatlantic radical Black activism for many reasons. It was the year of Martin Luther King's assassination, and the US Civil Rights and Black Power movements were in their ascendancy.

The conference was an arena for these radical socialists and Black nationalists from Canada, the UK the United States, and the Caribbean to debate topics such as 'what change would mean for people of African descent'.[23] It was an intergenerational conference, regarded as a 'passing of the torch, CLR James, to the younger generation, folks like Walter Rodney, Stokely Carmichael, Robert Hill from Jamaica'.[24] Conference attendees included Richard Small, a law student friend and associate of Walter Rodney. Small, now a prominent human rights lawyer in Jamaica, was a co-founder

---

[21]Errol Lloyd, interview with Claudia Tomlinson.
[22]David Austin, *Moving Against the System: The 1968 Congress of Black Writers*, Online video recording, 14 August 2018. Available at: https://www.youtube.com/watch?v=J7yhsDXBwDA.
[23]Ibid.
[24]Ibid.

of the Campaign Against Racial Discrimination (CARD), President of the Union of West Indian Students, and Secretary to C.L.R. James and was a leading member of the editorial group that produced *The Groundings with My Brothers* and wrote the introduction to the first edition.[25]

Prior to the start of the conference proceedings, Richard Small was taken aside by Walter Rodney for a private meeting. Rodney would have been aware of the significance of his attendance at the conference and the potential consequences for him. Rodney had taken his written lectures and speeches that he had been giving off-campus to disenfranchised Black people in Jamaica. Small recounted that at this meeting, Rodney 'handed to me these speeches, even before the start of the conference. I had taken them back with me to London.'[26] This suggests that Rodney was aware he was at risk of a banning order or some other political state sanction and wanted these papers transferred to his trusted supporters. These were his friends, associates and colleagues in London. While at the conference, Rodney was banned from returning to Jamaica by the Hugh Shearer government.

In fact, such was Rodney's reputation that the news spread rapidly around the Caribbean, London and of course Jamaica, where the students gathered in uprisings, dubbed the 'Rodney riots', on the campuses in the country. Small delivered the papers to Rodney's networks in London and reported that he had been given Rodney's papers with a view that Rodney wanted to see if they could be published in London. Rodney by this time knew of John La Rose and New Beacon Books was in its infancy as a publishing house having started operating in 1966. Perhaps Rodney hoped his papers could be published there.

Jamaican Prime minister Hugh Shearer quickly cast Rodney as a danger to the national security of Jamaica and gave his reason for the ban as due to the need to ensure the security of Jamaica and its nationals.[27] Shearer informed the Jamaican parliament that Rodney was a central player in a plot to bring about a communist revolution in Jamaica, in the style of Fidel Castro's Cuba. Shearer accused Rodney of adopting the guise of Black Power to mask his 'true' intentions of bringing a communist revolution to Jamaica that involved violence and burning down the university. Shearer attempted to suggest that Rodney's activities were not connected to Black Power. He said that Black Power 'to us and other well thinking Jamaicans does not mean rebellion, but rather the dignity of the black man'.[28] This was an attempt to persuade Jamaicans that Black Power was a polite, acquiescing debating

---

[25]Walter Rodney, *The Groundings with My Brothers; With an Introduction by Richard Small* (London: Bogle L'Ouverture Publications, 1969).

[26]Richard Small, interview with Claudia Tomlinson, 1 August 2020.

[27]'Shearer Tells House of Guyanese's "Castro Plot"', *The Daily Gleaner*, 18 October 1968.

[28]Ibid.

ideology. Shearer's action was widely viewed as an attempt to distort Rodney's purpose, which was for grassroots, revolutionary change, but he did not advocate violence. Shearer also sought to portray Walter Rodney as a communist, along the lines of Western capitalist formulation. Shearer chose to obscure the reality that Rodney's lectures and talks were addressed primarily to the Black underclasses in Jamaica. Jessica's next actions were to work with her associates to ensure the audibility and visibility of Rodney's message that Shearer sought to silence.

Collaboration with Walter Rodney – Raising Pan-Africanism

Walter Rodney was an important figure for Jessica and Bogle L'Ouverture Publications. His contributions to the formation of the publishing house were foundational. He was one of the contributing co-founders. However, his work with Bogle L'Ouverture Publications was a collaboration and partnership that brought wider renown both to himself and the publishing house. This collaboration was critical for the furtherance of their joint perspectives on Black Power and fighting neo-colonialism in the West Indies. Rodney was a personal friend of Jessica and Eric Huntley, and part of their social and political network in London. Rodney regularly stayed at the Huntleys' home and the two families were very close.

Jessica's long-established political involvement in the struggle for reform in the British Guiana was respected by Rodney. It was her history and standing, along with that of Eric's, that Rodney admired. As recalled by Jessica, 'when we came to live in Ealing, and because of the politics, Walter gravitated more towards us, plus he wanted to know a lot about our role in the Party, the PPP'.[29] The couple, she knew, enjoyed 'a kind of respect, and I suppose it came because of who we were in Guiana'.[30] Their association with Rodney was social as well as political. Rodney, who loved parties and socializing, played a full part in the Guyanese and West Indian 'liming' scene – West Indian style partying – in London at this time. On many weekends in London, he went with Jessica and Eric to parties which cemented the personal closeness between the friends.[31]

But it was Jessica in particular that Rodney formed an intellectual bond with and the two maintained regular correspondence. Jessica was the

---

[29]LMA, HC, LMA/4463/F/07/01/001/C, Eric and Jessica Huntley interviewed by Harry Goulbourne (Session Two), 27 May 1992.
[30]Ibid.
[31]Ibid.

FIGURE 10.3 *Jessica Huntley with Walter Rodney at Windermere Road, circa 1967. Courtesy of the Huntley Collection, London Metropolitan Archives.*

recipient of his correspondence that outlined his political journey during the 1970s in particular. Her courage, experience, intellectual ideas, charisma and influence in London meant she was one of Rodney's most important allies and sources of support at this time. She was also critically important to Rodney in several arenas, including activism, publishing, and the management of his personal affairs, such as storage and transportation of his personal belongings, banking and posting his property to him. She was one of the women who typed his PhD thesis when he was a student at the School of African and Oriental Studies (SOAS).[32]

She continued to provide him with general help once he had moved to Tanzania, and did so much for him that in jest, she asked him: 'don't know why you do not employ me as your Agent. I mean the fees will be quite small to do the work.'[33] Rodney therefore relied on Jessica to do these tasks for him. It also indicated a strong degree of personal trust to perform these tasks, some of which had security implications for her as Rodney was under constant secret service surveillance. He knew her to be fearless towards authorities and that she had many years of personal experience of evading the scrutiny of security services during her activism in British Guiana.

---

[32]Ibid.
[33]LMA/HC/ LMA/4462/C/01/092, Jessica Huntley Letter to Walter Rodney, 6 December 1974.

Many aspects of Rodney's successes, it could be argued, are more accurately viewed as a collaboration between himself, Jessica, Eric, Bogle L'Ouverture Publications and the many London-based Black friends, radicals and students who operated on his behalf, rather than viewed as Rodney's own personal and individual achievements. Walter Rodney's biographer, Rupert Lewis, has written that it was 'Bogle L'Ouverture's publication of his Jamaican lectures and speeches under the title *The Groundings with My Brothers*, that helped to shape his political reputation as the region's premier radical-intellectual-activist'.[34] Lewis also acknowledges that 'Rodney made his name with *How Europe Underdeveloped Africa*.'[35] Jessica said that her 'association with Walter is inextricably bound up with the building of a new society which we can all be proud'.[36] In fact, it was not Rodney's will that he would be viewed as an individual actor or that he would be personally celebrated, for example he clearly informed Jessica in relation to one of the many campaigns she led, that 'for both personal and ideological reasons, I would not like any protest to appear to be centred around me alone'.[37] In fact he prioritized the voice of the Black masses and he used his education and relatively privileged position for this purpose.

---

[34] Rupert Lewis, *Walter Rodney's Intellectual and Political Thought* (Kingston: University of the West Indies Press, 1998), p.117.

[35] Lewis, *Walter Rodney's Intellectual*, p.69.

[36] LMA, HC, LMA/4462/A/02/011, Notes of Speech by Jessica Huntley, 1968–75.

[37] LMA, HC, LMA/4462/C/01/092, Walter Rodney Letter to Jessica Huntley, 20 August 1974.

11

'A New Alternative in Publishing'

The years 1968 and 1969 were a watershed for Jessica – she consolidated the direction she wanted to take her life's work and mission in future. It was during these years that she stepped more solidly into a Pan-African identity for herself and Bogle L'Ouverture.

In October 1968 she was a co-signatory to a series of protest letters to the governments of West Indian nations criticizing the Jamaican government's action against Walter Rodney. These were addressed from the Huntley home in Windermere Road. The other co-signatories to the letters were Andrew Salkey and Richard Small. They were sent as part of the initial response to Walter Rodney's ban and criticized the Jamaican government's action. The letters denounced Jamaica for banning Rodney from Jamaica as 'a blow against the efforts towards unification of the territories in the area and a blow against the autonomy of the University of the West Indies, severely restricting academic freedom, and a blow against the traffic of ideas between Mother Africa and Ourselves'.[1]

Meetings of sympathetic activists were held at the Huntley home at Windermere Road, to organize their opposition to Rodney's ban and its implications for global Pan-Africanism. Those that attended the meetings were friends of Walter Rodney, fellow West Indian students, and associates from his years in London. They were also friends and associates of Jessica, made through years of activism at the West Indian Students Centre. They were fired up by what had happened to their friend and planned two protests at the Jamaican High Commission and the Jamaican Tourist Board in London. They started at the Commission where several people were arrested. Jessica recalled that 'while they were arrested three or four of us went into the Jamaican High Commission and of course we started to make

---

[1] LMA, HC, LMA/4462/A/02/011, Andrew Salkey, Richard Small and Jessica Huntley Letters to West Indian Governments, 23 October 1968.

our protest there, and they got the police to bodily take us outside'.[2] Jessica herself was not among those who were arrested, perhaps a testament of her experience in evading security forces and police in British Guiana. The next step was to decide what to do with Rodney's valuable papers.

Publishing *The Groundings with My Brothers*

An editorial group was formed from the loose original grouping of friends, associates and students, and the decision was made that they would work to publish Rodney's papers. Jessica's view was that the 'papers must be placed at the disposal of as many more people who were only able to read what the government had to say about Rodney'. She drew upon the friendship networks of those friends from the Caribbean, particularly from British Guiana, who had settled in Britain at the same time.

> We began through personal gifts and proceeds from parties, funds came from sisters, Waveney Bushell, Barbara Joseph, Sybil Phoenix, Natalie Stephenson, brothers Charles Patterson, Ray Eccles, Robert Hart, Ewart Thomas, Richard Small, Len Bushell, Cris LeMaitre, Franklin Johnson, and many other Black people. From those sources, we were able to print posters, and *Groundings*.[3]

These individuals were the Black friends, associates, students and workers who were part of the early networks and were in a position to donate. Jessica successfully obtained their co-operation to ensure *Groundings* was published. There were fragmented views amongst some of those who gathered to support Rodney, with not all agreeing about the way forward. Jessica described working with the opposing views and opinions amongst the initial supporters:

> At informal sessions we held, opinion was divided concerning our aims and how to achieve them. Doubts arose concerning raising of funds to achieve our objectives. Some felt that the source was immaterial. Others held the view that we should seek the support of only Black people. It was also suggested that we appeal to friends and relatives here and overseas for a donation, explaining to them the importance of these papers. Almost everyone at the meeting claimed that they do not like asking people for

---

[2]Philippa Ireland, 'Material Factors Affecting the Publication of Black British Fiction' (unpublished doctoral thesis, The Open University, 2012), p.240.

[3]LMA, HC, LMA/4462/A/02/011, p.5, 'A Brief Outline About the Development and Future of BLP', 9 February 1974.

money, that their friends were opposed to Black Power etc. Richard Small and I fully went along with the idea of raising funds from friends. Immediately I set about asking my friends and relatives.⁴

Jessica described the process of publishing *Groundings* after receiving the papers from Rodney: 'we began by the way and method we knew best as political activists, that is by typing and duplicating some of the talks which Rodney gave to the groups while he was in Jamaica. The quality was not very good as it took us many sleepless hours typing and duplicating. Since I was the one who had to do all the typing, and as women I'm sure we all recognise this role. The work of re-typing was very daunting. I suggested why don't we print the talks in a book form?'⁵ This was Rodney's desire, but no publishing company was available so Jessica's decision that the group would do what they could and publish the papers themselves moved the book closer to becoming a reality.

At this stage the group did not own a publishing company, and editor Ewart Thomas was involved in efforts to find a publisher for Rodney's book. He found that 'the other two Black publishers just didn't have the capacity, John La Rose had his own work cut out for him, and Allison & Busby'. According to Thomas, both existing publishers were supportive of Rodney's book but due to capacity issues another publisher had to be found. John La Rose declined to print it but agreed it was a good proposition and supported the idea of its publication.⁶

The question therefore can be legitimately posed about whether *Groundings* would have been published at this critical time if the London radicals had not made the decision to publish the lectures as a book. Whilst Rodney had a growing reputation as a young academic at this time, it is uncertain whether the publisher of the book derived from his PhD thesis, Oxford University Press (OUP), would have agreed to publish a work such as *Groundings*. Indeed, if Rodney had confidence in that publisher, he would have approached OUP to publish *Groundings*. It must be concluded that it was unlikely that they would have published, promoted and distributed a Black Power text.

John La Rose introduced Jessica to John Sankey of Villiers Publications who agreed to print an initial run of 2,000 copies of *Groundings* on account.⁷ The wider network of emerging Black publishers was crucial to the

---

⁴LMA, HC, LMA/4462/A/02/011, Notes on the Banning of Walter Rodney and the Foundation of Bogle, 1968–1975.

⁵LMA, HC, LMA/4462/A/02/011, p.5, 'A Brief Outline About the Development and Future of BLP', 9 February 1974.

⁶Ewart Thomas, interview with Claudia Tomlinson, 12 April 2021.

⁷Ibid.

establishment of Bogle L'Ouverture and in getting *Groundings* published. Margaret Busby and John La Rose had nurtured relationships with Villiers and Bogle L'Ouverture was also able to develop a relationship with John Sankey who was happy to print material with no demand for upfront payment. Jessica always acknowledged the strong support, advice and guidance provided by others such as John La Rose and Margaret Busby to the fledgling new publishers, which was very important in the early setting up phase.

Ewart Thomas became the editor of *Groundings* in 1969 after Richard Small completed his studies in London and returned to Jamaica. Thomas, a childhood schoolfriend of Walter Rodney's from British Guiana edited and provided a title for the book and designed the first company logo. The early co-founders of Bogle L'Ouverture Publications had no money, but Thomas recognized that it 'had a lot of intellectual resources as all of us were academic types'.[8]

Aware that the cover would be vitally important to the message of the book, Jessica asked Errol Lloyd to do the artwork. Lloyd, already a friend and associate through the West Indian Students Centre, and the Caribbean Artists Movement (CAM), was to become a close adviser. He became a prolific book cover artist, and a central player in the early establishment of Bogle L'Ouverture Publications. A law student from Jamaica at the time, he was also a gifted artist and writer, and became a long-standing friend of Jessica and Eric Huntley. He remembered how 'Jessica was very good at getting things moving. She was the one that asked me to do the cover, I had absolutely no idea what to do.'[9]

Lloyd's cover design of *Groundings* sketches of Black men, 'brothers', grouped together in joint reflective thought, appealed to conscious Black people, and proved to be an important element in the book's success. The concepts of self-reliance and self-independence in the production of this new enterprise was central. It was signalled by the employment of Lloyd, an important and highly talented Black artist.

To create the cover, Lloyd 'made thumb sketches of the people who were around me to form the images on that cover, so when the average person looks at it, they might think these are just invented faces, but when I look at it, I remember my friends, I can identify them by names'.[10] As well as Lloyd's contribution to advancing *Groundings*, it helped to develop him as an artist: the book was 'the first thing I had done which had any kind of public profile, so one felt was quite proud of it really'.[11]

---

[8]Ibid.

[9]Errol Lloyd, interview with Claudia Tomlinson.

[10]Ibid.

[11]Ibid.

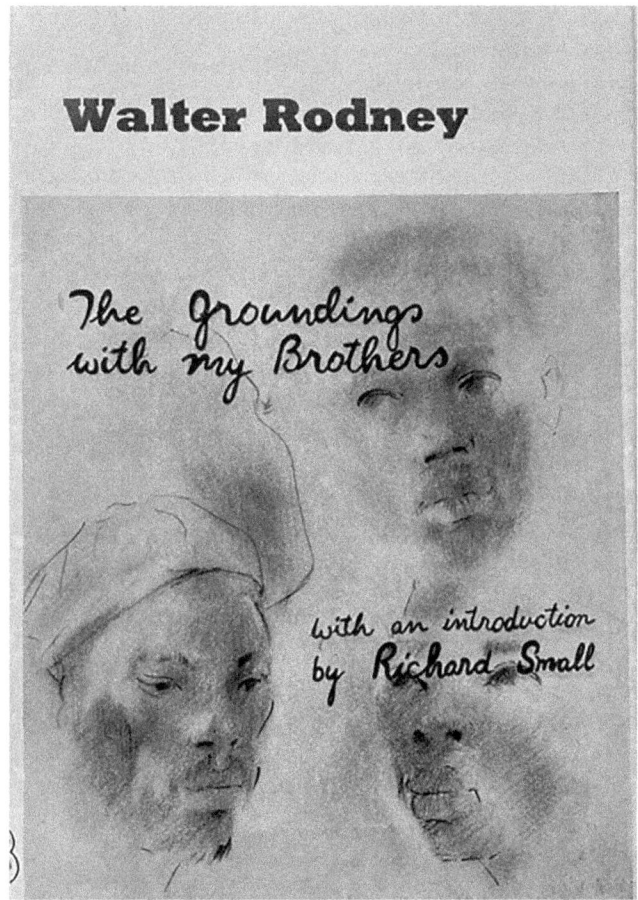

FIGURE 11.1 Cover of The Groundings with my Brothers, *illustrated by Errol Lloyd (1969). Image reproduced with kind permission from Errol Lloyd.*

Once the book was published, the group realized that the challenge of selling and promoting it would also fall to them. They followed the same self-help, self-reliance approach and Ewart Thomas has recounted that when distributing the books members of the group 'just recruited an army of friends, you might take three, another man might take six'.[12]

It was not important to receive the price of the book, and if someone did not have the full six shillings and six pence, 'you'd shrug your shoulders and say the most important thing is to get the word out, not to make a

---

[12]Ewart Thomas, interview with Claudia Tomlinson.

profit'.[13] As well as this direct selling, the group promoted the book through delivering talks, and there they found strong demand from their audiences, even though their own specialist subject wasn't African history and they had not previously know the information contained in Rodney's book. This group of young academics were being educated in African history for the first time, through their involvement with bringing *Groundings* to the world's attention.

Everyone working on the production of *Groundings* did so on a voluntary basis, no one got paid. Moreover, many had personally met some of the upfront costs of publishing the book and donated significant emotional and physical labour in producing the book, selling and distributing it. There was no sales outlet such as bookshops at the time that would stock the book, it was sold from the front room at Windermere Road, and from the handbags and briefcases of the friends and associates who were part of the network supporting Rodney and the struggle.

The book sold very well and funded several further re-prints and helped to establish the company. Rodney was aware that Jessica, his friends and associates were funding the first edition of of the book. He agreed that he would not be paid royalties for the book but the royalties would be used to build Bogle L'Ouverture Publications. He was paid for all future editions of the book.

Enormous effort was mounted by the editorial group, friends, and supporters, to distribute *Groundings* to universities, bookshops and organizations, and this occurred on an international scale. Orders were from British universities, overseas universities and bookshops in Britain, Europe, the United States, Canada, most of the West Indies including Guyana, Grenada, Dominica, Barbados, St Lucia, Jamaica, Trinidad and Tobago, Puerto Rico and Honduras. There were some small orders, but large orders of several hundreds were also placed. Once published, *Groundings* became a Black Power and Pan-African success that promoted Rodney's profile globally, presenting an invisible perspective on these ideas about Africa and Black history. It has been re-published many times and remains in print to this day.

The publication of *Groundings* was an exhilarating high point for Jessica, she has said that 'when the *Groundings* first came out, we were jolly, we were happy. It was a really wonderful experience.'[14] It was possibly her most exciting and satisfying political moment since the People's Progressive Party's (PPP) 1953 victory back home. She saw it as a triumph of the workers, students and supporters who had collaborated to get Rodney's papers published as a book.

---

[13]Ibid.

[14]Ireland, 'Material Factors', p.242.

Jessica had started this period, since 1958, as an extremely reluctant migrant, politically displaced into the belly of the capitalist beast she had been fighting for a decade in British Guiana. Homesick, with her children, beloved mother, and friends thousands of miles away, she would want to return home as quickly as possible, and missing no more than the one Christmas she had promised Chauncey she would be away for. Facing racism in boarding rooms, endless moves to escape this, and avoid eviction, and fighting open racism at work on a daily basis for years. It is remarkable that she progressed against this backdrop to establishing what would become one of the most famous Black publishers in British history during this short period. Her collaboration with husband, business partner and co-founder, Eric Huntley, as well as many other allies and supporters is something she nurtured and built as a strong network.

She overcame many hurdles on the journey to the birth of Bogle L'Ouverture Publications. The organizing and editorial committee for the development of *Groundings* was mostly all male, but she drew women in, not just as typists, although many performed that role for the company in its early days, but also as editors on the draft of *Groundings*, financial sponsors, and fundraisers. A greater hurdle was the bold confidence needed to start a new Black publishing house a mere two years after close friend John La Rose had founded his New Beacon Books. She was taking the bold step not just to publish *Groundings* but to talk about the necessity for another Black publisher that had a greater focus on Black history and heritage and one that was more radical and rooted in the lives of Black people and workers.

Jessica saw it as being about building 'a new alternative in publishing ... a hopeful, cultural idea to become a living reality and community example'.[15] She found the confidence to set this up, alongside, not in competition with, John La Rose, a titanic figure of political and academic intellectualism, much admired with strong connections and followers, with a strong Black, male, educated and middle-class constituency. Despite what La Rose had started a couple of years earlier, and Margaret Busby's vision with Allison and Busby in 1967, Jessica followed her own instinct, as she 'just knew that there was a vacuum in the black publishing market'.[16] She was to prove this was the case for decades to come.

---

[15]Jessica Huntley, Publisher's Note to *The Groundings with My Brothers* (London: Bogle L'Ouverture Publications, 1969).

[16]Ireland, 'Material Factors', p.243.

12

'To Re-Write Our Own History': A Black Publishing Strategy

After the publication of *Groundings* Jessica left her job determined to now work full time as a publisher of radical Black literature and as a full-time activist in the struggle. Between 1969 and 1975 she became more immersed in delivering her mission. This mission was steeped in celebrating and uplifting those of African heritage and driving their global fight for justice. Her struggle at this time was part of the struggle for decolonization which she viewed as the major impediment to Black liberation and freedom from oppression. This included decolonization of Black minds from centuries of embracing of eurocentrism. In her view, Black people were not sufficiently active in resisting aspects of their lives in which they faced the denigration of themselves, their history, culture and Africa. But beyond that, she embarked on self-decolonization and, as friend Norma Ashe-Watts said, 'I loved her because she always, most times, wore African clothes, she had these lovely African gowns and head-dress.'[1] By this time, she had ditched pressed hair, and was mostly sporting a short afro at this time.

The task of defining and refining the objectives of Bogle L'Ouverture was re-visited throughout the life of the company. Richard Small had proposed the new company be named after Paul Bogle, and Cris Le Maitre suggested Toussaint L'Ouverture, heroes of African and Caribbean resistance, and Bogle L'Ouverture was agreed upon. There was a clarity of vision at the outset as the company started with an early pledge in its Constitution to publish 'literature of educational, cultural, social and political nature for providing information for and assisting in the progressive advancement of

---

[1] Norma Ashe-Watt, interview with Claudia Tomlinson, 1 March 2021.

all Black People'.² The two initial areas of focus for publication were 'social and political commentary, and children's books'.³ Further, Jessica stated that 'we pledge to re-write our own history, from our own viewpoint'.⁴ This perspective followed on from the achievement and the success of *Groundings*, which Jessica viewed as defining the direction the company wanted to take. She said following the company's early publications: 'a pattern – a line was drawn – as it were', pointing to the direction that would be followed.⁵ This approach was rooted in Pan-Africanism and Black Power.

Defining the intended scope of Bogle L'Ouverture was required for the formal constitution of the company which was being established as a publisher. However, Jessica did not intend to abandon activism. Instead, she ensured that the publishing and the resistance activities of the company were developed in tandem. Bogle L'Ouverture married the resistance and protest during the Rodney ban with the publication of the book *Groundings*. One of the earliest campaigns under the banner of Bogle L'Ouverture Publications involved the validation of Black people's experience of oppression in Britain. Jessica explicitly acknowledged the extent of the racial injustices they faced. She stated in a publication that 'the forms of oppression and the intensity of oppression of the Black Community, in this country, are increasing to a frightening extent. One of the most significant and cruel attacks is the harassment of the entire Black community, and more especially Black Youth by police and by other agents of an overtly racist society.'⁶ For Black people to read or hear such a statement affirming the day-to-day realities of their lives was intended to be empowering and liberating.

Further, she accompanied this with a call to action, informing Black people that 'as a people, we have to move to organise NOW to resist by the most effective means, this attack before we are completely overwhelmed and destroyed by it'.⁷ She stressed the importance of Black unity, and the importance for Black people to adopt a strategic methodical approach in order to take on the system. She advised that:

> ... we cannot organise or mobilise pressure against the pressure of justice unless, and until we form a basis of knowledge. It is absolutely essential that all Black people in this country, as well as our brothers and sisters

---

²GPI, LRA/01/0127/01, 'Constitution of the Bogle L'Ouverture Publications', December 1969–May 1991.

³Ibid.

⁴Ibid.

⁵Philippa Ireland, 'Material Factors Affecting the Publication of Black British Fiction' (unpublished doctoral thesis, The Open University), p.242.

⁶GPI, LRA/01/0127/01, Bogle L'Ouverture Publications Flyer 30 November 1970.

⁷Ibid.

the world over, have clear and specific ideas exactly what we are facing as individuals and as a people. This knowledge we must have and share if we are to move.[8]

She launched this project under the auspices of Bogle L'Ouverture Publications that would 'provide a detailed and authentic account of specific experiences of Black people, of police harassment and victimisation as well as our failure to receive justice through the law courts. Such is the extreme nature of our oppression that we need no exaggeration or fictions to demonstrate our plight.'[9] She called on Black people to compile evidence and accounts of their personal experience of racial oppression, and indicated that Bogle L'Ouverture would catalogue, analyse and publish these records 'as the first weapon of resistance'.[10] This early call, through the distribution of these flyers in the community, as well as the later presence of a bookshop in the community, served as a magnet for Black people who were suffering and struggling to have a focused person and place where they could go for support and advice. In the late 1960s and early 1970s, there was an absence of such support, and advice, and this call would therefore have been extremely welcomed by Black people. These early themes were followed through with the series of publications that followed the publication of *Groundings* and were intended to follow in this template.

Publishing Black Greetings Cards and Prints

The first widespread production of greetings cards and prints featuring images of African descended people in Britain for popular commercial use is associated with Bogle L'Ouverture Publications from the late 1960s. Prints and cards were among the first publications offered by Bogle L'Ouverture Publications, and were part of the vision of Jessica, her close associates and co-founders as an important strand in Black liberation. Jessica believed that in the fight against global racialized injustice, Black people needed a sense of self-love and self-pride, and a strong understanding of what it means to be African, based on cultural and historical knowledge. She was aware that 'our people didn't like to see themselves'.[11] She worked to counter the self-dislike many Black people had of themselves and each other. She further said: 'they didn't like to see their skin and their faces on the cards. They

---

[8] Ibid.
[9] Ibid.
[10] Ibid.
[11] Carol Sidney, '60:60, Jessica Huntley, a Lifetime of Publishing', *Sable*, Spring (2005), p.95.

used to be embarrassed.'[12] The print and card series were therefore intended to bring change to these damaging Eurocentric perspectives on people of African heritage and the African diaspora.

Jessica was deliberate and bold in her strategy of exposing the African diaspora in Britain to their own authentic images and recalled the difficult experience of distributing the greetings cards and prints for the first time in the 1960s. She recalls her greetings cards 'in those days, were the first Black greetings cards'.[13] As well as selling the cards in the shop, she would carry them with her to parties and events, but they met with a negative reaction from some Black people. She recalled on one occasion 'trying to engage a Black woman. She didn't want to look. But then this white person said: "oh this is really lovely", and the Black woman comes very sheepishly and says "do you think so?"'[14] Having decided on this strategy, Jessica had the added difficulty of being an African diaspora woman, intrinsically viewed with suspicion and distrust, trying to promote Black self-pride amongst Black people in Britain at this time. To personally try to turn this tide was a feature of Jessica's bold and direct approach to decolonialization.

Her friend and close collaborator of many decades, Errol Lloyd, Bogle L'Ouverture co-founder, was the first and main illustrator of Bogle L'Ouverture's artwork that featured on the greetings cards. Lloyd recalls Jessica's breakthrough approach in commissioning and promoting Black images in the 1960s:

> Ras Daniel Heartman 'Mother and Child' published by Bogle L'Ouverture, that in a way forced people to re-evaluate their ideas about being black, because it was challenging back in the 1960s to have cards or posters of black images especially of Rastafarians, who had been denigrated to such the extent that the Prime Minister of Jamaica had more or less issued a carte blanche to the police to bring them in, dead or alive, which was totally out of order, but it goes to show the extent to which they were feared, that might have come from fear, misunderstood, denigrated and so on. Something like locs was anathema here to most people, those images began to challenge people's notions on how they can present themselves, you could present yourself in a more natural form. In addition to that of course we did cards that were produced by me and other artists, they were so shocking to some people that they sent them back to her, they were offended by receiving a black image through the post. So, a lot of her actions, I think people recognised, was a game-changing kind of

---

[12]Ibid.
[13]Sidney, '60:60', p.95.
[14]Ibid.

involvement she had with the black community. It changed white people's perceptions as well which was very useful.[15]

The early artists of the prints and greetings cards were Errol Lloyd, whose greetings card illustrations included the works *Boy, The Hunt, Sisters, Icon,* and *The Youth*. Lloyd's work *Boy* is a realistic depiction of an ordinary child of African heritage, proudly showcasing African facial features, in a reflective, questing expression. An image such as this, published around 1972, at the height of the oppression of Black children in British schools, brought an important, unspoken strand to the struggle.

The other important artists involved in the design of cards and posters included Lena Charles who produced *Nirvana*, Emmanuel Jegede, now a prominent Nigerian artist who produced *A Vision of Hope*. Kofi Kayiga, a Jamaican artist formerly known as Ricardo Wilkins contributed *Initiation North*. Over the subsequent decades, more artists contributed to the greeting cards series. The cards were very eventually very successful, despite initial resistance from some customers when they first appeared. They grew in popularity over decades and were sold through a wide network of distributors including some bookshops in London and the University of Tanzania.

One Love – The Cry for Black Unity, Andrew Salkey

The next book published by Bogle L'Ouverture after *Groundings* was *One Love*, in January 1971, an anthology featuring Black poets, edited by Andrew Salkey.[16] Salkey (1928–95), the Panamanian-Jamaican writer, BBC broadcaster, activist, editor and university academic, was a foundational member of Bogle L'Ouverture Publications. He was a close friend and comrade of Jessica, whom she relied on for editorial advice on book projects as well as the development of Bogle L'Ouverture.

He was at the centre of the company from its inception, and continually provided advice to Jessica and its associates until his death. He mentored many of the writers, and the final production of many of the books was shaped with his advice. He also donated several of his own books for publication by Bogle L'Ouverture, waiving royalties and any author payments which helped to grow and stabilize the company.

---

[15]Errol Lloyd, interview with Claudia Tomlinson.

[16]Audvil King et al. (eds), *One Love* (London: Bogle L'Ouverture, 1971), p.9. Huntley Collection, London Metropolitan Archives, LMA/4462/E/01/038/A.

FIGURE 12.1 *Jessica Huntley with Andrew Salkey, author, editor and founding member of Bogle L'Ouverture Publications, circa 1980. Reproduced with kind permission from Jason Salkey.*

The featured poets in *One Love* were Pam Wint, Audvil King, Althea Helps and Frank Hasfal. The anthology followed the publishing strategy pursued by Jessica in this period, to exclusively publish Black writers and works on Black themes. *One Love* is about Black unity, Black people coming together to show care, love, and an interest in each other, their culture and heritage. This was described as an unusual approach in a newspaper review which stated that '*One Love* is not, as one would have expected, directed towards unity between black and white, but rather between black people.'[17] The placing of a book review in the local press was an achievement and new departure that Jessica would use very effectively from this point. The very appearance of the review of a book about Blackness in a local paper at this time may have contributed to shaping perceptions of African descended people. It would certainly have made more Black people aware of the work of Bogle L'Ouverture and help promote the company. *One Love* reflected the Pan-African ideology at the heart of the publishing strategy pursued by Bogle L'Ouverture Publications.

---

[17]'Anthology of Work One Love', *County Times and Gazette*, 29 January 1971, p.8.

The idea of unity between Black people was one actively pursued by Jessica throughout her career as an activist in Britain. She specifically considered unity between people of African descent of great importance in delivering the objectives of eradicating racialized injustices to enable Black people to achieve full agency as a race of people globally. She pursued this objective in her personal life, as well as her activism. These ideas as expressed in *One Love* were not widely held in Britain at this time, and they were not the prevailing ideology held amongst Jessica Hunley's political associates. Indeed, it was an idea rejected by some Black people who did not hold the idea of Black unity as important and did not engage with it.

The work of Audvil King opens the books; 'A Word' is a narrative promoting self-reflection on identity, and the process of forming identities of being African or Caribbean and how Black people approach this task. King's poem 'Letter to a Friend' is a loving plea to a woman friend to examine identity through the practice of hair straightening among some Black women and its connection to Black liberation. It holds a gentle discourse about the Black liberation movements and about Rastafari as being close to pursuing the desired African ideals. The friend is engaged to help her gain a deepened understanding of the problematic nature of hair straightening.

The publication of *One Love* was ground-breaking as it featured writers publishing a political treatise with a clear revolutionary decolonial Caribbean literary stance. Andrew Salkey, in his introduction, wrote that the essence of the book was about 'the rightness and total desirability of the essential oneness of the love we should feel for one another, beginning, as it must, between the Black man and his Black woman'.[18] He particularly pointed to aspects of self-hate amongst Black people and cited the rejection of local Caribbean dialects by many Black people and their preference for standard English in Caribbean literature. *One Love* is written in local Caribbean dialect language and Salkey held the view that *One Love* 'with its definition of our new Caribbean alternative in language and life-style, will, I think, be remembered as the very first work of its kind, an Anthology composed by four of our writers, for all of us, and brought out by a publishing house of ours, with our readers, primarily, in mind'.[19] Jessica and Bogle L'Ouverture were unequivocally committed to resistance through a Pan-African decolonizing lens.

---

[18]LMA, HC, LMA/4462/E/01/038/A. King et al., *One Love*, p.9.
[19]Ibid.

13

Growing a Pan-African Publishing Tradition

During the 1970s, Jessica built Bogle L'Ouverture Publications into an effective organization of resistance to injustices towards the people of Africa and African-descended people. She was relentless in her quest to deliver a publishing programme of literature by, and for, Black people and children, their history and culture. She wanted to counter the legacy of colonial rhetoric which she believed underpinned the entire experience of Black people in Britain and the oppression of Black people worldwide. Her character, always strong and confident, strengthened. Alongside her charm, gregariousness, care and nurturing, she remained unwavering in her commitment to her work, as recalled by her friend Waveney Bushell:

> There were no half measures with Jessica, apropos forming groups in an impromptu way to raise money for places. Her whole manner showed that nothing was too big for her to undertake. She wouldn't be put off by anything which other people would feel 'oh gosh, that's too large something for me to get involved with'.[1]

Bushell expanded on her observations of Jessica's resolve to achieve her vision. If she was told that something was impossible, she would seek to find a solution:

> The more one told her that, the more determined she would be to focus on the topic and to be successful at it. That was her personality, there

---

[1] Waveney Bushell, interview with Claudia Tomlinson.

were no half measures with her. Her friendships showed that, she was a good friend. She could be a good friend, but equally she could dismiss one without batting an eye.[2]

In the early 1980s she started work on rolling out the programme of publishing books to be made widely available to children in Britain.

How the West Indian Child is Made Educationally Subnormal in the British Education System

In 1971, New Beacon Books published *How the West Indian Child is Made Educationally Subnormal in the British Education System*, by Bernard Coard. It was jointly published with Caribbean Education Community Workers Association (CECWA). CECWA was comprised of twenty-six Caribbean community organizations brought together by Jessica Huntley and John La Rose as a single organization. Waveney Bushell, who was considered by many to be the first Black educational psychologist in Britain, was a co-founder of CECWA and campaigner for the rights of Black children in the educational system kept the group informed with relevant information. She was particularly concerned about the psychological testing Black child arrivals were subjected to:

> The test that was used in those days was the Stanford–Binet test which is no longer used. One part of that test was called the Information, I think, we the psychologist stopped that test. I remember on my placement days, I remember seeing a lot of children who were black. Mainly because they started coming in, families started coming in since the 60s, and I used that very test and found that it was all wrong, that it was not relevant to that child. An example I gave is the word 'tap' was used. I would say to the child 'what's a tap?' and the child wouldn't know what's a tap. I found myself walking across the room, fortunately there was a pipe, what we at home would call a pipe. I said to the child, 'what's this then', and the child would say 'pipe', so I knew the child knew the concept, but didn't know the word that was used, what we called that, so I felt this is all wrong.[3]

---

[2]Waveney Bushell, interview with Claudia Tomlinson.
[3]Ibid.

Established publishers were approached as prospective publishers and distributors for Coard's book but all declined it. The twenty-six organizations run by Jessica Huntley and John La Rose agreed to raise the money themselves to publish the book and pay the printers. When the book was finally printed it was published under by New Beacon Books as the sole publisher. It was a major disappointment to Jessica that her significant input to the book's development was not recognized in the publishing arrangements. She raised the matter directly with John La Rose and Bernard Coard. According to Coard, Jessica 'thought the book that was coming out was a joint publication of New Beacon Books and Bogle L'Ouverture Publications'.[4] Jessica had been identified as the driving force behind the book's development and many feel that she was overwhelmingly responsible for its completion through her work with Coard.

Coard wrote the book as an act of resistance on behalf of the Black community in Britain.[5] CECWA had organized a conference in 1970 at which Coard presented a paper on the experience of Black children in Special Educational Needs schools. He was put under significant pressure by Black community leaders and the conference organizers to publish a book. He recalls that 'Jessica was part of the recruitment strategy, she was critical, a critical voice. She and John La Rose, there were a whole lot of other people, but they were the ones that were most insistent.'[6] He was given three months to produce the book, because of the sense of urgency.

The first print run of 10,000 copies quickly sold out, Coard said 'it was a sensation'. Chapter five of the book was published in *The Guardian* newspaper and the press in general was very sympathetic, and it received a lot of media attention. Almost every radio and TV programme gave it attention. There were over 200 phone calls and seventeen letters the day after the chapter appeared in *The Guardian*.[7] The fees from book sales and from media interviews were considerable, and Coard was paid in the region of £7,000 which he donated to Black youth and parents' organizations in Britain.[8]

Coard eventually decided to sign over the royalties of *How the West Indian Child* to Bogle L'Ouverture Publications, with Jessica advising him how these funds would be used. Coard said: 'she said to me, "I'm going to use it specifically for children's books … because black kids must be able to see people like themselves in the books, they read things that are historically

---

[4]Bernard Coard, interview with Claudia Tomlinson, 2 June 2021.
[5]Bernard Coard, 'Why I Wrote the 'ESN Book', *The Guardian*, 5 February 2005.
[6]Bernard Coard, interview with Claudia Tomlinson.
[7]Ibid.
[8]Ibid.

and culturally relevant".'⁹ She wanted to play a part in decolonizing Black children's literature. She felt that Britain, and much of the Western world, and in those countries colonized by Western nations either ignored Black themes, or presented distorted histories. She also wanted to correct what she perceived as the gaps, the silences and untruths about Black people and their histories.

Coard therefore recognized that many community organizations were being funded and financially benefitting from the book apart from Bogle L'Ouverture, despite Jessica's considerable role in its development. After the first print run, Coard changed publishers from New Beacon Books to Bogle L'Ouverture, informing New Beacon Books that future re-prints should be by Bogle L'Ouverture. This was explicitly requested of Bernard Coard by Jessica, in the presence of John La Rose, to encourage more equality between the two publishers and was in keeping with the open and transparent style she fostered.

Although Bogle L'Ouverture Publications was given approval to re-publish, a new print run did not appear from the company. It is not clear why Bogle L'Ouverture decided not to re-publish such a successful book, but at a 1974 meeting of Bogle L'Ouverture, Jessica indicated that royalties for *How the West Indian Child* had not been received by Bogle L'Ouverture Publications by that time.[10]

Getting to Know Ourselves – The First Children's Book

Getting to Know Ourselves, published by Bogle L'Ouverture Publications in 1972, was one of the earliest books dedicated to the education of Black children in Britain. It is possible that the idea for this book came from Guyana, as Jessica wrote to the Guyana Education Department around this time that she had 'seen one of your recent publications, *We Are One. They Came From Africa*, and would like to order 24 copies, urgently. If these are not for resale, please let us have as many as you can for use in Black Supplementary Schools.'[11] *Getting to Know Ourselves* was written by

---

[9]Ibid.

[10]LMA, HC, LMA/4462/A/02/011, p.5, 'A Brief Outline About the Development and Future of BLP', 9 February 1974.

[11]LMA, HC, LMA/4463/D/10/01/003, Letter from Jessica Huntley to the Guyana Education Department, 2 October 1972.

married couple Phyllis and Bernard Coard following on the very successful publication of Bernard Coard's *How the West Indian Child is Made Educationally Subnormal in the British School System*. In fact, *Getting to Know Ourselves* was intended to help address the issues raised in *How the West Indian Child*. The publishers wrote that:

> Bernard and his wife, Phyllis, herself a West Indian Mother, and a Psychiatric Social Worker with experience in Child Guidance work, have tried to help solve this most acute problem by writing a book specifically for children. This book is an introduction to African and Caribbean history which can be grasped by very young children.[12]

It was Jessica's view that this work would represent 'the first of a series of Children's books intended for readers between 3–7 years old. Our modest intention is that this book, together with the others in the series, will assist the young Black child in his search for his identity. They should help to bridge the gap between our peoples in the Old and New Worlds.'[13] The book features illustrations, intended to be used for colouring by young readers. Its narrative features a story about young children speaking about themselves and the lives and activities of their families in the Caribbean. Young children talk to each other about the achievements and contributions of their relatives in the building of roads, schools, hospitals and the infrastructure of the Caribbean and other countries, including America. It also informs young children of the contribution made by earlier generations of the African diaspora in the Caribbean to agriculture. It also covers Africa and informs young people that their roots are African and describes the culture including music and storytelling and that people in the Caribbean often shared stories about Africa. It gives children of African descent the simple message, 'so you see we are all African. We are all Brothers and Sisters, from Mother Africa. We are One People, and we are friends.'[14] This work continues to deliver Bogle L'Ouverture's commitment of re-writing Black history, an African history. It presented young Black readers of the era with a rare opportunity understand themselves and their history in a way that countered their racially oppressive everyday experiences in Britain.

---

[12]LMA, HC, LMA/4462, E/01/001-002, Phyllis Coard and Bernard Coard, *Getting to Know Ourselves* (London: Bogle L'Ouverture Publications, 1972), n.p.

[13]Ibid.

[14]Ibid.

Celebrating the Beauty of Creole Languages – *Rain Falling, Sun Shining*

Bogle L'Ouverture published its first book by a sole woman author, Odette Thomas, in 1975. Thomas' book was an early example of Jessica's resolve and commitment to achieving greater Black unity and uplift through books. This work celebrates and uplifts Caribbean language, music and rejects colonial legacies. Publishing Thomas' book can therefore be seen as an early act of decolonization by Jessica, who wrote that the book features musical rhymes, 'song-rhymes':

> Representative of Caribbean folk-culture, of its images, metaphors [sic], and music. They will appeal to people of all ages, especially the 4–7 year olds. To the grown-ups, the rhymes in Rain Falling, Sun Shining by Odette Thomas will bring back happy childhood memories, while to the young, this collection will help bridge the gap between their world and that of their parents.[15]

Thomas got the idea for her children's book, *Rain Falling, Sun Shining*, when visiting Guyana soon after her marriage to Ewart Thomas, the editor of *The Groundings with My Brothers* by Walter Rodney.[16] Spending time with family who had small children, she picked up and read their books of nursery rhymes. The books were a distorted blend of West Indian rhymes, set to the music of well-known British nursery rhymes.[17] For example, the rhyme 'Demerara Bridge is falling down' was set to the music of British children's rhyme 'London Bridge is falling down'. Considering this an appalling lack of authenticity with Guyanese music not available to accompany local lyrics, Thomas took the decision to take her own action to correct this situation. Then a student, Thomas 'decided to write some poems that depicted scenes and memories from my own childhood, e.g., looking out the window during a big rainfall and seeing the ducks in our yard eating up the juicy mangoes that were falling during the shower and wishing I could run out and get one before they got to it'.[18]

Thomas wrote these poems in West Indian dialect, often termed 'creole'. Describing how the book came to be published by Bogle L'Ouverture,

---

[15]LMA, HC, LMA/4462/E/01/054, p.7. Jessica Huntley, Preface, to Odette Thomas, *Rain Falling, Sun Shining* (London: Bogle L'Ouverture Publications, 1975).

[16]Odette Thomas, interview with Claudia Tomlinson (written responses submitted), 31 March 2022.

[17]Ibid.

[18]Ibid.

Thomas recalled that when Jessica was contacted about the book and 'she readily accepted the proposal to print it after having it reviewed by Andrew Salkey and others. It was Jessica's idea to add the musical score and procured a young musician, Chris Cameron, to put the words to music so that they could be sung. She also recruited her friend, Errol Lloyd to illustrate the book.'[19] Odette Thomas outlined her motivation for wanting to write the book: 'Our people have to study the foreign, out-moded non-standard English of Shakespeare and Chaucer, so does it make sense for them to be forbidden their own non-standard English in class? If there is a place for Shakespeare and Chaucer in schools, surely there is a place for West Indian language?'[20]

Thomas would have been pushing an open door with Jessica with this line of argument, as it accorded closely with Jessica's perspective on valuing Black languages and culture. The titles of the rhymes included in the book are games and dances entitled *Skipping*, *Tanti-Marie* and *Ice-Cream*. Other rhymes in the book are *Cane*, and *Rain and Sun*.

Publishing *How Europe Underdeveloped Africa*

Following the international success of *The Groundings with My Brothers*, Walter Rodney again needed a specialist radical Black publisher such as Bogle L'Ouverture Publications for his new work, *How Europe Underdeveloped Africa*.[21] He had a contract with a reputable publisher Oxford University Press (OUP) for his PhD thesis and was an emerging academic of international repute and could have probably attracted the interest of many traditional publishers for his historical research. It was very unlikely that OUP would have been interested in publishing *How Europe* as, unlike his PhD thesis, it was not a traditional academic historical work, it was a Pan-African critique of Western historiography, imperialism, colonialism and neo-colonialism. Rodney had also been branded a terrorist by the Jamaican government and banned from one of the most prestigious academic institutions – the University of the West Indies. His appeal to the international academies and publishers for *How Europe* was arguably more limited than it had been before October 1968. He was effectively a political exile. If a traditional publisher was interested in publishing *How Europe* at this time, it is unlikely they would have connected with the audiences

---

[19]Ibid.

[20]Ibid.

[21]LMA, HC, LMA/4462/E/01/034, Walter Rodney, *How Europe Underdeveloped Africa* (London: Bogle L'Ouverture Publications and Tanzania Publishing House, 1971).

Rodney wanted to reach. Rodney stated he wanted a book that was able 'to try and reach Africans who wish to explore further the nature of their exploitation, rather than to satisfy the "standards" set by our oppressors and their spokesmen in the academic world'.[22]

He was not seeking an academic publisher for the first edition of *How Europe*, even if one wanted to consider his new book. Given this circumstance, there was only one publisher in the UK that met this description – Bogle L'Ouverture Publications. New Beacon Books and Busby and Allison did not have a specific Pan-African publishing strategy, unlike Bogle L'Ouverture Publications. Rodney also wanted the 'volume as simply and cheaply as possible', which again would not appeal to publishers interested in profit.[23] Bogle L'Ouverture had declared disinterest in profit making as its primary purpose.

Rodney therefore needed Bogle L'Ouverture Publications to publish this seminal work, and he wanted it to be jointly published with Tanzanian Publishing House for the first print run. Bogle L'Ouverture was the senior publishing partner for the first edition, responsible for the production, printing and promoting of the book. There was disappointment on Jessica's part that Rodney had decided the book was to be jointly published as she regarded this as a missed opportunity for Bogle L'Ouverture to gain a foothold as a major publisher in Africa. However, she was aware that it was Rodney's view that *How Europe* was intended for an African audience primarily.

Bogle L'Ouverture influenced Rodney into shaping *How Europe* into the work it would become. The publishers, particularly Andrew Salkey, their principal editorial advisor, suggested a single authored manuscript. Jessica also supported Salkey's idea that *How Europe* should be a single authored book. This idea was initially rejected by Rodney who wanted to include the other authors 'who were good brothers, who had gone through the struggle', and had been imprisoned.[24] He eventually agreed to Salkey's suggestion and *How Europe* was first published in the UK in 1972 as a single authored volume, to enormous and enduring critical acclaim.

It is widely acknowledged as Rodney's most influential and well-known work. It provides a historical perspective of African history, starting with how the region developed up to the fifteenth century, its contribution to the European development in the pre-colonial period, and post-colonial periods. It also explores how colonialism underdeveloped Africa. Jessica has described that prior to the publication of *How Europe Underdeveloped*

---

[22]Ibid., 1983, p.8.

[23]Ibid.

[24]LMA, HC, LMA/4463/F/07/01/001/D, Eric and Jessica Huntley interview with Harry Goulbourne (Session Three), 28 May 1992.

Africa Rodney submitted a proposal for the book to Bogle L'Ouverture Publications, as a follow up to *Groundings*.

By 1974, Rodney appears to have widened his core objective for *How Europe* and agreed for future editions to be published by a traditional academic publisher. By 1973, Bogle L'Ouverture had published three editions of the book and the international demand was clear.

Jessica had established the worldwide success of the book, and by mid-1973, the 'heat' of 1968 surrounding Rodney had somewhat abated. Jessica wrote to Rodney that she was negotiating for the publication of *How Europe* by Howard University in the USA which published its own first edition in 1974. She wrote to Rodney saying 'as you know, we were through Ewart, negotiating with Howard for an American edition. In fact, only shortly before your letter arrived, I had written to them again I shall be giving Monthly Review rights to publish, since a final settlement is long overdue.'[25] Ewart Thomas, Rodney's childhood friend and US based academic was involved in the negotiations with Howard University. She also confirmed the negotiations she was leading on to publish the book in a large number of international markets, 'you will also wish to know I have been trying hard to find a French edition for the book'.[26]

Bogle L'Ouverture continued to reprint and publish the book until well after Rodney's assassination in 1980. In the publisher's note to the 1983 edition, Jessica described its success having been published in several languages and thousands of copies sold globally. She held the view that the book was essentially about a concern for modern Africa, and that its purpose was a 'tool in the struggles ahead aimed at reversing that process and for the complete social political and economic transformation of the continent'.[27]

A Voice for Black Youth – *Dread, Beat and Blood*

The mid-1970s in Britain continued to be hard environment for Black children and youth, and Jessica remained determined to intervene in this situation. When she was presented with the work of a young Jamaican born poet, Linton Kwesi Johnson, to consider for publication, she immediately recognized the value of the exciting new dub voice of a generation of youth that was hurting and being ignored. Johnson was a south Londoner in his early twenties when Bogle L'Ouverture published *Dread, Beat and Blood*

---

[25]LMA, HC, LMA/4462/C/01/092, Jessica Huntley Letter to Walter Rodney, 28 August 1973.
[26]Ibid. 1973.
[27]Rodney, *How Europe*, 1983, p.1.

in 1975. At this time, Black British youth, dubbed 'the first generation' was growing up and had become teenagers and young adults.

This was the generation born to parents who had worked around the clock to feed, clothe and house them, and had done so through the harsh background of racialized injustices. They had shed their disappointments of never achieving the education they had hoped they would get for themselves in England. They hoped their children would achieve the full extent of equality and dignity as respected Black British born citizens that they themselves had not experienced. They found their hopes were dashed, having been told their children were subnormal or just not as intelligent as the white children. They watched helplessly as their children were put into the bottom classes and entered into lower value exams that would ensure they didn't make it to university. Their children were put in detention, expelled or deemed unteachable. This new generation of Black children was headed for the welfare queues, where they would find themselves despised and denigrated for signing on and receiving the 'dole', or going to prison. They were targeted by police, constantly stopped and searched. Johnson himself described this position as a 'war of terror that the police was waging against black youth'.[28] This generation was the audience that *Dread, Beat and Blood* gave voice to. He has described this work as 'the book that established me as a poet in this country. I've been able to build upon that, my whole reputation was built around that book and everything happened after that.'[29] This theme formed the basis of Johnson's explosive new work.

Johnson had a friendship and comradely relationship with Jessica, and her husband Eric, over many decades, from the late 1960s, when he was introduced to the extensive network of radical Black political and cultural activism. These networks included John and Irma La Rose, Andrew Salkey, Oscar Abrams, and others. Johnson was initially mentored as part of the Caribbean Artists Movement (CAM), and specifically by Andrew Salkey who would read and comment on the work of the young poet. Salkey took Johnson's manuscript to Jessica for consideration, she agreed to publish it, recognizing the value of the work. After agreeing to publish Johnson, he was jointly mentored by Jessica and Eric Huntley, and he recalls that they 'both took me under their wings, probably saw some potential in me as a young activist and someone who was aspiring to become a poet'.[30]

Johnson reflects that simply to know the couple was transformational in his life, and that they were 'very nice people you know, the kind of people, you couldn't believe your luck that you had met people like them'. He described Jessica as 'a very inspirational person, a great motivator, a matriarch in the

---

[28]Linton Kwesi Johnson, interview with Claudia Tomlinson, 30 July 2020.
[29]Ibid.
[30]Ibid.

more social sense of the word, and she was someone you could look up to as a youngster'.[31] He reports his recollection of her personal attributes: 'She was extremely charming; she had this beguiling smile.'[32] Johnson is unequivocal about the influence Jessica and Eric had on him, and he mostly recalled the couple working jointly with him:

> They made a tremendous contribution to the black radical movement and the black liberation movement in this country, they provided the foundation for the information vacuum that was there before the intervention of New Beacon books, and then later on Bogle L'Ouverture. They provided the information, books on history, politics, culture, art and so on for the young up and coming activists of that generation. They were role models; they were inspirational they provided leadership and Jessica was very much at the forefront of that. They have left a solid foundation of political and cultural activism for the next generation that came along to build upon. I have a tremendous amount of respect for Jessica, and for Eric for that matter. There might have been ideological differences but on a personal level, I hope they were fond of me as I was of them.[33]

The Bogle Baby Writes – Works by Accabre Huntley

Accabre Huntley, daughter of Jessica and Eric Huntley, who became Accabre Rutlin after her marriage, was nine years old when she published her first book, *At School Today*, with Bogle L'Ouverture, in 1977, a poetry anthology. She published her second book with Bogle L'Ouverture in 1983, entitled *Easter Monday Blues*. By 1977 she had a clear identity, and it was this identity that was woven into the main themes of her books. Her poetry was about 'what it was like to be me, living in Ealing, Caribbean descent, born in Britain, the experiences I had in school'.[34]

In addition to her own identity and experiences she was the 'Bogle Baby', a babe-in-arms, and bounced on the knees of the greats of Black and Caribbean activism who converged on her parents' home. She was a toddler when *Groundings* was published and witnessed the joy and celebrations as the first copies arrived at her home. She grew up in the bookshop, reading the books, including the US authors, and witnessing first-hand what her

---

[31]Ibid.
[32]Ibid.
[33]Ibid.
[34]Accabre Rutlin, interviews with Claudia Tomlinson, 24 July 2020–27 October 2022.

parents were involved in. She learned about apartheid and the condition of most Black people around the world. But closer still, she witnessed what her parents and others were working to achieve. It was in 1977 that the attacks on the bookshop started, and her parents experienced many years of being threatened. Her writing, as described in the publicity material for her book *At School Today*, was rooted in her experience in Bogle L'Ouverture and 'underline the fact that her image of herself is firmly established = black, proud and hopeful'.[35]

Accabre was encouraged from an early age by her mother to write and perform poetry. It was not necessarily Accabre's own first desired activity, and she sometimes privately wondered whether her work would have been published if her parents were not publishers, and if she had benefited from her special position. From the age of nine, she performed her poetry, sharing platforms with the greats such as Linton Kwesi Johnson. When it was time for Accabre's poetry performance, her mother Jessica would coach and listen to her daughter practice her delivery, as she recalled: 'if I had a reading coming up, she would say "well you've read that one already, you haven't written anything else?" So, she was always encouraging me to write something.'[36]

In fact, Jessica's passion for encouraging her daughter to perform poetry led Accabre to wonder whether her mother had a hankering for performing on the stage herself, and whether she herself may have wanted to be an actress or performer. It is an interesting supposition as Jessica, it will be recalled, had a childhood that she regarded as wonderful for the times she spent performing in youth dramas, and reading poetry herself. Jessica's own mother, Hectorine, also had a love of verse, principally passages from the Bible and other poems, and would coach her daughter in this, for example as a gift for a friend's birthday. Nevertheless, Accabre's performances were powerfully delivered and very well received by audiences.

Celebrating Ten Years of Bogle L'Ouverture

In 1979 and 1980, Jessica led the establishment of a committee to formally mark the milestone of ten years of Bogle L'Ouverture Publications. The start date of Bogle L'Ouverture was therefore viewed as 1969, possibly in line with the publication of Walter Rodney's book, although as shown, publishing activity had taken place in 1968. The Friends of Bogle committee organized activities which ran from the spring of 1979 through to 1980. At one meeting,

---

[35]LMA, HC, LMA/4462/Q/01/003/001, Cover Notes on *At School Today*, 1976–7.
[36]Ibid.

FIGURE 13.1 *Jessica Huntley in 'Creation for Liberation', a film to celebrate ten years of Bogle L'Ouverture Publications (1979). Reproduced with kind permission from Ray Kril.*

it was clearly agreed that 'in addition to a book exhibition, including Black booksellers', publishers could also be invited.[37] The centrepiece of the celebrations was a Cultural Evening held at the Commonwealth Institute on 10 November 1979.

The evening was opened with a speech by Jessica, and then compered by Carmen Munroe. There were performances from actress Nadia Cattouse, the Cimmarons, Jimmy James and the Vagabonds, Keith Waithe, John Agard, Linton Kwesi Johnson, Steel 'N' Skin, Accabre Huntley and the Legba dance group. The vote of thanks was given by Errol Lloyd. Many of these people were the leading Black celebrities in Britain of this period, and were household names, recognized on the street. That Jessica was able to easily attract the contribution of such leading names is a testament to her standing, and the reputation of Bogle L'Ouverture. There was media interest from the national papers and magazines, local radio stations provided publicity for the events. There was a letter of congratulations from C.L.R. James: 'My Dear Jessica, congratulations on the splendid work of ten years.'[38]

---

[37]LMA, HC, LMA/4462/H/01/001/2 of 2, Minutes of the last meeting of the Tenth Anniversary, 26 October, year undated, circa 1979.

[38]LMA, HC, LMA/4462/H/01/001/1 of 2, C.L.R. James Letter to Jessica Huntley, 21 February 1979.

Black Parents Organizing

One of the most important areas of concern that Jessica was involved in was the resistance activities against the devastating oppression of Black children in Britain. From the early 1960s, Black parents increasingly had to contend with serious difficulties affecting Black children in the British education system. In 1969, activists focused activities on fighting the introduction of 'Banding' by Haringey Council. The Anti-Banding campaign was led by the North London West Indian Association (NLWIA), a committee of the West Indian Standing Conference, and headed by the Conference's secretary, Jeff Crawford.[39]

The Anti-Banding campaign arose when a report by an official working for Haringey Council in London recommended the introduction of a system of three separate streams in which to allocate children, based on school decisions about ability. The reason given in the council report for the introduction of the banding system was the perceived lower intelligence of Black children compared to white children, and it was argued that banding was necessary to separate Black children into lower bands. The NLWIA attacked the policy as being based on racism and demanded that plans to introduce it were abandoned. Haringey Council, at the time led by the Conservative Party, proceeded to implement the policy.

Jessica became a co-founder of the Black Parents Movement, on 20 April 1975. Its inception followed the arrest and subsequent conviction of seventeen-year-old Cliff McDaniel on 17 April 1975 on disputed charges of assaulting a police officer and insulting behaviour.[40] Organizations mounted a campaign against the verdict and organized a successful appeal won by the campaigners. An investigation was ordered into the police violence against Cliff McDaniel.[41] The Black Parents Movement agitated for action against police brutality faced by students and youth, educational injustices and all forms of harassment faced by Black youth in British society. They picketed public meetings of the council and police where Black youth was being discussed. Pickets were also held outside courts where its cases were being heard. The Black Parents Movement demanded that Haringey education department address their concerns over low literacy levels in their children after years in the British education system and the overtly racist behaviour

---

[39]LMA, HC, LMA/4463/B/02/01/002, p.1, Report of the Co-ordinating Council of the Black Parent's Movement, First Black Parents Movement and Black Students Movement Conference, 1978.

[40]Campaign Leaflet, 'The Police and the Black Student; The Case of Cliff McDaniel', 1975, Huntley Collection, London Metropolitan Archives, LMA/4463/B/02/02/001.

[41]Campaign Leaflet, 'Victory for the Black Parents and the Black Students Movements; Cliff McDaniel Wins, Hornsey Police Defeated', 1975, Huntley Collection, London Metropolitan Archives, LMA/4463/B/02/02/001.

of some teachers in the school environment. Activists further demanded that parents be given the right to be accompanied by representatives when attending school meetings to raise concerns. They also challenged the keeping of records on children, records which would follow them into their futures and which parents had no rights to access.[42]

Baroness Osamor, a member of the Black Parents Movement at the time recalled Jessica's influence at meetings of community members and parents:

> She's the kind of person that's welcoming, she's the kind of person that will encourage you to document what is happening to understand that you are dealing with a system, and to also understand that you have to form alliances, to understand that you have to form links, so all that is in the character of the person.[43]

The campaign by the Black Parents Movement was sustained and a commitment was given by the Labour Party to rescind the banding policy

FIGURE 13.2 *The Black Parents Movement, circa 1978, featuring Jessica Huntley, third left and John La Rose, second left. Courtesy of the Huntley Collections, London Metropolitan Archives.*

---

[42]Ibid.
[43]Baroness Lady Martha Osamor, interview with Claudia Tomlinson, 30 October 2021.

when they won the council government and they delivered on this, ending banding in Haringey.[44]

Many groups and organizations of Black parents started to become established and to organize to resist the emergence of this discrimination against Black children. Jessica was an important figurehead in these campaigns.

She was a founder member of CECWA in 1968. It started as the CEA (the Caribbean Education Association) but was eventually broadened to include workers as it was recognized that the oppression within the education system was connected to the experience of Black workers.[45] The gatherings that initially focused on oppression in the education system started to attract a lot of activists from across London and they determined that the focus of the original CEA was too narrow. CECWA therefore was formed, expanded from CEA, to look at racism in employment, policing and the treatment of Black children in the education system. Gus John was also an active founder member of CECWA which was established at the West Indian Students Centre and met once a fortnight.

An important part of the meetings was an opportunity for activists and community members to obtain literature of interest to their areas of concern. The meetings were provided with books published by Bogle L'Ouverture and New Beacon Books, on tables at the back of the hall for the London-based activists to consult and purchase. At this time, there was no access to the books that were being provided by the two publishing houses, and therefore the provision of these materials was an important part of the activism. According to Gus John, these two publishers provided a highly valuable resource at the meetings:

> So, we had something that was very rare in those days, a good collection of literature, and textbooks of various sorts, from the Caribbean, written by Caribbean people from Africa itself and from the United States. It was a time when there was something called the Heinemann African writers' series, and through that we were introduced to some fantastic African authors, Wole Soyinka, Chinua Achebe, Amos Tutuola, and a range of others. Having come from the Caribbean where we hardly saw anything written by black people, not even the novels of CLR James who was just round the corner from Grenada and Trinidad, I can't tell you how liberating it was to be able to actually have access to those books that Bogle L'Ouverture and New Beacon provided at those meetings.[46]

---

[44]Ibid.

[45]Gus John, interview with Claudia Tomlinson.

[46]Ibid.

Black Supplementary Schools

Jessica was a pioneer of the Black Supplementary Schools Movement in Britain since the middle of the 1960s, in its earliest forms in the West Indian Students Centre. In late 1971, working with a group of associates, Black parents and teachers, she founded the Kwame Nkrumah Black Supplementary school in Hackney, East London.[47] Its main aims were to 'educate black children to have pride and confidence in themselves, by teaching them about the history of their people and themselves – our history – the sort of thing they are not taught in their regular schools'.[48] It also aimed to provide classes in maths, English and science subjects. It also aimed to help 'organise ourselves as a black community to help ourselves, by working together to provide some of the facilities no one else can, or will provide for us'.[49] At its height, it appeared to have over fifty children in attendance and operated on weekday evenings, as well as on Saturdays. It was self-funded by fundraising events, such as dances. It relied heavily on the involvement and contributions of Black parents to operate. This was one of the areas that was problematic for the survival of the school given the significant demands on the time of parents of these children. The available records do not indicate how long this school survived, but it was struggling for survival in its first year of operation. It was at this time, 1971, that Jessica's childhood friend, Cecily Haynes-Hart emigrated permanently with her family to Britain. The two friends remained close, and Cecily worked in education and the Black Supplementary Schools in Britain for many years, as a shared interest with Jessica.

In 1972 Jessica co-founded the Marcus Garvey School in Shepherd's Bush, London, with other influential educators and activists such as Sandra Richards, Peter Moses and Tony Munroe.[50] It was founded as a school to supplement the education of Black children in the area, according to its stated objectives: 'because of the hypocrisies and subnormal attention that are being meted out to our children in classrooms (farcerooms), at school we decided to organise a school of our own, so as to enable our children to improve on the little education their school permits them'.[51] It also aimed to build children's confidence and pride to enable future power and prestige as people and a community. It was held on Saturdays, run by voluntary teachers, and taught basic school subjects including maths, English, history and science.

---

[47] LMA/4463/D/10/01/005 'Kwame Nkrumah Supplementary School', circa April 1972.
[48] Ibid.
[49] Ibid.
[50] LMA/4463/D/10/01/006 'Marcus Garvey School', 29 June 1972.
[51] LMA/4463/D/11/01/001 'Draft Report to Ealing Council on Peter Moses School', p. 1.

Moving into the 1980s, Jessica continued this work and established a new school. Together with Eric Huntley, and other supporters and organizers, she opened the Peter Moses School in 1986 in Ealing, London. The Bogle L'Ouverture Publications working group, The Friends of Bogle, founded the Peter Moses School on behalf of the company.[52] It was for pupils aged between nine and sixteen years old. Pupils met each Saturday morning at Ealing College and studied several subjects. They were taught maths, English, French, biology, physics, chemistry, history and creative activities by qualified and support teachers. An example of the cultural activities they participated in was their attendance at the First of August Marcus Garvey Centenary celebrations held at Ealing Town Hall. The curriculum included guest speakers, drumming lessons, school trips and speakers on Black history. There was a small fee charged to parents for the attendance at the school, and the school also received a grant from Ealing Council.

The selection of the name Peter Moses reflects the ideas and cultural objectives of the school. An Ealing resident, originally from Dominica, Moses was a member of the Black Liberation Front and also a pioneer of the Black Supplementary School Movement. In addition to the Marcus Garvey School, he was also a founding member of the Kwame Nkrumah School in Hackney, London. He died in 1973 due to leukaemia but struggled against the injustices faced by Black people despite his illness.

The overarching aim of the Peter Moses School was in keeping with the general objectives of the Black Supplementary school movement. It aimed to 're-adjust the inequality of education as meted out to black children'.[53] It was not exclusively for Black children, but 'organised primarily for black children'. The door was open to 'all children whose parents feel they can benefit from the service'.[54] There was an expectation that the organization of the school would be shared by parents and teacher and senior pupils so that it was a joint venture.

In 1991, the school learned that its grant from Ealing Council was to be reduced from £5,800 to £567 for the new academic year. Eric Huntley wrote to parents that this change in funding 'placed the school in a state of crisis for which we were not prepared'.[55] It was proposed that the shortfall be met by an increased charge to parents which some were unable to meet. The funding crisis, plus a gradual decline in attendance for a period, and reduced parental involvement meant that the school was no longer viable at this time. The decision was made to close in September 1991.[56] Throughout the 1970s all of Jessica's attention was focused on fighting racialized decolonization.

---

[52]Ibid.
[53]Ibid.
[54]Ibid.
[55]LMA/4462/C/01/092 'Eric Huntley Letter to Parents of Peter Moses School', 4 September 1991.
[56]Ibid.

14

'The Atmosphere Was Electric in the Shop': Bookshop Activism

In 1974 Jessica and Eric purchased a larger home at 141 Coldershaw Road, also in Ealing, which became the new permanent family home. Though it was firstly a family home, its threshold was crossed by many of the leading figures of international Black activism, arts, literature, socialist and left-wing politics. Its walls heard the tones and expressions of Andrew Salkey, John La Rose, Walter Rodney, Linton Kwesi Johnson, Maurice Bishop, Margaret Busby, Toni Morrison, Toni Cade Bambara, Kathleen Cleaver, Valerie Bloom, Bernard Coard, Lemn Sissay, the founders of Bogle L'Ouverture, Maya Angelou, Gus John and many others discussing literature, ideas of resistance, political and community organizing against racial injustices. Jessica was the central focus of this activity.

There were many callers to the home. Many were new arrivals to the country who only knew her name. Bogle L'Ouverture author Odette Thomas recalled that although Jessica was not expecting them: 'typically, these people arrived on her doorstep with only her name as reference and she would take them in, make them at home and provide them with contacts'.[1] These callers had heard about this space and would just call in for information, advice, to read literature that was rare at the time, and to talk about the Caribbean, Africa and global racialized injustices. The home would go on to be commemorated with a plaque in recognition of its cultural and historical importance.

---

[1] Odette Thomas, interview with Claudia Tomlinson.

The Bookshop in the Front Room Under Threat

Of the many local visitors who just turned up at Coldershaw Road, Steven Lewis, aged just sixteen, was pointed in the direction of the Huntley home by a teacher who spotted him wearing a Soledad Brothers badge:

> I happen to have a small badge I'd picked up somewhere that dealt with George Jackson and the Soledad Brothers. It had, I think was a fist with the chains, and I thought 'that looks pretty good', so I was actually wearing it at school, and he said to me 'Ah, do you know about Bogle L'Ouverture?', I said 'No'. He just explained that it was a bookshop, well it wasn't a bookshop as such, it was in the front room of the house in 141 Coldershaw Road, and he said 'You should go there, and meet the people'.[2]

The case of the Soledad Brothers involved the case of George Jackson, an African American man who in 1970 had been imprisoned in the California prison system for several years.[3] In 1970, Jackson was in Soledad Prison, and along with two other inmates was accused of the murder of a prison guard. These prisoners became known as the Soledad Brothers.[4] George Jackson's brother, Jonathan Jackson, became involved in a courtroom attempt to free the Soledad Brothers, an attempt which ended violently and led to his killing by authorities. In 1971, George Jackson was killed by prison guards when attempting to escape with other inmates.[5] His prison diaries were subsequently published and became an important document on the condition of Black men in America, incarceration and the experience of racism in all aspects of society in the United States.[6] Jackson's life and death was quickly adopted as an international campaign indicative of the struggle faced by Black people worldwide. The Soledad Brothers affair was a very high-profile campaign and continued to inspire activism for many years after the incidents.

The Soledad Brothers campaign was one in which Jessica was very much involved. She was able to obtain literature about the campaign that she would be able to display on her shelves for readers.[7] She also sent letters

---

[2]Steven Lewis, interview with Claudia Tomlinson, 4 December 2022.

[3]Zach Schrempp, George Jackson (1941–71), *Blackpast*, 4 October, 2010, https://www.blackpast.org/african-american-history/jackson-george-1941-1971/.

[4]Ibid.

[5]Ibid.

[6]George Jackson, 'Soledad Brother: The Prison Letters of George Jackson', *History is a Weapon*, https://www.historyisaweapon.com/defcon1/soledadbro.html.

[7]Letter from Jessica Huntley to the Friends of Soledad, 31 August 1971, Huntley Collection, London Metropolitan Archives, LMA/4463/B/17/01/001A.

of solidarity to other supporters of the campaign. Responding to campaign information from another supporter, she responded 'let me first of all say how profoundly shocked over the whole Soledad affairs [*sic*]. Your letters certainly convey to me that something need to be done now. I have been discussing the contents of the letter with some Brothers and as soon as our ideas are formulated, I will be writing to you again. In the meantime, we cannot afford to weaken as this will mean the enemies gain.'[8]

Steven Lewis has described why the Huntley home was such a magnetic draw for people like him in the early 1970s:

> In the front room, there was a typewriter, a desk, shelves everywhere, and books and magazines you name it, all over the place. We just started chatting casually basically, about education you know ... and then a few minutes later, a gentleman came in, he was rushing off somewhere, and that was Eric, he was working in insurance at that time, and then he left, you know, after a quick introduction, 'how do you do' an' stuff. It was all very friendly, they were very warm people, I thought 'this is

FIGURE 14.1 *The front room at Coldershaw Road, 1974, Jessica Huntley with Andrew Salkey (right) and Errol Lloyd (left). Courtesy of the Huntley Collection, London Metropolitan Archives.*

---

[8]Letter from Jessica Huntley, protesting the Soledad affair, 27 September 1971, Huntley Collection, London Metropolitan Archives, LMA/4463/B/17/01/001A.

interesting, I'd actually never met black folks like this', most black people were struggling, working, trying to make a living, you know, education was the priority, getting a good job, the usual stuff. But they were from a different angle in terms of, it was more the political and my eyes were opened and basically from there, the rest is history as they say.

Coldershaw Road also hosted multiple dinner parties and celebrations, and saw countless occasions of entertainment for family, friends and activists alike. Here, Jessica hosted cultural evenings, with literature readings from authors. By 1975, *Groundings* was on its fourth reprint, *How Europe* was on its second reprint and there were four other books in print, two for children. There were a number of posters and postcards available for sale, produced by artists working for Bogle L'Ouverture. The business was blooming.

These activities attracted the attention of a suspicious and unsympathetic neighbour who made an anonymous complaint to the local council that number 141 Coldershaw Road was being used to operate a business, in contravention of planning rules governing residential areas. In 1974 racial tensions were very high, and the neighbours' discomfort at a Black family moving into a white neighbourhood would have been discernible. But this was an important space for the family and their visitors for that very reason. With the continuing attacks on Black people, and after decades of being hounded out of rented boarding rooms, the settlers were now in a position to buy their own homes. Once acquired, they became safe refuges from a hostile outside world, and here, creativity, discussions, recreation and parties could take place. In fact, this was the very reason for the crowding of activists in the bedroom in their previous home.

It was a hard knock therefore when only a few months after the family moved in, the local council decided to take enforcement action against them. Jessica and Eric were given the option of closing down the business voluntarily or face its forcible closure. Despite being racked with worry, Jessica and Eric were clear that this was an unjust decision and challenged it. They were by this time very well known in Britain, particularly in London, as well as the Caribbean and beyond. They mounted a campaign to fight the council's decision, with Jessica describing the resistance activities: 'We mobilised support – we are politicals! Our friends outside, in Guyana and America, they wrote letters to the council.'[9] Ealing Council was flooded with complaints in the form of letters, petitions and telegrams from Britain and abroad, resulting in a highly publicized fight.

Jessica launched an appeal against Ealing Council's decision, and the proceedings were reported in the local media. A public inquiry was held

---

[9]Ireland, p.242.

in Ealing Town Hall, and it was reported that 'Mrs Jessica Huntley, who runs the Bogle L'Ouverture Bookshop, from the front room of her home at 141 Coldershaw Road, Ealing, was appealing against an Enforcement Notice served on her by Ealing Council demanding that she stop using the room for "office purposes".'[10] At the hearing, Jessica was represented by her friend, the lawyer and Trinidadian-born political and community activist, Cris Le Maitre. She answered questions directed at her by the Inspector of the Department of the Environment, from central government, prosecuting the case for the council. The newspaper reported her words: 'Bogle L'Ouverture, she said, was one of two bookshops in the country providing specialist children's literature to people who had been denied knowledge of their history and culture.'[11] She took the opportunity of the public hearing to inform local government officials of the importance of the political, historical and cultural importance of her work, and the importance of correcting this situation. She continued her public arguments, pointing out that 'both native and immigrant children benefitted from the educational matter she provided'.[12]

The case was presented and argued so passionately that it was clear that for Jessica it was her very vision for the Black struggle that was on trial and this is what she was defending in her statements. In addition to the presence of a central government official, there was an official presenting the case on behalf of Ealing Council. This council official enquired why Jessica had not sought to sell her material through established bookshops in commercial premises, and she responded she had 'approached W.H. Smiths with the literature but had received a very negative response'.[13] It appears she was also asked about meetings held at the home as 'she denied that the premises were used as a meeting place', but it is not clear why she was asked this as citizens could lawfully use their homes as meeting places. This is suggestive of concern possibly by security services that the home was being used for subversive political meetings, suggesting some surveillance of the home. In resting its case, the council said: 'it was not disputing the usefulness of the service Mrs Huntley provided in the community', but its objection was solely on the basis of a detrimental effect on the residential area.[14]

The council notified Jessica that the decision would be taken by central government, and that 'The Secretary of State for the Environment will notify

---

[10]The British Newspaper Archive, 'Bookshop in Front Room, "No Nuisance"', *The Gazette*, 11 April 1975, p.13, https://www.britishnewspaperarchive.co.uk/viewer/bl/0003289/19750411/236/0013.

[11]Ibid.

[12]Ibid.

[13]Ibid.

[14]Ibid.

interested parties of his decision.'[15] Several months later, Jessica received the news that she had lost the appeal, as 'the Department of the Environment Inspector who had attended the inquiry, recommended the dismissal of the appeal'.[16] Ultimately, it was a central government decision to back the local council's action. It may have been the case that all appeals against local planning decisions were heard centrally, however the question can be posed about the extent to which this was a political decision. Given the many high profile visitors to the home, the public inquiry may have reflected the security services concern about the activities of some visitors. Le Maitre successfully argued for a six-month period to allow time for Jessica to find new premises.

The professional trade magazine *The Surveyor* published a strong critique of the decision, stating that it was 'exactly the sort of case that gives planning a bad name', and that a more magnanimous approach should have been taken.[17] The ruling was also lamented by an Ealing school teacher, who, writing anonymously in the local paper, described the service provided by Bogle L'Ouverture Publications which was being conducted quietly from the family home. The author of the letter argued that teachers were at this time trying to make changes to the curriculum to meet the needs of a 'multi-cultural community' and 'a teacher like myself had been delighted to discover the existence of Bogle L'Ouverture and its books in our neighbourhood'.[18] They described the magnitude of the transformative change shepherded in by Bogle L'Ouverture and that: 'gradually, books reflecting the needs and interests of a multi-racial society are finding their way onto the library shelves of our schools'.[19] The teacher's letter continued, pointing out that 'parents and children too, are enjoying together the stories of many different cultures and, perhaps for the first time, hearing of the lives of the great men of Afro-Caribbean and Asian history' and the offer of 'an unrivalled supply of books for many who wish to know more about their origins and culture'.[20] Le Maitre's intervention was key as if the business was forced to stop operating immediately in the front room, this setback would have been enormous and potentially put the business entirely at risk of permanent closure.

---

[15]Ibid.

[16]Ibid.

[17]The British Newspaper Archive, 'Magazine criticises an Enquiry', *The Gazette*, 5 September 1975,p.10.https://www.britishnewspaperarchive.co.uk/viewer/bl/0003289/19750905/155/0012.

[18]The British Newspaper Archive, 'Good Cause Given Six Months' Notice', *The Gazette*, 5 September 1975, p.4. https://www.britishnewspaperarchive.co.uk/viewer/bl/0003289/19750905/052/0004.

[19]Ibid.

[20]Ibid.

Bogle L'Ouverture Bookshop at Chignell Place Opens

Following this ruling, Jessica and Eric made the decision to look for commercial premises. Chauncey Huntley, now a young man in his early twenties, had developed a love for Jamaican reggae music that was sold only in specialist shops that imported it from abroad. In 1975, imported Black music from the United States and the West Indies was beloved of Black youth of Britain at this time. It was also popular with white youth, and Black record shops did very brisk business in Britain at this time. One day Chauncey visited the record shop Greensleeves, where he went on a regular basis taking the route along the Uxbridge Road, past some of the staple sights of many British high streets in the 1970s. He passed the quintessentially English high street businesses, a launderette, a chip shop, a British Home Stores, a Marks & Spencer and a Woolworths.

As he turned off the Uxbridge Road, the reggae bass reached his ears before he turned into the secluded cul-de-sac, Chignell Place. On that day, as Chauncey walked into Greensleeves, he noticed that one of the shops opposite had become vacant and spoke to his parents about it.[21] He told them about the famous and busy record store that attracted customers from some distance away, saying those coming to the record shop would very likely be the same customers for a Black bookshop.[22] His parents, with only six months to find commercial premises took this opportunity.

The new bookshop opened with a launch event on 20 November 1975 at 5a Chignell Place, Ealing. The opening night was a joyous, happy occasion with Jessica hosting many friends and associates including artists, poets and musicians who were associated with Bogle L'Ouverture and Jessica herself. It was a combination of the launch of a business venture, but very much also took the shape of a loud and lively Caribbean social event with West Indian food and drink. The party spilled out onto the pavement as the small shop could not hold the large number of people who attended. Everyone arrived bringing a hot dish such as rice and peas or drinks like mauby. Among the guests was writer Samuel Selvon who entertained the packed venue, reading from his work, moving the audience to loud laughter into the Ealing evening. Walter Rodney also attended the launch event which was his only visit to the bookshop.

The shop had a glass front which displayed its goods of African art, jewellery, posters, cards, music and books. The interior was small with well stocked bookshelves on both sides of the main area. There was a

---

[21]Chauncey Huntley, interview with Claudia Tomlinson, 30 November 2020.
[22]Ibid.

FIGURE 14.2 *Opening day at Bogle L'Ouverture Bookshop, 20 November 1975. Reproduced with kind permission from the Salkey Estate.*

central island stand which displayed books. At the centre and in the space at the very back of the shop sat Jessica, on most days to be found at her typewriter.[23] Her typewriter continued to be an important tool of her activism, whether it was typing up her eviscerating campaign material, messages of support and solidarity to groups organizations and individuals around the world, drafting her speeches, or messages to her family and friends in Guyana. The bookshop grew to be at the centre of her work and the main point of contact for her and Bogle L'Ouverture once it opened. The sight of Jessica typing at her table at the back of the shop in the course of her daily activities was an image that belied who she was and shocked many as they discovered this extraordinary woman fronting a shop. For friend and musician Keith Waithe, it was 'mind-blowing to think how we can just see somebody sitting there in this bookshop and had such a history for Guyanese politics'.[24]

---

[23] Hazel Sawyers, interview with Claudia Tomlinson, 11 December 2021.
[24] Keith Waithe, interview with Claudia Tomlinson, 30 November 2020.

FIGURE 14.3 *Jessica Huntley seated in Bogle L'Ouverture Bookshop, circa 1976. Courtesy of the Huntley Collection, London Metropolitan Archives.*

The bookshop quickly became the centre of Jessica's daily schedule and bookshop worker and friend Hazel Sawyers has attested to her activities:

> She was there early every morning, always arriving before her staff to open up, and start work ... She'd go really early in the morning, 5 or 6 o'clock, the first thing she did was wash the front steps. The windows to the shop were quite long. She would open post, fulfil orders, type up orders, answer phone calls. People would often come asking to leave things to sell on their behalf, like craft, so she'd organise that. She'd liaise with other people, especially in Ealing, like fundraising. Or if someone's son was in trouble, get them legal help, when my niece was born she'd organise to get their hair done.[25]

The primary purpose of the Bogle L'Ouverture bookshop was to sell its own publications and make Black-themed publications as widely available as possible, through the provision of a high street shop where people could walk

---

[25] Accabre Rutlin, Interviews with Claudia Tomlinson, 24 July 2020–27 October 2022.

in and purchase products that they would be unable to find elsewhere at the time. Keith Waithe, Guyanese musician, friend and racial justice campaigner locates the bookshop as central to his education as he 'first met Jessica at the bookshop because I wanted to find out more about the lives of a lot of African musicians, African writers, poets, and that's the place to go'.[26]

The bookshop was also a space where the most well-known Black activists involved in writing, poetry, music and politics would meet each other, form alliances, friendships, creative collaborations and relationships. Linton Kwesi Johnson, the Jamaican author based in south London would make the special journey to west London occasionally. He said he 'used to go to the bookshop because they had books that New Beacon Books didn't have, which was John La Rose and Sarah White's publishing house and bookshop. They had other stuff, posters and drawings by Ras Daniel Heartman and stuff like that.'[27]

The bookshop became a central meeting place for comrades and associates involved in political work, and in supporting the community to deal with oppressive incidents with the police and in the education sector. For example, in 1979 Blair Peach, a white anti-racist teacher from East London was killed during a demonstration in Ealing against the National Front – a far right fascist political organization insurgent in Britain in the 1970s – after being hit by a police officer.[28] The community of supporters and comrades gathered at the Bogle L'Ouverture bookshop to discuss, bring meaning, share solace over the incident and plan support for any local campaigns. The shop was also a focal point for local activism, for example Hazel Sawyers recalled that Jessica helped local reggae band 'Misty in Roots because their manager got brutalised by the police at that point'.[29] This incident had also occurred in Southall Ealing when Ealing Council granted the National Front permission to march through the area which had one of the highest concentrations of Asians in the country. The lead singer of Misty in Roots was severely injured during this march.

Leading lawyers, such as Ian MacDonald and Gareth Pierce were to be found at the bookshop meeting with Jessica and others, discussing legal aspects of the many cases of injustices faced by Black people and others facing systematic oppression, particularly in the police and criminal justice system, including deaths in police custody. According to the observations of Hazel Sawyers, who worked in the bookshop for a number of years, part of her own role was to answer the phone in the bookshop for Jessica, taking

---

[26]Keith Waithe, interviewed.

[27]Linton Kwesi Johnson, interview with Claudia Tomlinson.

[28]Avtar Brah, 'The Scent of Memory: Strangers, Our Own, and Others', *Feminist Review*, 61 (1999), pp.4–26, esp.p.19.

[29]Hazel Sawyers, interviewed with Claudia Tomlinson.

messages if she was not present. Many of these callers would contact Jessica for advice, support and updates on the many campaigns and resistance actions that she was leading or involved with.

These calls came from around the world, and a regular caller was Mumia Abu-Jamal from the United States, in whose campaigns Jessica was a leading figure.[30] She met Abu-Jamal in the early 1980s at an American Libraries Association conference when he was a journalist. They remained friends and when he contacted her for support following his arrest for murder, a crime she was convinced he was innocent of, she became one of the leading international figures in the struggle to secure his freedom. The bookshop therefore developed in directions that she did not expect at the time of its opening. Jessica spoke of how, over time, the 'bookshop became like a community centre, because people wanted to know about housing, they have problems with the police and all different kinds of things like that. It was really like a centre point in the borough.'[31] There were visits by local schools and groups where young people could meet well known authors and performers.

FIGURE 14.4 *Bogle L'Ouverture Bookshop full of children and young people, circa 1976. Courtesy of the Huntley Collection, London Metropolitan Archive.*

---

[30]Film by George Fowokan Kelly, untitled, Jessica Huntley describing her association with the Mumia Abu-Jamal Struggle, circa 2008, personal communication.

[31]Jessica Huntley, interviewed at a Black History event, 2007, YouTube, https://www.youtube.com/watch?v=JQFCLvH6A8I.

She created the bookshop to be a space to showcase and platform the major writers and artists of the era, and one of them, Jamaican writer Valerie Bloom, described the atmosphere in the shop as 'electric, because the people who were performing would always be "names" if you like, everybody wanted to do something for Jessica because of the kind of person she was. She was so selfless and so committed to the struggle for human liberation.'[32] One of these 'names' that Bloom met as part of the Bogle L'Ouverture family was Linton Johnson, who went on to become Linton Kwesi Johnson. The bookshop, according to Johnson, 'always a good atmosphere, the place was always full, the shop was always very busy. They catered to black people from that part of London, Shepherds Bush, West London, they catered to a different crowd from New Beacon. If they put something on like a talk, their events were always well attended.'[33] A high point for Jessica was the visit to the bookshop by Sistren, the internationally acclaimed Jamaican women's theatre collective.

The bookshop became the new base from which Jessica operated after it opened, and she was there most days between 1975 and 1990, when it

FIGURE 14.5 *Sistren Theatre Collective visit the bookshop, pictured with Jessica Huntley (1983). Courtesy of the Huntley Collection, London Metropolitan Archives.*

---

[32]Valerie Bloom, interview with Claudia Tomlinson, 27 August 2020.

[33]Linton Kwesi Johnson, interview with Claudia Tomlinson.

closed. It provided her with an opportunity to significantly expand Bogle L'Ouverture's reach, but as it required her daily presence, it undoubtedly presented her with an enormous commitment. This was observed by some, such as Steven Lewis when he worked at the bookshop and saw how everything inevitably revolved around Jessica and that she shouldered the majority of the work. He considers that 'her role was actually the primary role, because Eric was still working in insurance at the time, I think he was part time around that time, Jessica was always there in terms of being the bookseller, but she was like manageress, but she was the actual key to the whole business really, yes it was always Jessica … Jessica was actually in the centre, and it was always Jessica.'[34]

Jessica created the bookshop as a place intended to inspire active resistance to injustices, a place for political learning, growth and development. It came to be central to her vision. Grace Quansah, a friend of the Huntley family said of Jessica's presence in the shop: 'she was also very keen to make sure you weren't wasting time. Don't be fooled. You were there for yourself, but you were also there for Jessica. You are there to get something out of it, you are there to enrich yourself, read book, come with something.'[35] Visitors to the shop who came to casually browse found an owner not interested in making profit as a priority, but primarily in the quest that they take something away with them from the experience to shape and improve their minds and their lives.

As the bookshop's international reputation grew, it became a magnet for the most well-known writers and artists, as well as those who were new and emerging. The bookshop really traded in the sale of ideas, self-improvement, and dreams of global freedom from oppression. In other words, Steven Lewis who spent many days working in the bookshop over several years concluded that 'what Bogle L'Ouverture and Jessica was actually selling, you couldn't put a price on it really, it was invaluable'.[36] The bookshop itself mainly sold the bestsellers in large quantities such as Linton Kwesi Johnson's *Dread, Beat and Blood*. The items purchased most frequently were the postcards, the greetings cards and posters depicting African themes. But, according to the observations of Steven Lewis 'the bulk of the business was with libraries, and schools and so on, library orders, one or two schools would purchase some books, most of it was overseas as well, the States, other parts of Europe, Africa'.[37]

The bookshop would also tour around London, organizations such as schools and colleges, educational institutions, and left-wing supportive

---

[34]Steven Lewis, interview with Claudia Tomlinson.
[35]Grace Quansah, interview with Claudia Tomlinson.
[36]Steven Lewis, interview with Claudia Tomlinson.
[37]Ibid.

groups would ask the bookshop to attend and set up a display. Many exhibitions were held by the bookshop at town halls. The political work of the bookshop, or bookshop activism, was spread through the mere presence of this new bookshop, and Jessica's prominence grew substantially during the 1970s to become one of the leading figures in Black activism in Britain. She said the purpose of the bookshop was 'not just the selling of books ... as booksellers, but it was really a community place where we organised readings'.[38] It was a draw for authors from around the globe, she said: 'our writers came from America, from Africa and from the Caribbean. Artists came. People came to ask for jobs, about jobs, if they wanted work. They were arrested, they came. They came after the riots in Notting Hill and Southall. And the young people would come into the shop as a pilgrimage. It was really a Mecca.'[39] The bookshop provided a momentous opportunity to building a political and publishing base and consolidated her renown as a major player. As such, she was central to the radical and progressive Black movements in Britain, and was in demand for collaborations and partnerships.

Bogle L'Ouverture Resisting Racist Attacks

On a quiet Sunday afternoon in February 1977, Eric went to check on the bookshop. He found the shop windows covered in painted slogans with words such as 'KKK' (the American white supremacist group Ku Klux Klan which also operated in Britain), 'White Power', 'Enoch Powell' (the white far right fascist sympathizer, anti-Black immigration campaigner and former conservative MP) and 'Niggers Out'.[40] He phoned Jessica to inform her and she immediately attended the shop. Jessica called the police, and two uniformed officers attended. Unknown to them, this was the start of a campaign of terror against Bogle L'Ouverture, and other Black and left-wing bookshops that would last into the 1980s, with its height in the late 1970s.

Jessica fought back against this campaign of violence with her customary unwaveringly courageous stance. She was vocal and energetic in ensuring that this outrage was confronted head on and with great visibility. She was interviewed in the local media on many occasions and was prominently photographed issuing robust refusals to be cowed or intimidated by these

---

[38]Carol Sydney, '60:60, Jessica Huntley, a Lifetime of Publishing', *Sable*, Spring (2005), p.97.
[39]Ibid.
[40]GPI, The Black Parents Movement, BPM/6/1/1/12, Jessica Huntley 'Statement of Witness' by Jessica Huntley, 8 March 1977.

FIGURE 14.6 *Eric Huntley at Bogle L'Ouverture Bookshop following a racist attack, circa 1978.* Courtesy of the Huntley Collection, London Metropolitan Archives.

series of attacks.[41] When Ealing police arrived after the first attack, Jessica and Eric had serious cause for concern at the police response. They reported that the visiting police officer remarked that they were 'not against middle-aged black people such as yourselves, but those young black thugs outside'.[42] This was possibly in reference to the Black supporters that had gathered outside the bookshop in a show of support. Following the first attack, the promised police action of visiting the bookshop to take prints, reporting the attack to Scotland Yard and arranging for CID officers to visit failed to materialize.

Jessica drew up a press release to alert her associates and the media what was happening, determined to shine a light on it, rather than cower

---

[41] The British Newspaper Archive, Dick Bower, 'Ku Klux Klan Terror to Shop', *The Gazette*, 7 December 1979, https://www.britishnewspaperarchive.co.uk/viewer/bl/0003289/19791207/006/0006.

[42] GPI, The Black Parents Movement, BPM/6/1/1/12, 'Summary of attacks on Bogle L'Ouverture Bookshop', undated, circa 1977.

in darkness. Bogle L'Ouverture Bookshop, along with community group 'Ealing Concerned Black Parents and Youth', convened a local meeting of supporters including teachers, social workers, lawyers and representatives of Black political organizations. The press statement published following the event revealed that 'there were two main speakers, Jessica Huntley, founder of Bogle L'Ouverture Bookshop, and Leila Hassan, assistant editor of *Race Today*, a member of The Alliance, and partner of Darcus Howe. Jessica described the bookshop's history and its services to the black community.'[43] In her speech, Jessica also informed the meeting about the lack of a police response and their failure to properly investigate the attack. Leila Hassan's speech covered the broader picture of 'unsolved fascist attacks on the black community'.[44] The meeting passed a resolution to entrust Bogle L'Ouverture management, Ealing Black Parents and Youth to form a delegation to carry out a number of actions. These included registering their discontent with the Home Secretary, suspending all fruitless meetings with local police until the local police had met with the Home Secretary and Police Commissioner. Hassan also told the audience that: 'whenever the black community has taken its own actions to deal with the fascists, the police have always arrested us and not the fascists. Therefore, we are not only having to oppose the fascist but the police who protect them.'[45] The meeting produced a petition and passed a resolution that 'those of us attending this meeting, and the undersigned, entrust the Bogle L'Ouverture Management and Ealing Concerned Parents and Youth, to form a delegation. We entrust the delegation to register to the Home Secretary the fact that the police have failed and neglected to do and carry out a proper investigation.'[46]

In June 1977, responses were received from the Home Office that the matter was being investigated, and one was also received from the Police Commissioner. It was clear to Jessica that these responses indicated that local police had not accurately represented the severity of the situation and she provided this information in her response to the Home Secretary and the Police Commissioner.

On a Saturday morning in July 1977 Jessica arrived to open the shop only to find it subject to a further attack. It was covered in pieces of paper that had been stuck to the glass with various racist messages including 'racially mixed couples pollute white race', 'negroes have a low IQ', 'negroes have

---

[43]LMA, HC, LMA/4462/J/01/001, Press Statement, undated, circa April 1977.
[44]Ibid.
[45]Ibid.
[46]Ibid.

small brains', 'negroes never created a single civilisation'.[47] A publication, *The Crusader – The Voice of the White Majority*, was left at the premises. Later on the same day, Eric answered the telephone in the bookshop and received a message: 'this is a warning. Move out or we will get you tonight you black bastards.'[48] On the occasion of these further attacks, the police appeared to take the investigation more seriously. On a Sunday, a worker at the bookshop discovered it had again been vandalized, with the bookshop's name covered in paint. Jessica was notified, and she called the Black community out to protest.

Anger mounted at the continuing inaction of the police, and there was a picket of the Home Office involving full participation of local groups, organizations and individual activists including the Black Parents Movement.[49] Interviewed in the local media early in January 1978, Jessica said: 'these attacks on black bookshops are part of a pattern of racist and fascist attacks that have been unleashed on the black community for some time now. We know that extreme right-wing organizations are trying to intimidate organizations like ours so that we close down. But we are not going to close, we are going to fight.'[50]

The police dismissed criticisms of inaction, claiming 'as far as these attacks are concerned, there is very little we can do. It only takes about five minutes to daub paint over a shop front or throw a brick through a window. Police officers can't be everywhere all the time.'[51] Jessica kept up the pressure on the Home Secretaries, Merlyn Rees, and William Whitelaw, and received several responses from the Home Office, in response to her many letters sent in protest and demanding action. She wrote to Whitelaw in 1979 that 'no one has been arrested in connection with any of the incidents ... we are therefore writing to you and requesting that you meet with us'.[52] In her correspondence, she always described the incidents as racist, fascist in nature and acts of terrorism. The Home Office and police, on the contrary, always described them as 'opportunist cases of vandalism' and a complete refusal to accept the racist nature of the crimes.[53]

---

[47] GPI, The Black Parents Movement, BPM/6/1/1/12, 'Summary of Attacks on Bogle L'Ouverture Bookshop', undated, circa 1977.

[48] Ibid.

[49] 'Race Leader Backs Fight Against Fear', *Gazette and Post*, 19 January 1978, p.2, https://www.britishnewspaperarchive.co.uk/viewer/bl/0002463/19780119/015/0002.

[50] 'We'll Fight Racist Attacks, Says Ealing Bookshop', *The Gazette*, 6 January 1978, p.3, https://www.britishnewspaperarchive.co.uk/viewer/bl/0002466/19780106/027/0003.

[51] 'We'll Fight Racist Attacks, Says Ealing Bookshop', *The Gazette*, 6 January 1978, p.3.

[52] LMA, HC, LMA/J/01/003, Jessica Huntley Letter to Home Secretary William Whitelaw, 4 October 1979.

[53] LMA, HC, LMA/J/01/003, Letter from Home Office to Jessica Huntley, 16 November 1979.

In 1978, with her associates and fellow activists Jessica was part of the formation of Bookshop Joint Action, a group established to pull together forces to fight the attacks on London bookshops and similar organizations. Speaking to the media again about the attacks, she said 'it is very worrying, bookshops in other parts of London have been the victims of arson. But we are not going to be terrorised out of existence.'[54] With this evidence of greater solidarity, the Home Office was forced to acknowledge that these were targeted attacks on the Black community. But it held firm in its expressions about vandalism rather than targeted attacks stating that these were 'acts of vandalism against the black community'.[55] Bookshop Joint Action was denied a meeting with the Home Secretary on the grounds that 'the Home Secretary has no power to give the Commissioner directions ... it would not be appropriate for the Home Secretary to receive a deputation to discuss these matters'.[56]

Later in January 1978, Jessica co-operated with the Mayor of Ealing in a joint local campaign to stamp out racist attacks on Bogle L'Ouverture, and other organizations identified as supporting and empowering Black people in the borough. This included the Ealing Community Relations Council offices which had been daubed with Ku Klux Klan insignia. The Mayor toured the affected sites, with the media saying, 'there have been a number of racist attacks all over the country, and they appear to be linked'.[57] They Mayor went on to say, 'I am shocked to think that anything like the Ku Klux Klan would come here and organise and finance this sort of activity.' Jessica was pictured in the local media, speaking out in determination.[58]

The attacks continued into the 1980s, and Jessica met a further attack when arriving for work on 26 August 1980, when the bookshop, now named the Walter Rodney Bookshop, was again daubed with paint used to spell out racist words such as 'Niggers get out'. 'Blacks go home', and 'keep Britain White'. This was the seventh attack on the bookshop in a campaign running over two years. Again, speaking openly in the local media, Jessica told the media that 'the slogans were signed "BM" the initials of the right-wing British Movement. It doesn't frighten me, I'm not surprised, one expects it because of the society that we live in.' Jessica and her associates concluded that fighting these attacks was one battle in the larger war against racial hatred in Britain.

---

[54]Ibid.

[55]LMA, HC, LMA/J/01/003, Home Office Letter to Jessica Huntley, 25 January 1978.

[56]Ibid.

[57]'My Fight Against Hate – By Mayor', *Gazette and Post*, 26 January 1978, p.7, https://www.britishnewspaperarchive.co.uk/viewer/bl/0002463/19780126/032/0007.

[58]Ibid.

15

'Matriarch of the Movement for Black Rights in Britain, the World'

It was in early July 1980 when Jessica arrived back in London from a week's visit to New York to attend the American Library Association (ALA) conference. She was on a high, her head full of ideas about possibilities for London and her networks, based on what she had just participated in. The first ALA conference she had attended was in 1978 in Chicago, where she met Coretta Scott King, American civil rights leader, and the wife of Martin Luther King, Jr. These conferences were founded in 1853 as a convention for librarians to meet, share ideas, research, and practice of their field. One of the most appealing aspects of the conferences was the exhibitions by publishers, arranged as a marketplace for the display and sale of books and other published material. Conference talks, evening events and tours were part of the programme. Jessica had not seen anything such as this before, and was very inspired to see some of these innovations brought to life in Britain. In 1979, as has been shown, the anniversary celebrations of Bogle L'Ouverture reflected some of what she had taken away from the 1978 conference, and it was extremely successful and popular with audiences. She recalled how the idea for the first International Book Fair of Radical Black and Third World Books was born in one of her regular telephone conversations with John La Rose.

Jessica's direct involvement in the political work of resisting racialized injustices and the oppression of African and African-descended people continued unabated. She was involved in many actions, but it was during this period that she was an important part of the activism that followed the New Cross Fire massacre that took place in London.

The International Book Fair of Radical Black and Third World Books

In 1980, after returning to London from the ALA conference, Jessica recalled that she 'came back to London with all these ideas, and one day John called', and she discussed with him how inspired she had been by the exhibitions. By the end of the phone call, John La Rose was as inspired as Jessica by what she had experienced in America, and the two friends had agreed to hold the first book fair. This was the start of what would become the unique International Book Fair of Radical Black and Third World Books. Jessica suggested a town hall would be the ideal venue. The first book fair was held at Islington Town Hall with Jessica Huntley and John La Rose as the co-directors. Later on, Race Today, led by Darcus Howe, was invited to participate as the third publisher that formed part of the first organizing committee.

The first book fair was held in early April 1982 at Islington Town Hall in London and was opened by C.L.R. James. The introductory speech was given by John La Rose, and the closing speech was by Jessica. The entire event was filled with names of the best in international Black and Third World literature, television, music, art, theatre and politics, with many household

FIGURE 15.1 *Jessica Huntley with John La Rose at the First International Book Fair of Radical Black and Third World Books, 1982. Courtesy of the George Padmore Institute.*

names in attendance. In addition to the fair, which was held during the day, there was a strong evening programme of films, such as the *Mangrove Nine* by Franco Rossi, *Blood a Goh Run* by Menelik Shabazz, *Riots and Rumours of Riots* by Imruh Cesar. The panel discussants included Labour party politician Diane Abbott and film-maker Horace Ove. There was a forum on Black theatre in Britain presented by theatre director Yvonne Brewster, agent Pearl Connor and prominent Guyanese actor Norman Beaton with panel contributions from writer Caryl Philips, activist and writer Farrukh Dhondy and novelist Earl Lovelace. An Evening of International Poetry was held at Camden Town Hall and included Linton Kwesi Johnson, John Agard, Valerie Bloom, Accabre Huntley and Cecil Rajendra. It also included Michael 'Mikey' Smith, who gave a wonderful performance. Jessica chaired a Forum on Racist and Fascist Attacks on Black, Left Wing, and Community Booksellers and Other Institutions in Britain. There were eighty-three international exhibitors at the first book fair including Allison & Busby, Black Ink Collective, Heinemann, Hansib Publishing, Oxford University Press, Tanzania Publishing House, Zed Press, the Women's Press and Yale University Press.[1]

Jessica's biggest contribution was the writers and artists she attracted to the book fairs. Because of her many contacts in the United States, made through the distribution of books and other published materials, as well as through the ALA conferences, she was extremely well connected. She had good connections with American publishers, universities, bookshops, and also through her relationships with American writers. Bogle L'Ouverture lays credible claim to being among the first, if not *the* first, publisher in Britain to import some American authors who then went on to become best sellers in Britain.

Through Jessica's contacts and activities in America with Bogle L'Ouverture, Eric Huntley recalls that:

> ... all the names that became household names in the '80s, their books were available in hardback in the States and we were the ones who imported them and sold them in the bookshop, we marketed them here and brought them to the attention of the public here, which gave Women's Press and Virago – who had the money – opportunity to print and have contracts with them and to publish paperback editions.[2]

---

[1] Sarah White, Roxy Harris, and Sharmilla Beezouhun, eds, *A Meeting of the Continents, History, Memories, Organization, and Programmes (1982–1995): The International Book Fair of Radical Black and Third World Books Revisited* (London: New Beacon Books, 2005), pp.78–85.

[2] Philippa Ireland, 'Material Factors Affecting the Publication of Black British Fiction' (unpublished doctoral thesis, The Open University, 2012), p.245.

FIGURE 15.2 *Jessica Huntley with Maya Angelou, approximately 1980, at a book launch in London. Courtesy of the Huntley Collection, London Metropolitan Archives.*

The explosion of American women writers in the 1980s into the consciousness of Black British women, and others, such as Toni Cade Bambara, Ntozake Shange, Maya Angelou and Alice Walker, was through a portal crafted by Bogle L'Ouverture and Jessica, who knew them all personally.

Some of the most popular writers showcased and performing at the book fair were those whose careers had first been launched by Bogle L'Ouverture. One example was Valerie Bloom, a very popular writer with a dynamic, lively and humorous performing style in Jamaican patois. Bloom is clear that one of the biggest impacts Jessica had on her career was that 'she put me on stage with all these people, it was very close to the time when I had just come over. There was James Berry, Linton, Michael, people from all over the world, it was huge, and that continued until '95'.[3] Bloom was unequivocal 'this was something she organised which was a worldwide movement of musicians with performers from all over the world, black and minority artists who used that platform to launch them into careers that are powerful'.[4]

---

[3]Ibid.

[4]Valerie Bloom, interview with Claudia Tomlinson.

Jessica played an equal role with John La Rose in the vision for the International Bookfairs and was substantially responsible for their inception and success. The interplay of gender, class and education had the effect of minimizing Jessica's significant contribution to the book fair. This could be seen in the decision for John La Rose to open the first book fair and introduce C.L.R. James as the keynote speaker, and with Jessica in the position of delivering the closing speech. It is not known how this decision was arrived at, or Jessica's view or choice in relation to this scheduling. It is known that she was not in the habit of foregrounding herself. However, this decision creates the impression of giving prominence to La Rose's contribution, and overshadowing Jessica's. As with the continued situation of male and female juxtaposition, it was, in this network, the male who was inevitably propelled by others, as well as themselves, into positions of power and visibility, with women more likely to be making contributions in the background that were monumental, but less recognized or acknowledged. Close witnesses recognized her as 'the one who organised it with Race Today and with the other black bookshop in London which was New Beacon, she organised the first Black British Radical and Third World Bookfair, there you can see how her organization was such a force to be reckoned with because we had people from all over the world'.[5]

At the end of the first book fair, Jessica made a powerful speech, that perfectly summarized her vision of the meaning of the event. Speaking to the audience of approximately 6,000 people who attended the first fair, she primarily contextualized it as a triumph for activism. She was careful not to take sole credit for the inspiration behind the fair, she spread this accolade through to her associates, activists and communities. However, she began by being clear that for her, the book fair was 'a celebration of our own filmmakers, a celebration of our writers and artists, a celebration of our poets … and it has also been a celebration of sections of the white community who share with us radical and revolutionary ideas in the furtherance of our struggles here in the Kingdom'.[6]

Jessica remained closely involved in the production of the book fair and was again joint co-director in 1982 with John La Rose for the second book fair. However, by the third book fair, she had stood down as its co-director leaving John La Rose as the sole director. She continued to attend and support the remaining book fairs which were now run between New Beacon Books and Race Today. Although various reasons have been suggested for Jessica's resignation from the Book Fair as joint director, it undoubtedly exposed some of the tensions between the comrades that had in reality existed from

---

[5]Valerie Bloom, interview with Claudia Tomlinson, 27 August 2020.
[6]GPI, The International Book Fairs of Radical Black, and Third World Books, BFC/01/05/01/02/02, Jessica Huntley, Closing speech, 2 April 1982.

the time of the formation of Bogle L'Ouverture Publications. The friends and publishers worked hard at remaining united, but some close to New Beacon Books and Bogle L'Ouverture Publications could recognize signs of growing tension. Linton Kwesi Johnson, for example, felt that the 'Bogle camp I guess was more nationalist, more orientated towards black nationalism, whereas the New Beacon camp were more closer to Marxism'.[7] This was certainly one of the differences between the two publishers, but unlikely to be at the root of Jessica's resignation as these ideological differences were present throughout their friendship which started in the 1950s and endured their full journeys together.

Jessica worked hard to nurture and sustain her highly valued relationships with long-standing and important associates and to overcome disputes and their differences. She rarely spoke about these difficulties, preferring to build partnerships and focusing on the strength in the unity of the partnerships, and she was 'very sensitive about relationships and didn't want these things misconstrued'.[8] By this she meant she wanted to avoid her specific concerns being misunderstood as broad and widespread fissures among allies. Speaking about the decision to step away from the co-directorship of the book fairs, she was clear that her collaborators sometimes made her and the work of Bogle L'Ouverture feel 'undermined. They treated us in a sense like, not so important. second class, who are we, always inferior to John and Sarah. Race Today treated us like that.'[9] She has spoken about how this perception of her position spread in a specific incident at the end of the second book fair when her status was challenged by a member of Race Today who challenged a request made for payment of one of the performers.

Given that she was a director on the organizing committee and a prominent figure, she should not have been challenged. She was forced to go to Darcus Howe to have her request validated by him, rather than on her own personal authority. Whilst Howe supported Jessica, he suggested it was her own responsibility to use her authority to stand up to the person and not let herself be denigrated. This was a failure to accept systematic patriarchy and class power at play and suggested that Jessica should draw on her personal power to dominate the person. It is true that Jessica had to rely on personal power all of her political life, but undoubtedly this was a harder form of power to draw upon continuously.

Jessica had to exercise this power in working with comrades in 'The Alliance', the partnership between Bogle L'Ouverture, New Beacon Books and Race Today. She was acutely aware of 'all the other things that were

---

[7] Linton Kwesi Johnson, interview with Claudia Tomlinson, 30 July 2020.

[8] LMA, HC, LMA/4463/F/07/01/001/E, Eric and Jessica Huntley interviewed by Harry Goulbourne (Session Four), 3 June 1992.

[9] Ibid.

happening, there were always meetings before the meetings, decisions taken before the meetings, I was conscious of these things happening, people thought I was so stupid I didn't know they weren't happening, but for the sake of unity one swallowed all these things.'[10] Her valued unity among collaborators also applied to her relationship with Darcus Howe, editor of *Race Today*. Jessica had a good relationship with Howe, but sometimes found his robust style of engagement and leadership was not as collaborative as her own leadership style. She also observed the close collaboration between John La Rose and Howe. She felt that 'Darcus had I believe had a tremendous influence over John and Sarah. Tremendous influence.'[11] Although Jessica Huntley, Darcus Howe and John La Rose were very close collaborators, the two men were widely viewed as leading male figures in the arena of Black activism. La Rose and Howe joined forces to play different, complementary roles in their subsequent leadership together, as evidenced by Steven Lewis:

> Darcus was like 'Malcolm' to John's 'Martin Luther King'. Darcus would talk about 'yeah, we're going go out there, and we're not taking no damn foolishness' you know, very down to earth, and John will say 'well look' and John will give you the history about the Notting Hill riots 1958, Kelso Cochrane, and bring in experiences of black people's struggle, how things happened and he would paint a slightly calmer picture, while Darcus rushes in, gnashing of teeth sort of thing.[12]

Once this partnership was consolidated between La Rose and Howe, Jessica had to revisit her fight against her old foe, patriarchy, in progressive, left-wing and radical Black activism.

Joining Hands to Heal After the New Cross Fire

In 1981, Jessica became a founding member of the New Cross Action Committee in response to a devastating fire at a children's party which killed thirteen young Black people, and to which there had been a lamentable response from the authorities and media. This was followed by the biggest mobilization of Black people in Britain at the time – uniting to give voice to decades of racialized oppression and injustice in Britain. Jessica was an instrumental figure in initiating and leading the community response. The

---

[10]Ibid.
[11]Ibid.
[12]Steven Lewis, interviewed.

response to the fire was massive and unified, by many who were at the forefront. Steven Lewis recalled that 'the politicals, John La Rose, Jessica, and the Race Collective, all decided well look something had to be done, people are angry'.[13] A series of meetings were organized, and actions planned from there.

It is recognized that histories of all those involved in the response cannot realistically be reflected in major biographies, however more acknowledgement and recognition of the contribution of leading figures such as Jessica Huntley should be documented as part of completing historical narratives. Linton Kwesi Johnson has identified that Jessica's role was as a key contributor to the response to the New Cross Fire:

> Jessica, and Eric and John La Rose and Darcus Howe and Roxy Harris, these were some of the first people on the scene, in the aftermath, on the Sunday morning after the fire. They were the people who initiated the Action Committee, John La Rose was the Chairman. The meetings were held at the Moonshot Youth Club which was run by Sybil Phoenix who was a friend of Jessica. So, we were involved in that, and helped to motivate about 20,000 people for the Black People's Day of Action on 2nd March '81.[14]

With the formation of the Action Committee, the decision was made to organize a Black People's Day of Action, and it the Steven Lewis observed that 'Jessica did not go up front, she was very much involved like myself with Eric, it was John … because John loved all that, him and Darcus, they loved the publicity, I don't know if it's a Trinidadian thing, they loved to be up front.'[15] Steven Lewis specifically recalls that a priority for the Black People's Day of Action march, was about 'getting the families, the bereaved families on board. So, both John and Jessica used to go up to these areas, and meet with and talk with the families, because they were so bereaved you couldn't get them to come down to travel to London, so they would go up, and it was a tremendous, tremendous achievement.'[16]

The bereaved parents were successfully supported to not only take part in the march but agreed to be positioned at the front of the march, with banners. Howe and La Rose were the public faces of the organization, and the evidence is that Jessica supported and encouraged this. The two men, according to Steven Lewis, 'were seen as the actual leaders of the Black People's Day of Action but in fact it wasn't just John and Darcus, Jessica was

---

[13]Ibid.

[14]Linton Kwesi Johnson, interview with Claudia Tomlinson.

[15]Steven Lewis, interview with Claudia Tomlinson.

[16]Ibid.

very, very instrumental in that, but like I said she never took centre stage, she would tell John or Darcus, "you go up, you go up"', when the opportunities to be interviewed on television and radio presented themselves.[17] There was also no evidence that La Rose or Howe denied Jessica the opportunity to become more visible. Whilst she wanted agency and power to influence and reform, she did not appear to wish to platform herself personally and was not interested in showcasing herself. She was very well known and recognizable at this time as a leading figure in Black resistance and her mere presence was an increasingly powerful symbol of support.

The Family and the Community

By the 1980s, Jessica's engagement and involvement with family in Britain and in Guyana continued. In Guyana, Hectorine was now very elderly and infirm and needed care. Jessica arranged for the care and payment of medical expenses for her mother.

Letters from the extended family in Guyana informed her of the ageing, infirmity of those she had grown up with. She maintained regular correspondence with cousins, nieces, nephews, brothers and friends in Guyana. She provided advice, encouragement and financial assistance, and sent items back home continuously. Her niece Kay Johnson described Jessica's generosity: 'She was kind, she'd give you her last penny if you needed it, the clothes off her back, the shoes off her feet if she felt that you would make use of it, she was that sort of person, she was very generous and giving.' Her daughter Accabre echoed these observations:

> Like I described her mother humming in the morning, mum used to hum and sing in the morning and hum. Dad used to take me swimming early in the morning and we'd come back home, and mum would have made bake and salt fish. She'd make bake and sweetbread for people, like for Keith [Waithe], I'd go there and this one would be for Keith, this one would be for so and so. And she loved to give, she couldn't keep anything, she had to give things away. She had to give things away like it would burn a hole in her pocket. She was so, so generous. If she got any money, she'd spend hours, if she got £50 she'd go 'If I give this much to my niece, give this much to so and so'. She got into trouble for giving away a gift that my aunt had given her.[18]

---

[17]Ibid.
[18]Accabre Rutlin, interview with Claudia Tomlinson.

Leaving for Britain in 1958 physically separated her permanently from those who had been part of her childhood, and she was now beginning to learn of their decline or demise.

Her standing in the community remained very strong, and she received regular requests to speak at events, or even to attend. Kay Johnson, daughter of Cecily Haynes-Hart, who Jessica regarded as a niece, said:

> Over the years she perfected the art of public speaking, even though she would be the first to admit she didn't have the posh education that was part and parcel of school life, but because she was passionate about what she did, it came effortlessly and people listened. And then of course she became a name, the name became known, and so that whenever you knew that Jessica Huntley would be there, you parted the waves and let her come to the front and say what she had to say. She had a lot of respect from people, not just black, white, she commanded that kind of attention because of the passion she had for what she did and what she believed in.[19]

In fact, people who respected her from her activism in British Guiana, were still seeking her services based on her work during that period. For example, in 1984, she was invited to speak at the Youth Conference on Racism, organized by the Caribbean Teachers Association (CTA). The CTA General Secretary wrote to Jessica that 'I shall be most anxious to see you again, for although you may not remember me, you made a tremendous impression on me as a child in Guyana in the first General Election of 1953.'[20] This accolade reflected appreciation for Jessica's past political activity in British Guiana. Although Jessica was no longer living in Guyana her activities as a fighter for the rights of exploited and abused working people back home remained constant throughout her life.

---

[19]Kay Johnston, interview with Claudia Tomlinson August 2020.
[20]LMA/4463/D/05/01/002 'Letter from General Secretary of the Caribbean Teacher's Association to Jessica Huntley', 7 January 1984.

16

Fighting for Decolonization in Independent Guyana

For much of the 1960s, British Guiana burned with colonial fires ignited by the raging political discourse on the road to independence when it would become the Co-operative Republic of Guyana, called 'Guyana' after it achieved independence in 1966. The cynical exploitation of workers from Northern India recruited to replace the labour of emancipated Africans caused a permanent schism in a workforce that should have united to defeat a joint oppressor. The original People's Progressive Party (PPP) sought to achieve unity between the descendants of Indian workers and the descendants of African enslaved peoples. This was the promise of April 1953 – a new political horizon that was ultimately crushed by Whitehall. The period between 1968 and 1983 was highly unstable in the newly independent Guyana. There was some mirroring in Guyana of worldwide movements in the 1960s against repressive state power, and in support of freedom for the individual rights and against suppression of exploited, grass-roots masses.[1]

This period in the Guyanese political landscape has also been described as part of the emergence of the 'New Left' period in the Caribbean. This can be defined as a struggle to implement an anti-imperialist, progressive socialist orthodoxy in the infrastructure of the new, independent Caribbean nation. The PPP won the national elections of 1957, in which Jessica had stood as a prospective MP. It further won the general election of 1961, but in the 1964 elections, despite the PPP winning the most seats, it did not secure a majority, and a coalition government was formed of the opposition People's National Congress (PNC) under Forbes Burnham, and the United Force. Cheddi Jagan's PPP was removed by the governor, on behalf of Whitehall,

---

[1] Nigel Westmaas, '1968 and the Social and Political Foundations and Impact of the "New Politics" in Guyana', *Caribbean Studies*, 37 (2009), pp.105–32, esp. p. 107.

the representative of the British government. The PNC won the crucial 1968 elections, the first in the post-independence period, but Burnham faced growing accusations of vote rigging and corruption in this and subsequent elections.

Guyana Emerging

The original PPP, co-founded by Jessica in 1950, was gradually perceived as having moved away from its original commitment to being a party for multi-ethnic cohesion of workers. By the 1970s, it was widely viewed as predominantly representing the interests of the Indian-Guyanese sections of the population. The PNC under Forbes Burnham had built a strategy widely viewed as being to provide representation for the African-Guyanese population. Thus, a racial division between the two ethnic groups, endemic since the introduction of Indian indentureship to defeat the employment rights claims of the newly freed Africans at the end of enslavement, was formalized into the political infrastructure of Guyana from 1964.[2] Political conflict became enshrined as racial conflict with different segments of the population perceiving their interests as either served or denied, and the other major racial group advantaged depending on which political party was in power.

This meant political campaigns and elections have since been rocked by inter-racial violence. Some political thinkers and theorists developed a view that 'the intervention of the Americans and the British in these disturbances and the participation of local politicians in that division had the effect of driving a concurrent racial and ideological wedge into society'.[3] Certainly, the period between the 1961 and the 1964 elections involved greater collaboration between American presidents Kennedy, and later Johnson, with Britain in various activities to prevent Jagan from winning power, particularly on the road to national independence.[4]

Walter Rodney made the decision to return home to Guyana in July 1974. He had been mostly teaching at the University of Dar-Es-Salaam since his 1968 ban from Jamaica. Before he left Dar-Es-Salaam, there were rumblings of emerging concerns about his presence in Tanzania. In a letter to her close friend Andrew Salkey, before Rodney's return to Guyana, Jessica expressed her anxieties about his plans: 'Walter's decision to return to a country, his own country, must be very worrying. In terms of security. Of course,

---

[2]Ibid., pp.109–10.

[3]Ibid., p.110.

[4]Robert Waters, and Gordon Daniel, 'The World's Longest General Strike: The AFL-CIO, the CIA, and British Guiana', *Diplomatic History*, 29 (2005), pp.279–307, esp. pp.287–9; Ibid., pp.114–15.

Walter, because of his politics, could also be in danger living in Tanzania, deportation for example.'[5] If Tanzania had thoughts of deporting Rodney, this was not clear. However, he certainly continued to receive the support of the University of Dar-Es-Salaam which advised his British supporters that 'the Dept. of History at the university of DAR would have liked Dr Rodney to renew his contract for a further two years. Dr Rodney, one of the most outstanding African historians, was more than welcome to continue teaching at the university. However, it was his wish to return home to be [sic] service the people of Guyana.'[6]

The Tanzanian university also moved to dispel rumours that Rodney was no longer welcome in Tanzania, arguing that:

> ... it has been alleged by authorities that he, that Dr Rodney was no longer welcome in Tanzania. This allegation is not only slander against Rodney personally, but also against the people of Tanzania. Let me make it quite clear that Rodney is always welcome in Tanzania, and we remember with deep brotherly feelings his service to the university, as well as, in the process, to the people of Tanzania.[7]

Whatever the position, Rodney's friends, including Jessica, had a sense of foreboding about the possible fate facing their friend in Guyana after his decision to return home.

The Committee of Concerned West Indians

Walter Rodney had returned to Guyana due to a job offer of Professor of African History at the University of Guyana which he accepted, in the expectation of starting work in the new academic year in 1974. When the job offer was subsequently withdrawn, there was widespread suspicion that Forbes Burnham had pressured the university to do so.[8] Rodney had maintained personal and professional correspondence with Jessica, as friends and comrades, and as publisher–author, from the late 1960s through to his murder in 1980, so she was kept up to date with the political situation at home.

---

[5]LMA, HC, LMA/4462/Q/01/001/002, Jessica Huntley Letter to Andrew Salkey, 17 February 1974.

[6]LMA, HC, LMA/4463/B/04/01, Message from University of Dar-Es-Salaam, 29 September 1974.

[7]Ibid.

[8]LMA, HC, LMA/4463/B/04, Campaign Leaflet Guyanese Government Panics, circa September 1974.

Rodney's regular correspondence with Jessica also included information about the position at the University of Guyana which had been withdrawn. She kept him informed about campaigns and resistance activities connected to Guyana and those involving him. In turn, he provided her with regular information which she disseminated at meetings, and in the many calls she frequently received for updates on Walter Rodney's situation. In his letters he provided Jessica with his interpretations of the position he found himself in:

> The Board of Governors reconvened and upheld their decision against the appointment. Once more, no reason was given, except to say that I refused to see them. Their request to see me was turned down by the University Staff Association, by the TUC and by myself. I'm including the relevant correspondence. It was obvious in the last week before the decision was given that the government had decided to stand firm but were delaying to let public outcry subside and to find some rationalisation, however thin. Presumably had I gone there the reason for my non-appointment would have been found in this interview. It seems as though they were quite upset that I didn't fall in line with their machinations. The Staff Association and the TUC are still protesting. Quite probably, the political struggle about the appointment as such will peter out, but at a more fundamental level it will remain to offer scope for political education.[9]

Following Rodney's ban from the University of Guyana, Jessica formed a resistance group in London, in August 1974, the Committee of Concerned West Indians, in response. She organized the first meeting at her home in Coldershaw Road on 28 August 1974. She informed those invited to this meeting that 'the appointment of Walter Rodney to teach at the University of Guyana has been revoked by the Governors of the University of Guyana. The Board of Governors of the University of Guyana is dominated by the Government of Guyana, and consequently can only be regarded as political victimisation of Brother Rodney.'[10] Following this meeting, the Committee of Concerned West Indians agreed its programme of activities.

The first of these was a large meeting, attended by 300 to 400 people at Conway Hall, in London, where a resolution was passed, on 13 September 1974, and then presented to the Guyanese Embassy in London, by a delegation led by Jessica. The resolution condemned the interference

---

[9]Ibid.

[10]LMA, HC, LMA/4463/B/04/01, Jessica Huntley Letter of Invitation to Meeting, 24 August 1974.

of the Guyanese government into the academic appointment of Rodney and demanded 'the immediate reinstatement of Dr Walter Rodney' to the position offered by the university, and an 'end to the ongoing harassment and persecution of the Guyanese people by the Burnham Government'.[11] Speakers included Jamaican-born academic Stuart Hall, John La Rose of New Beacon Books and others. Although the focus was on Rodney's situation, the meeting was broadened to include what was considered 'a general offensive by the notorious Burnham regime, directed against the oppressed masses and committed socialists'.[12] The meeting also adopted the position that 'this savage repression is not just peculiar to Guyana, but is rampant throughout the neo-colonial regimes of the Caribbean'.[13] The meeting further agreed that 'the struggle of our people for progress in the Caribbean is our struggle here also'.[14] The argument in the meeting literature was that: 'the same people who oppress us here, oppress our brothers and sisters back home through their agents, Burnham, Mauley, Williams, Gairy and the rest'.[15] This campaign lasted about one year. Its activities included picketing the Guyanese embassy in London. It also produced extensive campaign literature including leaflets and booklets providing information about the background to what she viewed as Forbes Burnham's abuse of political power.

Meanwhile, the opposition activists in Guyana were working to strengthen their power and influence in the country. In 1974, African Society for Cultural Relations with Independent Africa (ASCRIA) and Indian Political Revolution Associates (IPRA), along with other organizations, joined forces with each other to form the Working People's Alliance (WPA) and it was incorporated as a political party in 1979. The main activity fought by the WPA was Burnham's planned referendum to amend the constitution to extend the PNC's own right to remain in government, and it claimed victory in this referendum. Eusi Kwayana, Moses Bhagwan and eventually Walter Rodney after his return to Guyana in 1974, became actively involved in opposing Burnham's leadership which was viewed as increasingly oppressive. In July 1979 after two government offices, including that of the Guyana Sugar Corporation, were destroyed in an explosion, Walter Rodney was one of five arrested and the group was dubbed the 'Referendum Five'

---

[11] LMA, HC, LMA/4463/B/04, 'Resolutions', 13 September 1974.

[12] Ibid.

[13] Ibid.

[14] Ibid.

[15] LMA, HC, LMA/4463/B/04. Campaign Leaflet, 'Walter Rodney Banned Again!', undated, circa September 1974.

and were charged in relation to the explosion.[16] Those arrested were all academics and one student at the University of Guyana. The arrest of these opposition activists, all supported by Jessica, sparked a new campaign group. She formed the Committee Against Repression in Guyana (CARIG), in July 1979 with associates in London.

The Committee Against Repression in Guyana

CARIG's first action was on 17 August 1974 and was a picket of the Guyanese embassy in London to protest the first trial date of the Referendum Five in Georgetown.[17] The first public meeting of CARIG was convened by Jessica Huntley on 19 August 1974 at the Keskidee Centre in London, and attended by about seventy people. The meeting passed a resolution that 'we Guyanese, Caribbean, and other peoples present at this public meeting at the Keskidee Centre, London, support the struggles of the Working People's Alliance Party to bring about the downfall of Burnham's repressive regime'.[18] It called for the immediate release of the Referendum Five, and that the 'corrupt and repressive PNC regime led by Burnham resign'.[19]

CARIG had a core membership with Jessica as the convenor, and other regular members included Eric Huntley, Irma La Rose, who sometimes chaired the meetings, Leila Hassan, Pat Dick and John La Rose. Others that also attended meetings included Keith Waithe, Anne Braithwaite, Leland De Cambra, Harry Goulbourne, Andreas Jeffrey, son of Lionel Jeffrey and many others identified by their first name only in the meeting minutes. CARIG held many pickets and vigils outside the Guyanese High Commission in London, published regular bulletins and press statements, organized boycotts, and leafleting of PNC meetings, and disrupted a high profile public meeting at Battersea Town Hall in London held by Forbes Burnham.[20] Jessica therefore became the focal point for the provision of information about Guyanese

---

[16]LMA, HC, LMA/4463/B/03/01/002, Newsletter, 'The July (1979) Events in Guyana and Human Rights', International Committee in Defence of Political Prisoners in Guyana, July 1979.

[17]LMA, HC, LMA/4463/B/03/03/001, Campaign Leaflet, 'End Political Repression in Guyana – Free the Referendum Five', circa August 1974.

[18]LMA, HC, LMA/4463/B/03/01/001, Notes on Public Meeting Held in Protest of the Arrest and Charges Against the Referendum Five, circa July 1979.

[19]Ibid.

[20]LMA, HC, LMA/4463/B/03/01/001, Report of Meeting Addressed by Forbes Burnham at Battersea Town Hall, 23 January 1980.

political activity and this was disseminated into the work and activities of other organizations she was involved in, such as the Race Today Collective, the Black Parents Movement, and The Alliance.

It was not until several years after its formation that CARIG thrashed out its objectives, in a difficult meeting where it was clear that there were ideological differences in a number of areas, alongside a shared interest resisting political oppression in Guyana. The membership settled on three objectives for CARIG: '(1) CARIG is an anti-repression front, an alliance of individuals and organizations opposed to political repression in Guyana; (2) In carrying out this objective, CARIG will seek to mobilize others to support the struggle, and to put an end to the PNC regime in Guyana; and (3) CARIG seeks to maintain local and international contacts with other groups who share this objective'.[21]

Remarkably, despite the political turmoil in Guyana, and her successes in Britain, in January 1975 Jessica was seriously considering returning home to live permanently. She consulted with Walter Rodney on his views about the family's discussions about returning home:

> Hello Walter, this is a little note to ask you to feel out for me the possibility of opening a BLP in Guyana. Eric is meditating very hard about returning home in October and from some of the reports it sounds as if BLP will be trampled in a short period of time. Perhaps you can raise the matter with some of your comrades and let us know as soon as possible ... So many people have been saying not to return but Eric is quite tired of the hustle here and Accabre is demanding each day to return home. She has even begun saving for her return home, so I am thinking about the future of BLP.[22]

Rodney's response in a letter to Jessica recommended caution:

> I would still encourage many Guyanese abroad to return if they have certain commitments. Nevertheless, it would be pure romanticism to fail to take into account the narrow scope for establishing a base for opposition. In many respects, it would be easier for those who are not well known to return and work within the system and bide their time. Otherwise, one has to be in one of those few areas independent of immediate government control.[23]

---

[21]Ibid.
[22]LMA/HC/ LMA/4462/C/01/092, Jessica Huntley Letter to Walter Rodney, 8 January 1975.
[23]LMA/HC/ LMA/4462/C/01/092, Walter Rodney Letter to Jessica Huntley, 13 July 1975.

He had not long returned home himself and pointed out further realities to Jessica on her proposed plan of bringing the family home. He said:

> On the political front, one assumes things have changed for the worse since your visits. To have been identified with protests in London against the PNC clique would hardly have endeared you to them. More important still, the government is taking over as many things as possible so as to monopolize large areas of economic activity and silence opposition through this basic material threat.[24]

Rodney further advised: 'of direct relevance to yourself, is the new government proposal to control the import of all books through a bookstore which they have set up. This is probably aimed at the Michael Ford Bookstore in the first instance, but it will also keep everyone else in line.'[25] Responding to her friend Rodney's advice, Jessica informed him of the decision eventually reached:

> With regard to BLP, from the general reports, it seems unlikely that it will be allowed to be developed, so I have changed courses in terms of setting it up at home. I will, however, make certain that BLP has a firmer base in London with sisters and brothers who will be prepared to work harder on it that I did. It cannot die.[26]

Jessica approached the Communist Party of Great Britain for support in CARIG's campaigns. It readily agreed it would cooperate 'in any activities in solidarity with the people of Guyana and against repression'.[27] Attempts were made to establish branches of CARIG in Trinidad and Tobago and Barbados, with John La Rose leading on and reporting activities in those two countries and also activities in New York and Massachusetts where Jessica's friend Andrew Salkey was now living.[28] News of overseas resistance towards the Burnham government was suppressed by his government. Rodney confirmed this in his correspondence with Jessica that:

> No news of overseas protest has been allowed to reach the Guyanese public, except through roundabout strategies. For instance, the U.S resolution was passed in Washington and circulated for a large number

---

[24]Ibid.
[25]Ibid.
[26]LMA, HC, LMA/4462/C/01/092, Jessica Huntley Letter to Walter Rodney, 28 July 1975.
[27]LMA, HC, LMA/4463/B/03/01/002, Letter from Jack Woodis, International Department of the Communist Party of Great Britain to Jessica Huntley, 20 October 1979.
[28]LMA, HC, LMA/4463/B/03/01/002, Minutes of a Meeting of CARIG, 24 September 1979.

of signatories ... the Committee sponsoring the support then purchased an advertisement in the Graphic ... This caused quite a stir ... Therefore you would need to do something similar.[29]

CARIG was active until into the late 1980s, and its concern grew for the safety of Rodney and opposition supporters. Rodney and two associates who had been arrested, but released on bail were now due to stand trial. CARIG acknowledged that the situation for Walter Rodney was now very perilous as he was due to stand trial at the end of January 1980. The meeting noted that 'Omowale, Rodney, and Roopnarine were due in court on 30/31 January there was serious concern they would be found guilty and then assassinated in jail'.[30] There had been a number of suspicious killings of opposition sympathizers or supporters at the hands of Guyanese police or security services. On one occasion, Rodney was in very close vicinity to one of the suspected individuals who had died due to possible state sanctioned assassination, and he was clearly at risk.[31]

Word from Rodney himself, in his correspondence to Jessica, signalled his intention of intensifying his bid for the leadership of Guyana, with the WPA:

> Little has changed at this end, except perhaps a steady deterioration – economically and with a political reflection. The WPA has been doing a lot internally to reorganise itself for the challenges ahead. We feel ready to offer more definitive leadership towards a new political system. Some of our proposals will soon be made public.[32]

There was discussion of CARIG sending observers from London to witness the trials. By May 1980, the uppermost issue for CARIG was the fate of Rodney and his co-accused who were still awaiting trial at this point, and they noted it would not be a jury trial but a magistrate trial. Shockingly, within weeks of this observation, CARIG's fears for the life of Walter Rodney were realized when he was killed on 13 June 1980.

CARIG's statement on Rodney's death was unequivocal about the course of events, advising the world that 'Rodney was murdered by the Burnham regime. He was murdered on June 13th by a car bomb in Georgetown, Guyana.'[33] The statement was also an obituary for Rodney, giving a history

---

[29]LMA, HC, LMA/4462/C/01/092, Walter Rodney Letter to Jessica Huntley, 20 September 1974.
[30]LMA, HC, LMA/4463/B/03/01/002, Minutes of a Meeting of CARIG, 24 September 1979.
[31]LMA, HC, LMA/4463/B/03/01/002, Minutes for CARIG, 21 November 1979.
[32]LMA, HC, LMA/4462/C/01/092, Walter Rodney Letter to Jessica Huntley, 7 March 1978.
[33]LMA, HC, LMA/4463/B/03/01/002, p.1, 'Walter Rodney Murdered by Burnham Regime in Guyana', 15 June 1980, CARIG.

of Rodney, a history of his participation in struggles for working people's rights and of his recent involvement in the opposition of Burnham's regime. It informed supporters that Rodney had been killed in an explosion while travelling in a car. It said 'the Committee Against Repression in Guyana mourns the loss of one of the finest voices in the Caribbean revolutionary tradition. We promise the Burnham regime our concentrated attention, our vigorous opposition until this cancerous presence in the Caribbean body politic is eliminated.'[34]

This was one of the lowest points in Jessica's life. The pain of losing a close friend and precious comrade such as Rodney was a major loss that was difficult to recover from. The loss of what he represented to the struggle that she herself had spent a lifetime fighting for, was a very heavy body blow. The paths of the Rodneys and the Huntleys had been closely joined for almost twenty years at the time of his death. He was like a member of the family, they worried about almost every day. With Eric, she acknowledged that throughout Rodney's 'political life, his activities have somehow been bound up with ours, first as friends, prior to the formation of Bogle L'Ouverture Publications, and subsequently as publishers and activists'.[35]

The couple reflected on their long relationship with Rodney, first meeting him in London in the early 1960s when he was a PhD student at the School of Oriental and African Studies (SOAS), and they were working in jobs and engaged in 'overseas Caribbean politics'.[36] Due to Rodney's quest for knowledge about the politics of Guyana in the 1950s, which Jessica and Eric were part of, he spent endless sessions in discussion with them about their previous political work in Guyana. With the deteriorating political situation in Guyana following the 1964 elections, Guyanese abroad were very concerned, and Jessica, Eric and other parties organized the Guyana Symposium and provided the young Rodney with a platform to speak on the situation.

Once Rodney was banned from Jamaica in 1968, Jessica and Eric recalled that 'many of us who had participated in the Symposium, and others, came together and organised protest action against the ban'.[37] They protested on the streets and risked their own liberty for the Rodney cause. They formed an editorial committee that included Jessica, and published *Groundings*, and later *How Europe Underdeveloped Africa*. Jessica and Eric jointly summarized the loss of Rodney:

---

[34]Ibid., p.2.

[35]LMA, HC, LMA/4462/E/01/032, Jessica Huntley and Eric Huntley, 'Publisher's Note to the Fifth Edition of *The Groundings with My Brothers*', 1983, Huntley Collection, London Metropolitan Archives, LMA/4462/E/01/032.

[36]Ibid.

[37]Ibid.

Our relationship with Walter Rodney, who we regard to have died in active combat, could be seen to have continued through four re-prints of The Groundings with my brothers and four reprints of How Europe Underdeveloped Africa as well as the most active and formative [sic] of his political life covering a period 1964–1980. At each crucial juncture, we were expected, and did in fact rally much needed personal and political support. With his assassination we not only mourn the passing of an author, but also a friend and comrade.[38]

This statement goes a long way towards illuminating the period of almost two decades of political collaboration between Rodney, Jessica and Eric Huntley. The fascinated 22-year-old student in 1964 learned from and was inspired by the story of the older couple's participation in a critical period of revolutionary change in Guyana, something he would later try to achieve himself in his homeland. There can be no doubt that Jessica and Eric Huntley were viewed as intellectual icons by Rodney, as well as providing him with support over many years to assist and help him, the provision of essential support in fact. In turn, they regarded him as a beloved member of their family.

On 20 June 1980, CARIG organized a 'Memorial Meeting' for Walter Rodney at Conway Hall, in London. Bogle L'Ouverture Bookshop was renamed the Walter Rodney Bookshop as a tribute to Rodney from 1980 until it closed in 1990. Jessica was part of the upsurge of protests that followed Rodney's death, and a range of events and activities followed. The most prominent of these was the Walter Rodney Memorial. She led on the organizing of demonstrations against the Burnham government outside the Guyanese embassy in London.

Jessica held the belief that the overturning of colonization was incomplete. Like other activists, Jessica held the belief that too many of the West Indian countries were emerging as 'client-states' of the former Western colonial powers, and Black people, particularly the poor and disenfranchised, would continue to experience oppression and the elites would continue to profit. She connected the decolonizing work she was doing with Bogle L'Ouverture, its publications and her political activities in Britain with her work as a Guyanese overseas political activist. She believed that Forbes Burnham was shaping the independent Guyana in this direction, and that from 1964 through to his death in 1985, she saw his operations as that of an authoritarian ruler that she continued to oppose.

---

[38]Ibid.

17

Publishing Activity in Bogle L'Ouverture's Later Period

Moving into the 1980s, Jessica continued her publishing activity by developing new voices. Her insistence on respect and acceptance for non-standard English in publishing remained and this was seen in her work with new authors in this period, such as Valerie Bloom. Bogle L'Ouverture Publications validated the 'creole' and 'patois' languages as spoken by Black people in Britain and in many global majority countries. These languages were often ridiculed in favour of Standard English, in Britain, Europe and the United States, and in the West Indies and Africa.

Valerie Bloom and Bogle L'Ouverture Publications

When Valerie Bloom arrived in Britain in 1979 she was already a recognized author in Jamaica as she had been published there since the age of twelve and taken part in the national writing festivals. On arrival in Britain, she soon started contributing poems to a touring Jamaican folk group. Her unique and popular poetry led to the demand for a published poetry collection. Based in Manchester at this time, in the north of England, she was informed about Jessica Huntley and Bogle L'Ouverture Publications, and travelled to London to meet with the publisher. In 1981, armed with a handful of poems, Valerie had a meeting with Jessica in the bookshop. Jessica read through the poems and there and then, informed Valerie that she would like to publish an anthology of her poetry.

Valerie returned to Manchester, after she had obtained agreement that Bogle L'Ouverture would publish the book, and continued with her activities. These included a radio programme where she would read a new poem each week to her audience and was building up her collection for publication in that manner. She was also working in a school, teaching Jamaican folksongs and poetry to children in schools. Time passed, and the poetry collection was slowly building to an anthology. One evening, when packing for a holiday to Scotland, Valerie received a call from Jessica asking for the manuscript of the promised book, saying 'where is the book? I've been waiting for the book!' Startled, Valerie spent the rest of that evening working on her book which she completed that very night: 'I panicked, and I spent all night, sitting up all night writing poems for this collection.'[1] Despite the pressure from Jessica that had spurred her into action, Valerie appreciated this approach, saying 'Bless her, she was very good. I sent that off and eventually she published that.'[2]

This book by Valerie was *Touch Mi! Tell Mi!* eventually published in 1983. Following this, Valerie was brought into the Bogle L'Ouverture family, and her work was regularly promoted in what she considered an ideal situation:

> I would go to the bookshop to do performances, she used to put on performances every so often in the bookshop and that was such an amazing situation because there were all these people who were legends who used to come to the bookshop who would come to the bookshop and you'd be performing in front of them, rubbing shoulders with them. People like Gus John, Darcus Howe, Linton Kwesi Johnson, Keith Waithe and so on, who would also be performing some of them. It was just an amazing, amazing time.[3]

Jessica was closely involved with the development and production of Valerie's book and oversaw all production aspects. Her friend and main editorial advisor, Andrew Salkey, had at this time moved to Massachusetts to take up an academic role.

Once her book was published, Valerie said Jessica 'promoted it left, right, and centre, everywhere. Whenever they were putting on a programme of any sort, she would invite me to come and read. She got Linton to do the introduction, which was amazing.'[4] 'Linton' was poet and Bogle L'Ouverture author Linton Kwesi Johnson, and this act by Jessica of securing his services as an established and well-known author to help launch a new but less well-known talent in Britain became her trademark approach.

---

[1] Valerie Bloom, interview with Claudia Tomlinson.
[2] Ibid.
[3] Ibid.
[4] Ibid.

Valerie's view on Bogle L'Ouverture's publishing strategy is that Jessica's decision to publish her book for Black children and families held importance beyond herself as an author. It is a book written in Jamaican creole. She argued that it was unlikely that any other publisher in Britain at the time would have accepted this book. Valerie has suggested that Jessica was building on the strategy launched over ten years earlier with the publishing of Rodney's *The Groundings with My Brothers*, and that she was 'always the one who would publish books which wouldn't really get published unless she really did it. Books on all these black activists but also black writers'.[5] Valerie was clear that when Bogle L'Ouverture published her book, no other British publisher 'would know what to make of it, yet the fact that she published it is what launched my writing career here'.[6]

In fact, the partnership and friendship between Valerie and Bogle L'Ouverture grew and continued until the end of Jessica's life. The publication of *Touch Mi! Tell Mi!* came to the attention of Cambridge University Press (CUP), and because of the Bogle L'Ouverture book, CUP asked Valerie if she would publish a book with them; *Duppy Jamboree* was published in 1992. The demand for Valerie's work grew and other publishers wanted her work. She described this growing interest: 'Macmillan saw the Cambridge book and asked if they could use one of the poems as a children's book.' Informed of this, Jessica made Valerie a counter-offer which she accepted, and Jessica published Valerie's next book, based on Macmillan's offer. Jessica agreed the concept with Valerie who recalled that 'I had this poem written which was *Alphabet*, she said "let's do that"'. Bogle L'Ouverture eventually collaborated with Macmillan to jointly produce the book.

The book was subsequently published in 1999 titled *Ackee, Breadfruit, Callaloo: An Edible Alphabet*. Jessica also identified a Black woman illustrator for the cover, Kim Harley, who she commissioned to produce a highly visually appealing illustration of a Black girl eating a piece of Caribbean fruit. Valerie felt that this was part of 'the way she goes about promoting black women and she said "Kim will do the illustration", so we would meet and go through it, this was not usual with other publishers you know, that you would get such a big say in the artwork of your book, they would say "here is the artwork, we think it's great, I hope you like it"'. Jessica's work, partnership and friendship is a strong exemplar of how she commissioned authors, most went to her, she sought out very few. She expected delivery, and worked co-operatively, almost as comrades, to respectfully produce something that was for the author, and the reader but that which had a purpose for something that was beyond the author's vision and intention. Valerie Bloom became one of Bogle L'Ouverture's

---

[5]Ibid.
[6]Ibid.

most popular authors, in terms of performances, book sales and broader appeal to other mainstream publishers, and has received multiple awards and honours for her work.

Valerie was also very well-liked by Jessica, not only for her talent and the trust and friendship they forged, but she provided Jessica with the opportunity to publish more women authors, something she struggled to do: 'out of every ten manuscripts we get now, only one will be by a woman. The women didn't write or think of themselves as writers. It was considered a male thing. The women were always active They made intellectual contributions, but they are missing when things come to be recorded'.[7]

Lemn Sissay Joins the Bogle Family

Later in the 1980s, Jessica started to work with new young author, Lemn Sissay, who was introduced to the Bogle L'Ouverture stable by Valerie Bloom. Lemn appears to be the first Black British-born author published by Bogle L'Ouverture, apart from Accabre Huntley whose first book was published in 1977. With the passage of time, a new generation of young Black people were starting to come through as poets and writers in Britain all seeking an outlet. Bogle L'Ouverture was still a major destination for new authors, more than twenty years after it was established.

Lemn was born in 1967 in Lancashire, in the north of England, to an Ethiopian mother who had arrived in Britain as a student. He was named Norman, and fostered by a white British family, but was eventually returned to the children's home by the family, and he lived out the remainder of his childhood there. In care, he was mistreated, experienced abuse and racism. One of the biggest injustices he suffered was the mishandling of his separation from his birth mother and his subsequent thwarted efforts to be reunited with her. Lemn was around nineteen or twenty years old, and not long out of the children's home, he was writing poetry regularly when he set about launching his writing and performing career.

One day, he went into the office of North West Arts, an agency based in Manchester working to develop art and culture in the region, with a pamphlet that featured a collection of his poetry, *Perceptions of the Pen*, that he had self-published in 1985 as a seventeen- or eighteen-year-old. He was seen by then Arts Officer Valerie Bloom who had a publishing contract for her first book with Bogle L'Ouverture, although it had not yet been published at this time. Valerie looked at Lemn's pamphlet and spoke with him. He told Valerie he had another collection of poetry completed and

---

[7]Jessica Huntley, interview with Sandra Courtman, 5 June 1995.

wanted to publish them as a book. Valerie had the immediate thought: 'the best person to nurture him would be Jessica'.[8]

Valerie introduced Lemn to Jessica, who, according to Lemn immediately 'adopted him'.[9] Jessica agreed to publish Lemn's non-self-published first book, *Tender Fingers in a Clenched Fist*. Valerie felt that Jessica was very energetic in publishing and then promoting Lemn's book, and Valerie was asked to write the introduction. Valerie and Lemn have remained friends ever since.

Tender Fingers in a Clenched Fist was first published by Bogle L'Ouverture in 1988, with a second edition published in 1998. A substantial anthology of sixty-one poems written for performance, Lemn's work is a strong reflection of the concerns of Black youth in general, and Black people more broadly, their representation, and experiences in London, Manchester, and their global experiences. On the publication of the second edition, Lemn acknowledged the part played by Jessica and Bogle L'Ouverture, and Eric Huntley in moving his career to a larger platform:

> It is now ten years since *Tender Fingers in a Clenched Fist* – and it is still the best book I have ever chosen. I was twenty years old when it first hit the shops and sold out. I am now thirty years old. I, like many other black writers in England am eternally grateful to Jessica and Eric Huntley, who nurtured me from those days and whose mere presence inspired many other crucial developments in Britain. They inspired a generation, and I am proud to be part.[10]

He wrote about class, race and colour, British politics in the 1970s and 1980s, particularly Thatcherism, AIDS and South African oppression. Today Lemn Sissay is an established, multi-award-winning poet, author and performer. He is a former Chancellor of the University of Manchester, the holder of several honorary degrees including doctorates. He is currently an Honorary Chair in Creative Writing at the University of Manchester. He also founded 'The Christmas Dinner' charity in 2013, to provide young people leaving the care system with a warm and welcoming Christmas Day experience.

---

[8] Valerie Bloom, interviewed.

[9] Ibid.

[10] Lemn Sissay, *Tender Fingers in a Clenched Fist* (London: Bogle L'Ouverture, 1988), LMA, HC, LMA/4462/E/01/052, p.xvii.

18

The Bookshop Goes Back Home

The Walter Rodney Bookshop at Chignell Place closed in 1990. Jessica blamed a combination of factors including the downturn in sales partly on the rise of Thatcherism from 1979. It was her view that this 'affected a lot of the radical booksellers. A lot of them couldn't continue because people weren't buying the radical books. The temperature in Britain had changed quite a lot.'[1] She also pointed to the austerity shepherded in by Prime Minister Margaret Thatcher's economic policy and funding cuts made to public libraries reduced their budgets so that their purchase of books was limited. There were also increased demands for higher presentation levels for the books and demands by the libraries that all books needed to have jackets which added to the costs for the publisher.

After the bookshop closed, Jessica lived more quietly with Eric at Coldershaw Road but did not ever retire from her mission. The bookshop activities and services were once again centred in the family home.

The loss of the bookshop was felt acutely, and Jessica said: 'after we went into liquidation, there was a lull, and people really have been calling and saying, "when are you going to start something else?" and so on. We continue to publish, modestly, but we do, and also, we do book services. The schools, and libraries, organizations.'[2]

Despite its closure, Bogle L'Ouverture Publications continues to publish and sell its books regularly at events today. In 1993, it was rebranded and became BLP. The most recent new publication at the time of writing is *You Can't Cut Down a Green Heart Tree with Just a Grand Idea*, by Eric

---

[1] Philippa Ireland, 'Material Factors Affecting the Publication of Black British Fiction' (unpublished doctoral thesis, The Open University, 2012), p.244.

[2] Jessica Huntley, interviewed for a Black History event, 2007, https://www.youtube.com/watch?v=JQFCLvH6A8I.

Huntley.³ Many of the titles published after 1990 were sold at various book events, at the Annual Huntley conference and through the website of the Friends of the Huntley Archives at the London Metropolitan Archives.

The Publishing Mission: Changing Yet Remaining the Same

Jessica maintained her commitment to the original strategy of Bogle L'Ouverture in her focus on publishing on Black history, politics, arts and literature. In this later period, she continued to validate the importance of lessons from the 1960s for contemporary audiences. As an example, Bogle L'Ouverture re-published *Journey to an Illusion* by Donald Hinds in 2001 after it was originally published by Heinemann in 1966.⁴ Originally from Jamaica, Hinds arrived in Britain in 1955 and worked in several jobs before joining the West Indian Gazette, owned by Claudia Jones, the Trinidadian born activist as a reporter. In *Burning an Illusion: The West Indian in Britain*, Hinds explodes the myth of Britain as a Mother Country for West Indian migrants. He argues that the sole British interest in the West Indies was for profit and enrichment of itself, not for any interest in the culture or people it brought there through processes of enslavement, indenture, and immigration. Presenting the testimonies of the journeys of many West Indians, Hinds argues that the main source of the shattering of this illusion is one part of the experience of West Indian migrants to Britain, particularly as they tried to obtain jobs and accommodation. Moving beyond the stage of describing the disillusionment, Hinds also scopes what he describes as the 'counterattack', or the resistance to anti-Blackness encountered by West Indian migrants during the 1950s. The decision to re-publish and promote this book two decades after it was first published, indicated that Jessica considered the themes that were relevant in 1966 continued to be significant for Black people's lives in the twenty-first century.

Bogle L'Ouverture also re-published Beryl Gilroy's *Black Teacher* in 1994 which had been out of print for some years. A pioneering head teacher from British Guiana, Gilroy wrote about her experiences as one of the first Black teachers working in Britain. After the book went out of print, she struggled to find a new publisher, and was in contact with Jessica who agreed to re-publish this important work. Bogle L'Ouverture marketed it as a book

---

³Eric Huntley, *You Can't Cut Down a Green Heart Tree with Just a Grand Idea* (London: Bogle L'Ouverture Publication, 2022).

⁴LMA, HC, LMA/4462/E/01/009, Donald Hinds, *Journey to an Illusion: The West Indian in Britain* (London: Bogle L'Ouverture Publications, 2001).

'located within the genre of biography and its own time – the 1950s'. Bogle described it as essential reading for professionals, particularly teachers, and social workers who would learn from the book issues of 'education of minorities, race, class, the role and purpose of the curriculum'. Gilroy's book was published again in 2022 by Faber and Faber.

Friends of the Huntley Archives at the London Metropolitan Archives (FHALMA)

One of the main activities Jessica was involved in during the last years of her life included the establishment of the Huntley Archives, and the work of the Friends of the Huntley Archives at the London Metropolitan Archives (FHALMA), which included development of the archives, the annual conference and the educational and charity work of the organization. In 2005, the collection of personal and business records, amassed over decades was donated as an archival collection to the London Metropolitan Archives in London.

FIGURE 18.1 *Jessica with sculpture by George Fowokan Kelly at the LMA, 2007. Reproduced with kind permission from George Fowokan Kelly.*

Jessica's sculpted image, and the Huntley name are currently an integral part of the Huntley Archive at the LMA. An exhibition room is named The Huntley Room which holds a sculpture of Jessica by artist, writer and filmmaker George Fowokan Kelly. She has described Kelly's role in building this legacy:

> He came to see me once and he said he was commissioned to do some masks for some people in America. He persuaded me that I must sit for this mask. And after a lot of 'not me', 'somebody else' and so on, I agreed to sit and then halfway through that he said that he wanted to do something bigger, with myself. He did this piece of sculpture, it's fantastic. It's now at the London Metropolitan Archives, and in fact they have named a room on behalf of both Eric and myself.

Jessica Goes Home

Jessica Huntley died in Ealing Hospital following several years of ill health. Her death was sudden and unexpected, despite a background of ill health including triple coronary by-pass surgery in 1998. Although often in pain, she continued her participation in several campaigns until her death, prompting the figurative remark from Grace Quansah that 'she was going out on marches till the day she died'.[5]

Her periods of ill health prior to her passing meant some hospital admissions. One evening after she had attended a film screening of a documentary about Mumia Abu Jamal, she became ill, and an ambulance was called. As she lay in the ambulance, word circulated that she was being taken to hospital. Groups of young people who had attended the documentary, joined hands in a circle around the ambulance and prayed for Jessica's life to be spared. When she arrived at the hospital and was receiving treatment, these young people travelled there and waited in a vigil all night until they knew she had been safely treated. She left the hospital the next day to resume her usual activities. The young of the next generation were not prepared for her to depart this life. When she later learned what had happened, she found it 'very touching ... that to me will be a very lasting moment of appreciation and of respect that you all showed me that night'.[6]

She hosted a dinner party at home with her husband, attended by five or six longstanding friends and associates on the evening of her death. As was well known, activism was part of the fibre of her being and it is likely that

---

[5] Grace Quansah, interview with Claudia Tomlinson.
[6] Jessica Huntley, filmed by George Fowokan at Coldershaw Road, circa 2011.

the friends would have discussed the international political scene and what they were doing. They may have well discussed her recent attendance at a reception at the Jamaican High Commission in London as part of the 2013 UK tour by Dr Julius Garvey, son of Marcus Mosiah Garvey. Linton Kwesi Johnson recalled that: 'The last time I saw Jessica, was at the Jamaican High Commission actually, she had been ill, it might have been after some hospitalisation, I was glad I saw her because she died soon after that, so I was glad I saw her, and I gave her a little kiss, and she had that beguiling smile as usual.' Friend Grace Quansah also recalled: 'She did say in that email, I remember it vividly, that she and Eric were not well and I shouldn't come round, they both had flu, it was literally after they had attended, which I had, this gathering with Julius Garvey, he came from Jamaica, it was at the Foreign Office, 2013. It was somewhere in October, she died on the 13th, it would have been the week before.' Jessica died that night, following the dinner party held at Coldershaw Road.

Her death was reported and lamented in the communities in which she worked, predominantly by Black organizations and leaders. Her funeral reflected the life she had lived, and although she left no instructions for her funeral, those around her made sure she had a transition based on her beliefs, and provided her favourite readings, music and African drumming. Her casket was borne aloft by female bearers.

By the time of her death, she had received multiple awards and honours, some of these awarded posthumously. She was a grandmother and a great grandmother. She accepted an honorary doctorate from the London South Bank University, which holds a film and a photograph of her receiving the award. Jessica's lifelong struggle against imperialism and colonization in Britain and globally has been illuminated by the legacy she leaves in her friends, families and communities, and her words. At a book exhibition in 2007, Jessica said 'what we have to be sure of, that we must publish things that are relevant to our struggle, so that will keep us going, and keep that struggle we talk about on'.

What is the future of the legacy of Jessica Huntley? To a great extent this remains in the hands of her family and community. For her family, granddaughter Marika Efea Rutlin adopts the position that:

> Everything granny and grandad did in some ways is to make my life and the life of my generation easier. We should receive that gift and keep pushing further so that generations after us can have that luxury ... It feels like there is a momentum I should carry forward into the world ... my grandparents are political activists and they owned one of the first black publishing houses in the UK and that's something I can really be proud of.

Recalling her friend and comrade, Baroness Martha Osamor sent a message of appreciation to the Pan-African realm where many believe Jessica is now residing. Osamor said: 'wherever you are Jessica, we heard you, we did what you were asking for, we continue to do it in your name, and you will be remembered for being this strong African black woman which you've always been, we appreciate it and we're grateful for having had your company, so thank you Jessica'.

APPENDIX: ORAL HISTORY INTERVIEWS

Original unpublished interviews conducted by the author featured in this publication:

Norma Ashe-Watts: Founder member of Islington Card, co-founder of the Keskidee Centre, associate and friend of Jessica Huntley.

Moses Bhagwan: Member of the People's Progressive Party of Guyana, Member of the IPRA and WPA organizations in British Guiana. Friend and associate of Jessica Huntley and Eric Huntley.

Valerie Bloom: Bogle L'Ouverture author and trustee, friend and associate of Jessica Huntley.

Margaret Busby: Founding publisher with Allison and Busby, associate and friend of Jessica Huntley and Bogle L'Ouverture.

Waveney Bushell: Teacher and Educational Psychologist, friend and associate of Jessica Huntley, co-founder of CECWA.

Bernard Coard: Bogle L'Ouverture Author and activist with New Beacon Books, Bogle L'Ouverture, and CARD member in Britain, associate of Jessica Huntley.

Leila Hassan Howe: Assistant Editor of *Race Today*, activist, associate of Bogle L'Ouverture and friend of Jessica Huntley.

Chauncey Huntley: Youngest son of Jessica Huntley and Eric Huntley. Musician, educator, Bogle L'Ouverture bookshop worker.

Eric Huntley: Co-founder of the People's Progressive Party of Guyana and party official. Business partner, political collaborator and husband of Jessica Huntley. Owner of the Huntley Collection at the London Metropolitan Archives. Member of CARIG.

Patrick Huntley: Retired reverend, brother of Eric Huntley.

Gus John: Educator, activist and author. Bogle L'Ouverture Publications cataloguer, associate and friend of Jessica Huntley and Eric Huntley, co-founder of CECWA.

Anne Johnson: Writer, former Ealing teacher, member of Friends of Bogle, friend and associate of Jessica Huntley and Eric Huntley.

Eusi Kwayana: Co-founder and government minister of the People's Progressive Party of 1953. Teacher, poet, author and historian. Friend and Comrade of Jessica Huntley and Eric Huntley.

Linton Kwesi Johnson: Bogle L'Ouverture author, activist, associate of Jessica Huntley and Eric Huntley.
Steven Lewis: Activist, worker at Bogle L'Ouverture, member of the Friends of Bogle, Black Supplementary School teacher.
Errol Lloyd: Co-founder of Bogle L'Ouverture. He is a writer, artist and book cover illustrator including *The Groundings with My Brothers*. He is a former member of the Caribbean Artists Movement. He is a former friend and associate of Jessica Huntley.
Sir Woodville Marshall: Former West Indian Student Union member, Member of the West Indian Students Centre in the 1950s.
Grace Akuba Quansah: Friend and mentee of Jessica Huntley, storyteller, writer, poet, educator and activist.
Accabre Rutlin, née Huntley: Daughter of Jessica Huntley and Eric Huntley. Bogle L'Ouverture author, worker in Bogle L'Ouverture bookshop, event organizer, Trustee of FHALMA.
Efea Marika Rutlin: Granddaughter of Jessica and Eric Huntley, events volunteer with Bogle L'Ouverture.
Ewart Thomas: Co-founder and editor of Bogle L'Ouverture. Editor of *The Groundings with My Brothers*. Friend and associate of Jessica Huntley and Eric Huntley.
Odette Thomas: Bogle L'Ouverture author (provided written responses to questions).
Ngugi wa Thiong'o: Author, Distinguished Professor, friend, associate of Jessica Huntley and Bogle L'Ouverture Publications.
Martha Osamor, Baroness Osamor, the Baroness of Tottenham in the borough of Haringey, and Asaba in the Republic of Nigeria. Labour Party Peer. Former member of the Black Parents Movement and other community organizations in north London during the 1970s, 1980s, and an associate of Jessica Huntley.
Hazel Sawyers: Former worker at Bogle L'Ouverture bookshop in the 1970s and 1980s.
Richard Small: Former official of the West Indian Students Centre and the West Indian Students Centre. Co-founder of CARD Co-founder of Bogle L'Ouverture, author of Introduction of *The Groundings with My Brothers*. Associate of Jessica Huntley and Eric Huntley. Former Secretary to C.L.R. James.
Keith Waithe: Flautist, composer, band member of the Macusi Players, Member of the Board of Directors of FHALMA. Associate and friend of Jessica Huntley and Eric Huntley.
Ansel Wong: Former official of the West Indian Students Centre House Committee and West Indian Students Union (WISU). He is a former member of the Caribbean Artists Movement. He is also an associate and friend of Jessica Huntley and Eric Huntley.

Oral History Interviews Conducted by Other Researchers:

Jessica Huntley and Eric Huntley were interviewed by Harry Goulbourne in 1992 and this series of interviews are available at the London Metropolitan Archives as part of the Huntley Collection.

Jessica Huntley was interviewed by George Fowokan Kelly in 2010. This is a filmed record in the personal collection of Mr Kelly. Kelly also filmed Jessica Huntley on several occasions and holds these within his personal collection.

Cecily Haynes-Hart was interviewed by Dr Margaret Andrews in 2011.

Dr Sandra Courtman kindly donated notes of an interview conducted with Jessica Huntley in 1995.

Original, unpublished interviews are in the personal records of the interviewers.

BIBLIOGRAPHY

'Action Group to Fight Race Attacks', *Gazette and Post*, 15 June 1977.
Adi, Hakim and Sherwood, Marika, *Political Figures from Africa, and the Diaspora Since 1787* (London: Routledge, 2003).
Adi, Hakim, *Pan-Africanism: A History* (London and New York: Bloomsbury, 2018).
Adi, Hakim, *African and Caribbean People in Britain: A History* (London: Penguin Random House, 2022).
Akala, 'The Great British Contradiction', *RSA Journal*, 164 (2018), 18–21, 19–20.
Alleyne, Brian, *Radicals Against Race: Black Activism and Cultural Politics* (Oxford: Berg 3PL, 2002).
Altink, Henrice, *Public Secrets: Race and Colour in Colonial and Independent Jamaica* (Oxford: Oxford University Press, 2019).
Anderson, Clare and others, 'Guyana's Prisons: Colonial Histories of Post-Colonial Challenges', *The Howard Journal of Crime and Justice*, 59 (2020), 335–49.
Andrews, Margaret, *Doing Nothing is Not an Option: The Radical Lives of Eric and Jessica Huntley* (Middlesex: Krik Krak, 2013).
'Anthology of Work One Love', *County Times and Gazette*, 29 January 1971.
Basdeo, Sahadeo, 'The "Radical" Movement Towards Decolonization in the British Caribbean During the Thirties', *Canadian Journal of Latin American and Caribbean Studies*, 22, no. 44 (1997), 127–46.
Bates, Thomas, R., 'Gramsci and the Theory of Hegemony', *Journal of the History of Ideas*, 36 (1975), 351–66.
Benn, Dennis, 'Introduction', *Report of the West India Royal Commission: The Moyne Report* (Kingston: Ian Randle, 2011), 436.
Bhabha, Homi, 'Of Mimicry and Man: The Ambivalence of Colonial Discourse', *October*, 28 (1984), 125–33.
Bhattacharya, Sabyasachi, 'History from Below', *Social Scientist,* 11, no. 4 (1983), 3–20.
Bloom, Valerie, *Touch Mi! Tell Mi!* 1983, LMA, HC, LMA/4462/E/01/002.
Bloom, Valerie, *Ackee, Breadfruit, Callaloo: An Edible Alphabet*, 1999, LMA, HC, LMA/4462/E/01/002/A.
'Bookshop in Front Room, "No Nuisance"', *The Gazette*, 11 April 1975.
Boyce Davies, Carole, *Left of Karl Marx: The Political Life of Black Communist Claudia Jones* (Durham, NC and London: Duke University Press, 2008).
Brah, Avtar, 'The Scent of Memory: Strangers, Our Own, and Others', *Feminist Review*, 61 (1999), 4–26.
Bryan, Beverley, Dadzie, Stella, and Scafe, Suzanne, *Heart of the Race: Black Women's Lives in Britain* (London: Verso Books, 2018).

Bunce, Robin E.R., and Field, Paul, *Darcus Howe: A Political Biography* (London: Bloomsbury Academic, 2013).
Bunce, Robin, and Field, Paul, 'Michael X and the British War on Black Power', *History Extra*, 14 October 2017. https://www.historyextra.com/membership/michael-x-and-the-british-war-on-black-power/ (last accessed 13 April 2024).
Cantres, James G., *Blackening Britain: Caribbean Radicalism from Windrush to Decolonization* (Lanham, MD: Rowan and Littlefield Publishers, 2020).
Carpen, Mel, 'In Memory of the Enmore Martyrs', *Guyana Journal* (2008). http://www.guyanajournal.com/Enmore_Martyrs_melcarpen.html (last accessed 14 March 2023).
Cleall, Esme R., 'Emancipation, Slave-Ownership and the Remaking of the British Imperial World', *History Workshop Journal*, 75 (2013), 307–10.
Clover, David, 'Dispersed or Destroyed: Archives, the West Indian Student's Union and Public Memory', *The Society for Caribbean Studies*, 6 (2005), 1–14.
Coard, Bernard, 'Why I wrote the "ESN book"', *The Guardian*, 5 February 2005.
Coard, Phyllis, and Coard, Bernard, *Getting to Know Ourselves* (London: Bogle L'Ouverture Publications, 1972),
Cook, Anne Patricia, 'Social Policy and the Colonial Economy' (unpublished doctoral thesis, The University of Surrey, 1985), 9.
Courtman, Sandra, 'Lost Years: West Indian Women Writing and Publishing in Britain 1960–1979' (unpublished doctoral thesis, University of Bristol, 1998).
Critchlow, Hubert, 'Greetings from British Guiana', *The Voice of Coloured Labour*, ed. by George Padmore (1945). https://www.marxists.org/archive/padmore/1945/labour-congress/ch07.htm.
Critchlow, Hubert, 'History of the Trade Union Movement in British Guiana', in *The Voice of Coloured Labour*, ed. by George Padmore (1945) https://www.marxists.org/archive/padmore/1945/labour-congress/ch12.htm.
Da Costa, Michael, *Colonial Origins, Institutions and Economic Performance in the Caribbean: Guyana and Barbados* (International Monetary Fund, 2007), 1–37, 5.
De Haan, Francisca, 'The Women's International Democratic Federation (WIDF): History, Main Agenda, and Contributions, 1945–1991', in *Women and Social Movements (WASI)* Online Archive, ed. by Kathryn Kish Sklar and Thomas Dublin (2012).
DeSouza, Sanchia, and Belliappa, Jyothsna Latha, 'The Positionality of Narrators and Interviewers', in *Beyond Women's Words Feminisms and the Practices of Oral History in the Twenty-First Century*, ed. by Katrina Srigley, Stacey Zembrzycki, and Franca Iacovetta (London: Routledge, 2018).
Engerman, Stanley L. and Higman, B.W., 'The Demographic Structure of the Caribbean Slave Societies in the Eighteenth and Nineteenth Centuries', in *The General History of the Caribbean*, ed. by Franklin W. Knight (London and Basingstoke: Unesco Publications, 1997), The Slave Societies of the Caribbean, 45–104.
Farley, Rawle, 'The Rise of Village Settlements in British Guiana', *Caribbean Quarterly*, 10 (1964), 52–61.
Flinn, Andrew, 'Cypriot, Indian and West Indian Branches of the CPGB, 1945–1970: An Experiment in Self-Organisation?', *Socialist History 21 Red Lives* (London: Rivers Oram Press, 2002), 47–66, esp. 57–61.

Garvey, Marcus, 'Speech at the Ward Theatre, Kingston Jamaica', *Negro World*, 7 January 1928, in *Race First*, ed. by Tony Martin (Baltimore, MD: Black Classic Press, 2020).

Gibsone, Harriet, 'Lemn Sissay and Valerie Bloom Look Back: "I Was a Wild Child When She Met Me"', *The Guardian*, 26 February 2022.

Gilroy, Beryl, *Black Teacher* (London: Bogle L'Ouverture Publications, 1994).

Gilroy, Paul, *The Black Atlantic, Modernity and Double Consciousness* (London: Verso, 1993).

Gilroy, Paul, *There Ain't No Black in the Union Jack: The Cultural Politics of Race and Nation* (London: Routledge, 2002).

Goolsarran, Samuel J., *The System of Industrial Relations in Guyana* (Trinidad and Tobago: International Labour Office, 2003).

Goulbourne, Harry, *Caribbean Transnational Experience* (London: Pluto Press, 2002).

Gradskova, Yulia, 'Women's international Democratic Federation, the "Third World" and the Global Cold War From the Late-1950s to the Mid-1960s', *Women's History Review*, 29 (2020), 270–88.

Green, Hannah, and Hanna, Kathleen, 'Oral History', in *The Houses of History: A Critical Reader in History and Theory* (Manchester: Manchester University Press, 1999).

Guba, Egon G. and Lincoln, Yvonna S., 'Competing Paradigms in Qualitative Research', in *Handbook of Qualitative Research*, ed. by N.K. Denzin and Y.S. Lincoln (Thousand Oaks, CA: Sage Publications, Inc, 1994), 105–17.

Hall, Stuart, *Familiar Stranger: A Life between Two Islands* (London: Allen Lane, 2017).

Healey, Michael S., 'Colour, Climate and Combat: The Caribbean Regiment in the Second World War', *The International History Review*, 22, no. 1 (2000), 65–85, esp. 65–6.

Heuman, Gad, 'The Social Structure of the Slave Societies in the Caribbean', in *The General History of the Caribbean*, ed. by Franklin W. Knight, 6, 3, The Slave Societies of the Caribbean (London and Basingstoke: UNESCO Publications, 1997).

Higgs, Michael, 'Malcolm X's Visit to Britain', *Institute of Race Relations* (27 February 2014), https://irr.org.uk/article/malcolm-x-oxford-union/ (accessed 10 April 2024).

Hinds, Donald, *Journey to an Illusion: The West Indian in Britain* (London: Bogle L'Ouverture Publications, 2001).

Hogsbjerg, C.J., '"A Thorn in the Side of Great Britain": C.L.R. James and the Caribbean Labour Rebellions of the 1930s', *Small Axe: A Caribbean Journal of Criticism*, 15 (2011), 24–42.

House of Commons, *Hansard's Parliamentary Debates: The Official Report* (24 July 1849 vol. 107, cc920-).

Huntley, Eric, *You Can't Cut Down a Green Heart Tree with Just a Grand Idea* (London: Bogle L'Ouverture Publication, 2022).

Huntley, Jessica, 'Nostalgic Moments', *Kunapipi*, 17, no. 1 (1995), 56–7.

Huntley, Jessica and Cheddi Jagan Research Centre, 'Call to Our Women', *Thunder*, 9 February 1958.

Ireland, Philippa, 'Material Factors Affecting the Publication of Black British Fiction' (unpublished doctoral thesis, The Open University, 2012).

Ishmael, Hannah, 'The Development of Black-Led Archives in London' (unpublished doctoral thesis, University College London, 2020).

Ishmael, Odeen, 'The Guyana Story', https://www.landofsixpeoples.com/TheGyStory.html.

Jackson, Jackson, 'Soledad Brother: The Prison Letters of George Jackson', History is a Weapon. https://www.historyisaweapon.com/defcon1/soledadbro.html (last accessed 14 April 2024).

Jagan, Cheddi, 'Bitter Sugar', Cheddi Jagan Research Centre, c.1950.

James, C.L.R., *Black Power, Its Past, Today, and The Way Ahead* (London: Bogle L'Ouverture, 1968).

James, C.L.R., *The Making of the Caribbean Peoples* (London: Bogle L'Ouverture, 1968).

James, C.L.R., *The Black Jacobins, Toussaint L'Ouverture and the San Domingo Revolution* (Dublin: Penguin Modern Classics, 2022), 15.

Jayawardena, C., *Conflict and Solidarity in a Guianese Plantation* (Oxford: Berg, 2004), 14–27.

Johnston, Kay, 'Cecily Haynes Hart Obituary', *The Guardian*, 24 March 2022.

Josiah, Barbara P., *Migration, Mining, and the African Diaspora: Guyana in the Nineteenth and Twentieth Centuries* (New York: Palgrave Macmillan, 2011).

Kipping, Matthias, R., Wadhwani, Daniel, and Bucheli, Marcelo, 'Analyzing and Interpreting Historical Sources: A Basic Methodology', *Researchgate* (2013), 305–29, esp. 313–16.

King, Audvil, Helps, Althea, Wint, Pam, Hasfal, Frank and Salkey, Andrew (eds), *One Love* (London: Bogle L'Ouverture, 1971), p.9. Huntley Collection, London Metropolitan Archives, LMA/4462/E/01/038/A.

Labott, Susan M., et al., 'Emotional Risks to Respondents in Survey Research: Some Empirical Evidence', *Journal of Empirical Research on Human Research Ethics: An International Journal*, 8 (2013), 53–66.

Lambert, Laurie R., 'Black Power and/as Patriarchy', *Small Axe*, 24, no. 3 (2020), 206–17.

Lewis, Gordon K., *The Growth of the Modern West Indies* (Kingston: Ian Randle Publishers, 2004).

Lewis, Rupert, *Walter Rodney's Intellectual and Political Thought* (Kingston: University of the West Indies Press, 1998).

Lewis, Rupert, *Marcus Garvey* (Barbados: The University of The West Indies Press, 2018).

'Marcus Garvey's Son Arrives for UK Tour', *Operation Black Vote*, 1 October 2013.

Martin, Tony, *Race First: The Ideological and Organizational Struggles of Marcus Garvey and the Universal Negro Improvement Association* (Baltimore MD: Black Classic Press, 2020), 3–21.

Nehusi, Kimani S.K., *A People's Political History of Guyana, 1838–1964* (Hertford: Hansib, 2018).

Nelson, Renee A., 'The West Indian Press and Public: Concepts of Regionalism and Federation, 1944–1946', *Journal of Caribbean History*, 54 (2020), 82–105.

Padmore, George, 1902–59, *Pan-Africanism or Communism? The Coming Struggle for Africa* (London: Dennis Dobson, 1956).
Palmer, Colin A. *Cheddi Jagan and the Politics of Power: British Guiana's Struggle for Independence* (Chapel Hill, NC: The University of North Carolina Press, 2010).
Palmer, Colin A., 'The Slave Trade, African Slavers and the Demography of the Caribbean to 1750', in *General History of the Caribbean*, ed. by Franklin W. Knight (London and Basingstoke: Unesco Publications, 1997), 3: The Slave Societies Of The Caribbean, 9–44.
Payne, Anthony, 'One University, Many Governments: Regional Integration, Politics and the University of the West Indies', *Minerva*, 18 (1980), 474–98.
Perry, Kennetta Hammond, *London is the Place for Me: Black Britons, Citizenship, and the Politics of Race* (New York: Oxford University Press, 2015).
Phillips, Mike, and Philips, Trevor, *Windrush: The Irresistible Rise of Multi-Racial Britain* (London: HarperCollins, 1998).
Rabe, Stephen G., *U.S. Intervention in British Guiana: A Cold War Story* (Chapel Hill, NC: University of North Carolina Press, 2006).
Ramcharan, Lilowatti, 'The Cold War in British Guiana, 1953–1966: A Case Study of Anglo American Cooperation/Lilowatti Ramcharan' (doctoral thesis, University of Kent at Canterbury, 2003).
Ramdin, Ron, *The Making of the Black Working Class in Britain* (London: Verso, [1987] 2017).
Roberts, Maureen, 'The Huntley Archives at the London Metropolitan Archives', in *The Future of Literary Archives*, ed. by David C. Sutton and Anne Livingstone (Leeds: Arc Humanities Press, 2018), 33–40.
Robertson, James, and others, 'Report of the British Guiana Constitutional Commission 1954 (The Robertson Commission Report)'.
Robinson, Cedric J., *Black Marxism: The Making of the Black Radical Tradition* (London: Penguin Classics, 2021).
Rodney, Walter, *The Groundings with My Brothers* (London: Bogle L'Ouverture Publications, 1969).
Rodney, Walter, *How Europe Underdeveloped Africa* (London: Bogle L'Ouverture Publications and Tanzania Publishing House, 1971).
Rodney, Walter, *A History of the Guyanese Working People, 1881–1905* (Baltimore, MD: The Johns Hopkins University Press, 1981).
Rodney, Walter, 'Plantation Society in Guyana', *Review*, 4 (1981), 643–66.
Rose, James G., 'British Colonial Policy and the Transfer of Power in British Guiana, 1945–1964' (unpublished doctoral thesis, King's College London, 1992).
Sands O'Connor, Karen, *Children's Publishing and Black Britain, 1965–2015 – Critical Approaches to Children's Literature* (London: Palgrave Macmillan, 2018).
Sands O'Connor, Karen, *British Activist Authors Addressing Children of Colour* (London: Bloomsbury Academic, 2022).
Sanghera, Sathnam, *Empireland: How Imperialism Has Shaped Modern Britain* (Penguin Random House UK, 2021).
Schwartz, Bill, ed., *West Indian Intellectuals in Britain* (Manchester and New York: Manchester University Press, 2003).

Schrempp, Zach, 'George Jackson (1941–1971)', *Blackpast*, 4 October 2010, https://www.blackpast.org/african-american-history/jackson-george-1941-1971/.
Sherwood, Marika, *Claudia Jones: A Life in Exile* (London: Lawrence & Wishart, 1999).
Sherwood, Marika, 'Peter Blackman, 1909–1993', *History Workshop Journal*, 37, no. 1 (1994):266–7.
Shiwcharan, Clement Toolsie, 'Indians in British Guiana, 1919–1929: A Study in Effort and Achievement is a Substantial and Important Work on this History' (unpublished doctoral thesis, University of Warwick, 1990).
Sidney, Carol, '60:60, Jessica Huntley, a Lifetime of Publishing', *Sable*, Spring (2005).
Sissay, Lemn, *Tender Fingers in a Clenched Fist* (London: Bogle L'Ouverture, 1998).
Smith, Evan, 'National Liberation for Whom? The Postcolonial Question, the Communist Party of Great Britain, and the Party's African and Caribbean Membership', *International Review of Social History; Cambridge*, 61, no. 2 (2016), 283–315.
'Stokely Carmichael speaking at the Dialectics of Liberation, 1967', British Library, Black Power – Address to Black Community.
Tate, Shirley Anne, 'The Dark Skin I Live In: Decolonizing Racial Capitalism's Aesthetic Hierarchies in the Diaspora', *Caribbean Review of Gender Studies*, 13 (2019), 173–98.
Teixeira, Gail, 'History of Struggle of Guyanese Women, The People's Progressive Party, Forward with the Women's Struggle. A Publication of the Women's Progressive Organisation in Honour of its 30th Anniversary', *WPO Publications* (1983), 9–16.
Thierens, Clyde W., 'Winifred Gaskin – An Early Guyanese Politician', *Stabroek News*, 10 December 2009. Available at: https://www.stabroeknews.com/2009/12/10/features/winifred-gaskin-an-early-guyanese-politician-2/.
Thomas, Odette, *Rain Falling, Sun Shining* (London: Bogle L'Ouverture Publications, 1975).
Tuck, Stephen, 'Malcolm X's Visit to Oxford University: U.S. Civil Rights, Black Britain, and the Special Relationship on Race', *The American Historical Review*, 118 (2013), 76–103.
Walker-Kilkenney, Roberta, 'Women in Social and Political Struggle in British Guiana 1946–1953', *History Gazette* The University of Guyana, 49 (1992). https://www.yumpu.com/en/document/view/54522448/women-in-social-and-political-struggle-in-british-guiana1946-1953 (last accessed 10 April 2024).
Walmsley, Anne, *The Caribbean Artists Movement, 1966–1972; A Literary and Cultural History* (London and Port of Spain: New Beacon Books, 1992).
Waters, Robert, and Daniel, Gordon, 'The World's Longest General Strike: The AFL-CIO, the CIA, and British Guiana', *Diplomatic History*, 29 (2005), 279–307.
Westmaas, Nigel, 'Gertie Wood: Pioneer Women's Rights Activist', *Stabroek News*, 2018.
Westmaas, Nigel, '1968 and the Social and Political Foundations and Impact of the "New Politics" in Guyana', *Caribbean Studies*, 37 (2009), 105–32.

White, Sarah, Harris, Roxy and Beezouhun, Sharmilla, eds, *A Meeting of the Continents, History, Memories, Organisation, and Programmes (1982–1995): The International Book Fair of Radical Black and Third World Books Revisited* (London: New Beacon Books, 2005).

Wild, Rosalind Eleanor, 'Black Was the Colour of Our Fight. Black Power in Britain, 1955–1976' (unpublished doctoral thesis, University of Sheffield, 2008).

Williams, Eric, *Capitalism and Slavery* (London: Penguin Modern Classics, 2022).

Wylde Carter, Martin, 'I Come From the Nigger Yard', *New World Journal*. https://newworldjournal.org/volumes/volume-1-1963/i-come-from-the-nigger-yard/.

INDEX

Page numbers in italics refer to photographs.
The full form of abbreviations that appear in subheadings can be found either by looking up the abbreviated form in the index or by using the abbreviations list on page 15 of the text.
The initials 'JH' and 'EH' have been used as an abbreviation for Jessica Huntley and Eric Huntley respectively.

Aaron, Burchell 55
Abbott, Diane 179
Abrahms, Oscar 108
Abu-Jamal, Mumia 169
Achebe, Chinua 156
Ackee, Breadfruit, Callaloo: An Edible Alphabet (Bloom) 201
Adi, Hakim 2
African facial features 21, 97, 137
African Society for Cultural Relations with Independent Africa (ASCRIA) 191
Agard, John 153, 179
ALA conferences *see* American Library Association (ALA) conferences
Alleyne, Doris 86
Allison & Busby 127, 131, 148, 179
American Library Association (ALA) conferences 177, 179
androcentrism *see* patriarchy
Angelou, Maya 159, 180, *180*
Anti-Apartheid Movement of Britain 109
Anti-Banding campaign 154–6
anti-colonialism
    labour rebellions (across the West Indies, 1930s) 10
    Marcus Garvey (Jamaica) 3
    neo-colonialism 4, 76, 105, 106, 121, 147, 191, 197
    political imprisonment 32

PPP 35, 40, 43, 46, 51, 60, 74
trade unions 15, 27, 34–5
West Indian Federation, plans for 100
West Indian groups in Britain 89, 90, 91, 92–3
West Indian regionalism 99
WIDF 74
and women's rights 61–2
see also decolonization
anti-intellectualism 108–9
anti-plantation movement 34, 39
archives *see* Huntley Archives
ASCRIA (African Society for Cultural Relations with Independent Africa) 191
Ashe-Watts, Norma 133
Atkinson airbase 54
At School Today (Accabre Huntley) 151, 152
Aukland, M.H.A. 47

Baez, Joan 93
Bagotstown 9
Bambara, Toni Cade 159, 180
Beaton, Norman 179
Benn, Bridley 59, 61, 66, 67
Berry, Chuck 71
Berry, James 180
BGFA (British Guiana Freedom Association) 89

BGLU (British Guiana Labour Union) 15, 16, 34
Bhagwan, Moses 63–4, 72, 191
Bishop, Maurice 104, 159
Black hair 71, 113, 133, 139
Black Ink Collective 179
Black Liberation Front (BLF) 109
Blackman, Peter 91
Black Panther Party 109
Black Parents Movement 154–6, *155*, 174, 175
Black People's Day of Action (2 March 1981) 184
Black Power, its Past, Today, and the Way Ahead (James) 116–17
Black Power Movement
  anthems of 97
  C.L.R. James's papers, publication by BLP 116–17
  Congress of Black Writers (Montreal, 1968) 119, 120
  contextual impetus for BLP 106, 110, 113, 121
  Jamaican government's stance 105
  key figures visit Britain 106–8, 109–10, *110*, 117
  Groundings With My Brothers (Rodney) 127, 130
  Walter Rodney's Jamaica ban 120–1
Black Supplementary Schools 24, 104, 144, 157–8
Black Teacher (Gilroy) 206–7
Black Youth 97–8, 134, 149, 150, 154
  see also children's literature; education system (Britain)
BLF (Black Liberation Front) 109
Blood a Goh Run (Shabazz) 179
Bloom, Valerie 159, 170, 179, 180, 199–202, 202–3
  Ackee, Breadfruit, Callaloo: An Edible Alphabet (Bloom) 201
  Duppy Jamboree and Other Jamaican Poems 201
  Touch Mi! Tell Mi (Bloom) 199–201
BLP *see* Bogle L'Ouverture Publications (BLP)
Bogle L'Ouverture Bookshop
  closure (by now Walter Rodney Bookshop) 205

  in Coldershaw Road *161*, 162–4
  feminist publishers 179
  JH's daily routine 166, 167, *167*, 170–1
  launch event 165–6, *166*
  as a meeting place for Black activists 168–70, *170*, 171, 172
  and New Beacon Books, differences 182
  racist attacks on 152, 172–6, *173*
  renamed Walter Rodney Bookshop 176, 197
  on tour 156, 171–2
Bogle L'Ouverture Publications (BLP)
  American authors 179
  and Andrew Salkey 137, *138*, 147, 148, 200
  At School Today (Accabre Huntley) 151, 152
  Black advancement, vision for 114–15, 133–5, 141, 206–7
  books for CECWA meetings 156
  cards and prints 115, 117–19, *118*, 135–7, 162
  children's literature 143–5, 162, 163, 201
  in Coldershaw Road 160–4, *161*, 205
  contextual impetus 99, 106, 110, 111, 113, 115, 121, 127
  Dread, Beat and Blood (Johnson) 149–50
  earliest publications 115–19, *118*
  feminist publishers and Black women writers 146–7, 179, 180
  Guyana, possible relocation (1975) 193, 194
  How Europe Underdeveloped Africa (Rodney) 147, 148–9, 196, 197
  How the West Indian Child is Made Educationally Subnormal in the British Education System (Coard) 143, 144
  intellectual resources 108, 128
  later publications (from 1980s) 199–203, 205–7

One Love (Salkey, editor) 137–8, 139
Pan-Africanism 125, 134, 138, 139, 148
and the Peter Moses School (Ealing, London) 158
rebranded as BLP (1993) 205
ten year celebration (1979) 152–3, *153*, 177
value to teachers in multicultural Britain 164
in Windermere Road 111–13, *112*, 116, 130
see also *Groundings With My Brothers, The* (Rodney)
Booker Group 34
see also Enmore Sugar estate
Bookshop Joint Action 176
Braithwaite, Anne 192
Braithwaite, Eddie 104
Brethren Church 22
Brewster, Yvonne 179
Britain
    Black Power Movement, key figures visit Britain 106–8, 109, 110, *110*, 117
    Committee Against Repression in Guyana (CARIG) 192–6, 197
    house ownership 162
    Huntley family
        Accabre Huntley, birth of 96
        early life, Caribbean friends 79–80, 93–5, 98
        EH's migration to 62, 64
        family reunited 85, 86–8, *87*
        Friends of the Huntley Archives at the London Metropolis Archives (FHALMA) 206, 207–8
        JH's final illness and death 208–10
        JH's migration to 62, 65–6, 68–9, 71, 72
        racial discrimination 80–1, 97–8
    immigrant workers, life of 78, 80, 81–2
    International Book Fairs (of Radical Black and Third World Books) 177, 178–83, *178*
    New Cross Fire, aftermath 177, 183–5
    political organizations (BFGA, CPGB and WICP) 5, 89–93, 194
    right wing/fascist groups 172
    suburbia 96–7, 162
    see also Bogle L'Ouverture Bookshop; Bogle L'Ouverture Publications (BLP); education system (Britain); racism (in Britain); West Indian Students Centre (London)
British Guiana
    Buxton Village activism 38–41, 43–4
    class prejudices 35, 36
    EH and JH's courtship and wedding (1950) 30–1, 33–4, 35–7, *38*
    EH's arrest and imprisonment 54–7, 82
    EH's childhood and family background 31, 33
    Friendly and Burial Societies 23
    geography of 9
    Gertie Wood 25–6
    independence, organizations (in Britain) 89, 90, 91, 92–3
    JH's childhood and family background 9–11, 12, 13, 16–18, 21–5, 33, 35
    labour rebellions (1930s) 10–11, 99–100
    plantations 10, 15, 22, 32, 34, 39, 62
    prison system 31–2
    representation at the Fourth WIDF Congress 73, *73*, 75–7, 78
    spectrum of 'Blackness' 10
    tenement yards 12–15, 17–18
    trade unionism 11, 14, 15–16, 27–8, 29, 30, 34–5
    voting rights 37, 44–5, 46, 76
    Women's Political and Economic Organization (WPEO) 45–6
    Women's Progressive Organization (WPO) 46–9, 52–3, 61, 74, 76, 77
    see also People's National Congress (PNC); People's Progressive Party (PPP)

British Guiana Freedom Association
    (BGFA) 89
British Guiana Labour Council 27
British Guiana Labour Union (BGLU)
    15, 16, 34
British Road to Socialism, The (CPGB)
    91
British West Indies Battalion 27–8, 100
Brown, James 97
Bumbo (WISU newsletter) 104
Burnham, Forbes
    coalition government (following the
        1964 election) 187
    election (1968) 188
    opposition activism 191, 192, 194,
        196, 197
    and the original PPP 40
    PPP-Burnham (split, 1955) 59, 67–8
    and racial politics 40, 67, 188
    and Walter Rodney 189, 191, 195–6
Burnham, Jessica 61
*Burning an Illusion: The West Indian
    in Britain* (Hinds) 206
Busby, Margaret 128, 131, 159
Bushell,, Len 126
Bushell, Waveney 14, 79–80, 126,
    141–2

Cambridge University Press (CUP) 201
CAM (Caribbean Artists Movement)
    105, 115, 128, 150
Cameron, Chris 147
CARD (Campaign Against Racial
    Discrimination) 105, 120
cards and prints 115, 117–19, *118*,
    135–7, 162, 168, 171
Caribbean Artists Movement (CAM)
    105, 115, 128, 150
Caribbean Education Community
    Workers Association
    (CECWA) 142, 143, 156
Caribbean Teachers Association (CTA)
    186
CARIG (Committee Against
    Repression in Guyana)
    192–6, 197
Carmichael, Stokely 105, 106, 107–8,
    117, 119

Carroll, Elleise *see* Huntley, Jessica
Carroll, Hadden 19
Carroll, Hectorine
    approval of EH 31
    care of the children (when JH left
        for Britain) 82, 83–5
    Caribbean matriarch 16–18, 22–3,
        31, 57
    Christian views/biblical adherence
        9, 16, 17, 22, 84–5
    coming to England 85–6, *87*, 88
    community resistance activity 44–5
    family background 11
    generosity of 16–17, 23
    JH's upbringing 9, 16, 17–18,
        21–4
    love of verse 152
    old age 185
    return to Guiana 88
    support of JH whilst EH in prison
        56–7
Carroll, James 9, 11–12
Carroll, Munroe 19, 23, 29, 30, 85,
    87, 88
Carroll, Robert 19
Carter, Keith 60
Carter, Martin 30, 59, 60, 63, 91
    'I Come From the Nigger Yard of
        Yesterday' 14
'catting' 16, 32
Cattouse, Nadia 153
CECWA (Caribbean Education
    Community Workers
    Association) 142, 143, 156
Cesar, Imruh, *Riots and Rumours of
    Riots* 179
Charles, Lena, *Nirvana* 137
Checker, Chubby 71
children's literature 143–5, 162, 163,
    201
Cimmarons 153
Circle of Sunshine Workers 25–6
Civil Rights Movement (US) 93, 97,
    106, 119, 177
Cleaver, Eldridge 106, 109
Cleaver, Kathleen 106, 109, 159
C.L.R. James School for Black Youth
    104

INDEX

Coard, Bernard 104, 159
   Getting to Know Ourselves 144–5
   How the West Indian Child is Made Educationally Subnormal in the British Education System 142, 143, 145
Coard, Phyllis, *Getting to Know Ourselves* 144–5
colonialism 10, 14, 16, 27–8, 31–2, 75
   see also anti-colonialism; decolonization; plantations
Committee Against Repression in Guyana (CARIG) 192–6, 197
Committee of Concerned West Indians 190
Communism
   JH's interest in 4, 5–6, 40–1, 47, 48, 89–92
   and the PPP 51, 52, 55, 60
   and Walter Rodney 120, 121
   WPO and WIDF 74
Communist Party of Great Britain (CPGB) 5, 89–90, 91, 194
Comrie, Loxley 113
Congress of Black Writers (Montreal, 1968) 119, 120
Connor, Pearl 179
Co-operative Republic of Guyana *see* Guyana
Courtman, Sandra 115
CPGB (Communist Party of Great Britain) 5, 89–90, 91, 194
Crawford, Jeff 154
creole (and patois) languages 199, 201
   Rain Falling, Sun Shining (Odette Thomas) 146–7
creole people 28, 33, 45
Critchlow, Hubert Nathaniel 14, 15, 16, 27–8, 34
CTA (Caribbean Teachers Association) 186
CUP (Cambridge University Press) 201

Davis, Angela 106, 109–10, *110*
De Cambra, Leland 192
decolonization 4, 133, 136, 139, 144, 146, 197
   see also anti-colonialism

De Freitas, Michael (Michael X) 106, 107
Dhondy, Farrukh 107, 179
Dialectics of Liberation Congress 107, 117
Dick, Pat 192
dock worker strikes (British Guiana, 1905) 15–16
Doiley, June 102
Dread, Beat and Blood (Johnson) 149–50, 171
Duncan, Virgil ('Mums') 98
Duppy Jamboree and Other Jamaican Poems (Bloom) 201

Easter Monday Blues (Accabre Huntley) 151
Eccles, Ray 126
education system (Britain)
   Black Parents Movement 154–6, *155*, 174, 175
   Black Supplementary Schools 24, 104, 144, 157–8
   BLP books 164, 171–2
   intellectualism and Black liberation 108
   literary canon 147
   racism 95, 142, 143, 150, 154–5, 156
enfranchisement 37, 43, 44, 45, 46, 76
Enmore Sugar estate 34–5, 39
Esbrand, James Maxton 11
Esbrand, Jr., James Maxton 11
Esbrand, Thomas 11

facial features 21, 97, 137
FHALMA (Friends of the Huntley Archives at the London Metropolis Archives) 206, 207–8
Fitzgerald, Ella 93
Friendly and Burial Societies in British Guiana 23
Friends of the Huntley Archives at the London Metropolis Archives (FHALMA) 206, 207–8

Garvey, Amy Ashwood 3
Garvey, Amy Jaques, messages by
 115–16
Garveyism 3
Garvey, Julius 209
Garvey, Marcus Mosiah 3, 105, 209
Gaskin, Winifred 45
gender *see* women
George Padmore Institute 6
Georgetown prison 32, 55–6
Getting to Know Ourselves (Coard, P.
 and Courd, B.) 144–5
Gilroy, Beryl, *Black Teacher* 206–7
GIWU (Guyana Industrial Workers
 Union) 34, 54
Goulbourne, Harry 7, 192
Greensleeves record shop 165
Greenwood, Earl 113
Griffiths, Fitzroy 113
Groundings With My Brothers, The
 (Rodney)
 in Bogle L'Ouverture's schedule
  115, 118
 editorial team 120, 126, 128–9,
  130, 131, 196
 front cover (Lloyd) 128, *129*
 funding 126–7
 publishers 127–8
 and Rodney's reputation as a
  radical-intellectual-activist 123
 sales and success of 129–30, 134,
  162
 and the vision of Bogle L'Ouverture
  134, 201
Guardian, The 143
Guyana
 general election (1968) 188
 JH's possible return to (1975)
  193–4
 'New Left' 187
 overseas resistance 190–3, 194–7
 racial divisions across the PPP and
  PNC 188
 Walter Rodney's return 188–9, 190
Guyana Industrial Workers Union
 (GIWU) 34, 54
Guyana Sugar Corporation 191
Guyana Symposium (London, 1965)
 92–3, 196

hair 71, 113, 133, 139
Hall, Stuart 191
Hansib Publishing 179
Harder They Come, The 117
Harley, Kim 201
Harris, Roxy 184
Harris, Wilson 30
Hart, Robert 126
Hasfal, Frank 138
Hassan, Leila 174, 192
Haynes-Hart, Cecily 24–5, 30, 67,
 68–9, 72, 82, 84, 157
Heartman, Ras Daniel 115, 117–18, 168
 'Mother and Child' 118, *118*, 136
Heinemann 179, 206
Heinemann African writers' series 156
Helps, Althea 138
Hill, Robert 119
Hinds, Donald
 *Burning an Illusion: The West
  Indian in Britain* 206
 Journey to an Illusion 206
Hodge, Merle 103
Howard University Press 149
Howe, Darcus 107, 178, 182, 183,
 184, 185, 200
How Europe Underdeveloped Africa
 (Rodney) 123, 147–9, 162,
 196, 197
*How the West Indian Child is Made
 Educationally Subnormal in
 the British Education System*
 (Coard) 142, 143, 145
Huntley, Accabre (married name
 Rutlin)
 At School Today 151, 152
 as a baby 96, *96*, *112*, 151
 Bogle L'Ouverture, publication by
  151, 152, 202
 desire to return to Guyana 193
 Easter Monday Blues (Accabre
  Huntley) 151
 on her mother's generosity 185
 poetry performances 152, 153, 179
Huntley Archives 6, 206
Huntley, Chauncey
 birth 37
 and Bogle L'Ouverture Bookshop
  165

in British Guiana (in the period
when JH and EH were in
Britain) 82, 83, 85, 86, 131
following EH's imprisonment 56
life in England 88, 95, 95, 97–8,
108, 112
and preparations to reunite the
family in Britain 85, 86, 87
Huntley, Eric
awards and tributes 73
birth of his children 37, 96
Bogle L'Ouverture Publications
(BLP) 179, 196, 203
childhood and family background
31, 33
correspondence with JH between
Britain and British Guiana
62, 64–6, 67, 68
courtship and wedding (1950)
30–1, 33–4, 35–7, 38
decision to bring Hectorine and the
boys to Britain 85, 86, 87
decision to move to Britain 62
desire to return to Guyana (1975)
193
and the Huntley collection 6
JH's letters from the WIDF
Congress (1958) 75–6
life in England 80, 81–2, 83, 93–4,
95, 95, 96–7, 121
on the loss of Walter Rodney 196–7
Peter Moses School (Ealing) 158
political activism
against repression in
independent Guyana 192
arrest and imprisonment 54–7,
82
and the Buxton progressive
study group 40
CPGB 89, 90
Guyana Symposium 92, 196
New Cross Fire, aftermath 184
security service surveillance 53–4
'Three Small Boys', association
with 38–9
trade unionism 35, 43, 54
and the 'Ultra Left' PPP 59, 60,
63
WICP 91, 92

and the racist attacks on the
bookshop 172, *173*, 175
social and political networks 93,
121, 150, 151, 159, 161
working life in British Guiana 35,
44, 52
*You Can't Cut Down a Green
Heart Tree With Just a Grand
Idea* 205
Huntley, Frank 31, 32–3, 35–7, 55–6
Huntley, Jessica
and Accabre's poetry 152
appearance 21, 71
awards and tributes 73, 209
birth of her children 37, 96
Bogle L'Ouverture Bookshop
bookshop activism 166, 167,
168–9, 171, 172, 176
in Coldershaw Road *161*, 162–4
on its closure 205
JH's daily routine 166, 167, *167*,
170–1
opening in Chignell Place 165
response to racist attacks 172–4,
174–5, 176
Sistren Theatre Collective 170,
170
Bogle L'Ouverture Publications
Black publishing strategy
114–15, 133–6, 138, 139,
141, 146, 206–7
book reviews 138
children's books 142, 143–4,
145, 201
Dread, Beat and Blood
(Johnson) 149, 150
early books (1968) 115, 116,
117–18
foundation 111–15, *112*, 121,
128, 131, 137, *138*
*How Europe Underdeveloped
Africa* (Rodney) 148–9, 196
later books (1980s) 199, 200,
201, 202, 203
Rain Falling, Sun Shining
(Thomas) 146, 147
ten year anniversary 152, 153,
153
and the British education system

Huntley, Jessica (cont'd)
    Black parents' groups 154–6, 155
    Black Supplementary Schools 104, 144, 157–8
    CECWA 142, 143, 156
    childhood and family background 9–11, 12, 13, 16–18, 21–5, 33, 35
    courtship and wedding (1950) 30–1, 33–4, 35–7, *38*
    decision to bring Hectorine and the boys to Britain 85, 86, 87
    early married domesticity 37–8
    and EH's departure for Britain 62–5
    and EH's imprisonment 56–7
    final illness, death and legacy 1, 7, 207, *207*, 208–10
    first job (garment factory) 28–30
    gender power relations within marriage 44, 65
    Huntley Archives 6, 207
    International Book fairs (1980s) 177, 178–83, *178*
    'Jessica Goes Home, A Poetic Tribute' (Ngugi wa Thiong'o) 1, 7
    life in England 78–82, 83, 88, 93–4, 95, *95*, 96–7, 98, 159
    migration to England 62, 65–6, 68–9, 71, 72
    Pan-Africanism 1, 2, 4, 5, 7, 96, 125, 139, 210
    personality
        generosity 185
        musical taste 93
        passion and commitment 7, 141–2, 170
        selflessness 170
        warmth 71–2, 150–1, 161
    political activism
        against neo-colonialism 4, 76, 105, 106, 121, 197
        against repression in independent Guyana (CARIG) 192–3, 194, 196, 197
        on behalf of Walter Rodney 125–6, 190–1, 192, 196
    Black Power Movement in Britain 106–10, *110*, 121
    early inspiration and education (in British Guiana) 25–6, 29, 30
    and EH's association with the Ultra Left PPP 60–1, 63
    finding a foothold in Britain (BFGA, CPGB and WICP) 5, 89–93
    first strike (at the garment factory, British Guiana) 29, 30
    following the New Cross Fire 183–5
    and the New Politics (Buxton village) 39, 40–1, 43–4
    in the PPP during EH's time alone in Britain 62–4, 65, 66–8, 187
    security services (in British Guiana) 54, 64
    Soledad brothers campaign 160–1
    WIDF's Fourth Congress, PPP representative (1958) 73, *73*, 75–7, 78
    WPO 46, 47–9, 52, 53, 103
    public speaking skills 25, 30, 44, 186
    racism, experiences of 80–1, 131
    religion 22, 84–5
    self-decolonization 2, 71, 133
    voting rights (in British Guiana) 37, 44, 45
    and Walter Rodney
        activism for 125–6, 190–1, 192, 196
        Guyana, possible return to (1975) 193–4
        his return to Guyana (1974) 188–9, 190–1
        leadership bid 195
        publication of his books 126–7, 128, 130, 131, 148–9, 196
        relationship with 121–2, *122*, 123, 196, 197
    West Indianism, West Indian Students Centre and Union

INDEX

99, 100–1, 102–3, 104, 105, 108–9, 116, 125
Huntley, Ken Karl
  birth 37
  in British Guiana (in the period when JH and EH were in Britain) 82, 83, 85, 86
  following EH's imprisonment 56
  life in England 88, 95, 95, 97–8, 112
  and preparations to reunite the family in Britain 85, 86, 87
Huntley, Patrick 32, 33, 36
Huntley, Selina Thorne 31, 33
Huntley, Stella 37
Huntley, Vera 37

'I Come From the Nigger Yard of Yesterday' (Martin) 14
imprisonment *see* prisons
indenture system 32, 40, 188
Indian Political Revolution Associates (IPRA) 191
Initiation North (Kayiga, formerly Wilkins) 137
International Book Fairs (of Radical Black and Third World Books) 177, 178–83, *178*
IPRA (Indian Political Revolution Associates) 191

Jackson, George 109, 160
Jackson, Jonathan 160
Jagan, Cheddi
  background 39–40
  JH's association with 43
  and political groups in Britain 90, 92, 93
  political imprisonment 56
  and the PPP's anti-religion stance 37
  and PPP splits (1955–1956) 59–60
  on racial unity 40, 59–60
  Western powers' opposition of 187, 188
Jagan, Janet Rosenberg
  background 39–40
  and JH's departure to Britain 72
  and the PPP 39, 43, 47

  PPP's first meeting (1950) 43
  Thunder 47, 72
  and 'Ultra Left' PPP 60, 61
  Women's organizations 45, 46, 47, 61, 74, 75
James, C.L.R. 102, 115, 116–17, 120, 153, 178, 181
  Black Power, its Past, Today, and the Way Ahead (James) 116–17
  The Making of the Caribbean Peoples 116
James, Jimmy 153
Jeffrey, Andreas 192
Jeffrey, Lionel 59, 60, 79, 82, 91, 93
Jeffrey, Pansy 79, 91, 93
Jegede, Emmanuel, *A Vision of Hope* 137
'Jessica Goes Home, A Poetic Tribute' (Ngugi wa Thiong'o) 1
John, Gus 94, 104, 156, 159, 200
Johnson, Anne 6
Johnson, Franklin 126
Johnson, Kay 185, 186
Johnson, Linton Kwesi
  on BLP and New Beacon Books, differences 168, 170, 182
  Dread, Beat and Blood 149–50, 171
  on his final meeting with JH. 209
  International Book Fair of Radical Black and Third World Books (1982) 179
  on the mentorship from JH and EH 150–1
  poetry performances 152, 153, 200
  and Valerie Bloom 170, 200
  as a visitor to Coldershaw Road 159
Jones, Claudia 206
Joseph, Barbara 126
Journey to an Illusion (Hinds) 206
juveniles
  delinquency in British Guiana (1955–1957) 77
  see also Black Youth; children's literature; education system (Britain)

Karran, Ram 56
Kayiga, Kofi (formerly Ricardo Wilkins), *Initiation North* 137
Kelly, George Fowokan, sculpture of JH *207*, 208
King, Audvil 138, 139
   'Letter to a Friend' 139
King, Coretta Scott 177
King, Martin Luther 119
King, Sidney 59, 60, 63
   see also Kwayana, Eusi (born Sidney King)
Ku Klux Klan 172, 176
Kwame Nkrumah Black Supplementary school (Hackney, East London) 157, 158
Kwayana, Eusi (born Sidney King) 13–14, 35, 39, 40–1, 43, 61, 191
   see also King, Sidney
Kwe Kwe dances 23

language dialects 139, 146–7, 180, 199, 201
La Rose, Irma 72, 91, 92, 93, 94, 192
La Rose, John
   background 94
   CARIG 192, 194
   CECWA 142
   Committee of Concerned West Indians 191
   friendship with the Huntleys 72, 93–4, 159, 181, 183
   and the International Book fairs 177, 178, *178*, 181–2, 183
   and Malcolm X 107
   New Beacon Books 94, 120, 131, 143, 144, 168
   New Cross Action Committee 184, 185
   and the publication of *The Groundings With My Brothers* 127, 128
   West Indian Students Centre 102, 104
   WICP membership 91, 92

Legba dance group 153
Le Maitre, Cris 104, 126, 133, 163, 164
Lenin, Nikolai 5
'Letter to a Friend' (King) 139
Lewis, Gordon K. 99
Lewis, Rupert 123
Lewis, Steven 94, 160, 161, 171, 183, 184–5
Lloyd, Errol
   on Daniel Heartman's poster series 117–18, 119, 136–7
   on the gatherings in Windermere Road 113
   illustrations for BLP 117, 128, *129*, 136, 137, 147
   as visitor to Coldershaw Road *161*
   West Indian Students Centre 104
logging and timber industry (British Guiana) 28–9
London Metropolitan Archives 6, 207, *207*, 208
London South Bank University 209
Lonely Londoners, The (Selvon) 79
Lovelace, Earl 179

McDaniel, Cliff 154
MacDonald, Ian 168
MacMillan Caribbean 201
Making of the Caribbean Peoples, The (James) 116
Malcolm X 105, 106
Mangrove Nine (Rossi) 179
Marcus Garvey School (Shepherd's Bush, London) 157
Marshall, Woodville 100
Marxism 5, 6, 39–40, 41, 43, 60, 116, 182
Marxism and the National and Colonial Question (Stalin) 5
Mazuruni prison 56
Michael Ford Bookstore 194
Michael X 106, 107
Misty in Roots 168
Mitchell, Joni 93
Monroe, Tony 157
Morrison, Toni 159
Moses, Peter 157, 158

'Mother and Child' (Heartman) 118,
    118, 136
Movement for Colonial Freedom 105
Moyne Commission and report 10–11,
    34, 100, 116
Muhammed, Elijah 105
Munroe, Carmen 153
Munroe, Tony 157

National Front 168
Nehusi, Kimani 60, 61
neo-colonialism 4, 76, 105, 106, 121,
    147, 191, 197
Neuville, Elaine 113
New Amsterdam Prison 32, 33
New Beacon Books
    archives 6
    BLP, differences 148, 168, 170, 182
    CECWA meetings 156
    *How the West Indian Child is Made
        Educationally Subnormal in
        the British Education System*
        142, 143, 144
    International Book Fair of Radical
        Black and Third World Books
        181
    and JH's decision to form BLP 131
    in La Roses' living room 94
    Walter Rodney's papers 120
New Cross Fire, aftermath 177, 183–5
'New Left' (in Guyana) 187
Ngugi wa Thiong'o, 'Jessica Goes
    Home, A Poetic Tribute' 1, 2
'Nigger Yards' 15
    see also tenement yards
Nirvana (Charles) 137
NLWIA (North London West Indian
    Association) 154
non-standard English 139, 146–7, 180,
    199, 201
North London West Indian Association
    (NLWIA) 154

OAAU (Organization of Afro-
    American Unity) 106
One Love (Salkey, editor) 137–8, 139
Organization of Afro-American Unity
    (OAAU) 106

Osamor, Martha (Baroness) 155, 210
OUP (Oxford University Press) 127
"Our Black Women Speak" (West
    Indian Students Centre,
    London, 1969) 102–3
Ove, Horace 179
Oxford University Press (OUP) 127,
    147, 179

Padmore, George 5
Pan-Africanism
    Amy Jaques Garvey 115
    BLP strategy of 125, 134, 138, 139,
        148
    and Communism 5
    congresses 2
    defined 2
    and Garveyism 3
    JH 1, 2, 4, 5, 7, 96, 125, 139, 210
    One Love (Salkey, editor) 138
    Walter Rodney 121, 125, 130, 134,
        147
patois *see* creole (and patois) languages
patriarchy
    and Black activism (in Britains) 101,
        102–3, 104, 181, 182, 183
    in marriage 44, 65
    in the PPP 59, 61–2
Patterson, Charles 126
Peach, Blair 168
People's National Congress (PNC) 187,
    188, 191, 193
People's Progressive Party (PPP)
    anti-colonialism 35, 40, 43, 46, 51,
        60, 74
    and the CPGB 90
    election performance 46, 48, 59,
        187
    first meeting (1950) 43
    Frank Huntley's views on 36–7
    general election (1953) 45, 46, 48,
        59
    Janet Jagan 39
    JH's political activism before
        joining EH in Britain 62–4,
        65, 66–8, 187
    journal (*Thunder*) 47, 48, 52, 68, 72
    party splits (1955–1956) 59–60

People's Progressive Party (*cont'd*)
   racial division 40, 67, 187, 188
   removal of and period of military
      suppression 51, 52, 53, 54,
      55, 56, 57, 59, 74, 80
   travelling comrades, support for 72
   'Ultra Left' PPP 59–62, 63
   and WIDF 73, 74
Peter Moses School (Ealing, London) 158
Philips, Caryl 179
Phillips Gay, Jane 47
Phoenix, Sybil 126, 184
Pierce, Gareth 168
plantations 10, 15, 22, 32, 34, 39, 62
PNC (People's National Congress) 187, 188, 191, 193
police
   harassment and violence (in Britain) 134, 135, 150, 154, 168
   response to racist attacks on Black bookshops 173, 174, 175
   suppression of strikes (in British Guiana) 16, 34–5
   surveillance of EH's parents' home 55
posters 115, 117–19, *118*, 126, 135–7, 162, 168, 171
Post Office Journal, The 54
Post Office Workers Union 35, 54
pressed (straightened) hair 71, 113, 133, 139
prints and cards 115, 117–19, *118*, 135–7, 162, 168, 171
prisons
   Angela Davis's release 109
   as colonial domination 31–2
   EH 55–7, 57, 62, 82
   Frank Huntley 31, 32–3, 35, 55–6
   military suppression (following 1953 election) 51, 52, 77
   Soledad brothers 160
Providence sugar estate 54

Quansah, Grace 171, 208, 209

Race Today 178, 181, 182, 183
racism (in Britain)
   attacks on Bogle L'Ouverture Bookshop 172–6

BLP campaign 134
   education system 95, 142, 143, 150, 154–5, 156
   the Ministry of Pensions 80–1
   National Front 168
   police harassment and violence (in Britain) 134, 135, 150, 154, 168
   in rented accommodation 81, 131
   white neighbourhoods 97, 162
Rain Falling, Sun Shining (Odette Thomas) 146–7
Rajendra, Cecil 179
Rastafarians 117–19, 136
Rees, Merlyn 175
'Referendum Five' 191–2
reggae music 165, 168
Rhodesia 94
Richards, Sandra 157
Riots and Rumours of Riots (Cesar) 179
'Rodney riots' 120
Rodney, Walter
   advice to JH on her possible return to Guyana 193–4
   assassination of (1980) 195–7
   background 92–3
   Bogle L'Ouverture Bookshop opening (1975) 165
   collaboration with JH 121–3, *122*, 196, 197
   How Europe Underdeveloped Africa 123, 147–9, 162, 196, 197
   Jamaican ban (1968) 105, 111, 119–21, 125–6
   Pan-Africanism, Walter Rodney 121, 125, 130, 134, 147
   return to Guyana (1974) 188–90, 190–2, 195–6
   on tenement yards 15
   and Virgil Duncan 98
   as a visitor to Coldershaw Road 159
   see also Groundings With My Brothers, The (Rodney)
Rossi, Franco, *Mangrove Nine* 179
'rude boys' 97

Rutlin, Accabre *see* Huntley, Accabre (married name Rutlin)
Rutlin, Marika Efea (JH's granddaughter) 209

Salkey, Andrew
  background 137
  and BLP 137, *138*, 147, 148, 150, 200
  CARIG 194
  JH's letter on fears for Walter Rodney's safety (1974) 188
  JH's letter on her connection to Mrs Garvey 115
  and Linton Kwesi Johnson 150
  Malcolm X meeting 107
  One Love (editor) 137–8, 139
  protests following Rodney's Jamaican ban 125
  as a visitor to Coldershaw Road 159, *161*
  West Indian Students Centre 103, 104
Sankey, John 127, 128
Sawyers, Hazel 167, 168
Second World War 27–8, 100
self-decolonization 2, 71, 133
Selvon, Samuel 79, 165
  Lonely Londoners, The (Selvon) 79
Shabazz, Menelik, *Blood a Goh Run* 179
Shange, Ntozake 180
Shearer, Hugh 120–1
Singh, A. Judah 68
Sissay, Lemn 159, 202–3
  Tender Fingers in a Clenched Fist (Sissay) 203
Sistren Theatre Collective 170, *170*
Small, Richard 104, 113, 117, 119–20, 125, 126, 127, 128, 133
Smith, Ian 94
Smith, Michael (Mikey) 179
Soledad brothers 160
Soyinka, Wole 156
Stalin, Joseph, *Marxism and the National and Colonial Question* 5
Stanford-Binet test 142
Steel 'N' Skin 153

Stephenson, Martin 39
Stephenson, Natalie 126
strikes 15–16, 29, 30, 34, 54
students *see* West Indian Students Centre (London)
sugar estates 10, 16, 34–5, 39, 54
Surveyor, The 164

Tanzanian Publishing House 148
Taylor, Cleston 91
Tender Fingers in a Clenched Fist (Sissay) 203
tenement yards 12–15, 17–18, 48
Thatcherism, impact on the radical book market 205
Thomas, Ewart 126, 127, 128, 129, 146, 149
Thomas, Odette 159
  Rain Falling, Sun Shining 146–7
'Three Small Boys' 39
Thunder (PPP journal) 47, 68, 72
  'Call to Our Women' 48
  'Women and Peace' (JH) 47, 52
Touch Mi! Tell Mi (Bloom) 199–201
trade unions
  British Guiana Labour Union (BGLU) 15, 16, 34
  Guyana Industrial Workers Union (GIWU) 34, 54
  Hubert Critchlow 14, 15, 16, 27–8, 34
  logging and sawmills (in British Guiana) 29, 30
  Ministry of Pensions (England) 81
  Moyne Report 11, 34
  Post Office Workers Union (British Guiana) 35, 54
Tutuola, Amos 156
TWTUC (World Trade Union Conference) 27

'Ultra Left' PPP 59–62, 63
UNIA (Universal Negro Improvement Association) 3
University of the West Indies 100, 119, 125

Vagabonds 153
Vaughn, Sarah 93

Villiers Publications 127, 128
Virago 179
Vision of Hope, A (Jegede) 137
voting rights 37, 43, 44–5, 46, 76

Waithe, Keith 153, 166, 168, 185, 192, 200
Walker, Alice 180
Walmsley, Anne 115–16
Walter Rodney Bookshop 176, 197, 205
  see also Bogle L'Ouverture Bookshop
West Indian Communist Party (WICP) 89, 90–2, 93
West Indian Federation 59–60, 100
'West Indianism' ('West Indian regionalism'/West Indian Nationalism) 99–105
West Indian Standing Conference 105
West Indian Students Centre (London)
  anti-intellectualism 108–9
  background 101
  C.L.R. James 116
  Errol Lloyd 128
  JH 100–1, 102–3, 104, 105, 108–9, 116, 125
  Woodville Marshall 100
West Indian Student Union (WISU) 100, 101, 102, 103, 104
Westmaas, Richard "Rory" 59, 60, 63, 95
Whitelaw, Willie 175
White, Sarah 94, 168, 182, 183
WICP (West Indian Communist Party) 89, 90–2, 93
WIDF (Women's International Democratic Federation) 73, 73, 74, 75–7, 78
Wilkins, Richard (later Kogi Kayiga), *Initiation North* 137
Williams, Aubrey 104
Williams, Henry Sylvester 2–3
Wilson, Jackie 71
Wint, Pam 138

WISU (West Indian Student Union) 100, 101, 102, 103, 104
women
  appearance of 21, 71, 139
  Black stereotyping (in British Guiana) 36
  Caribbean matriarchs 16–18, 22–3, 24, 31, 57, 98
  editors at BLP 131
  formal political participation (British Guiana) 37, 44–9, 59, 60–2, 68
  gender power relations within marriage 44, 65
  Gertie Wood 25–6
  patriarchy and Black activism (in Britain) 101, 102–3, 104, 181, 182, 183
  voting rights (British Guiana) 37, 44, 45, 46, 76
  WIDF 73, *73*, 74, 75–7, 78
  as workers 25–6, 29, 30, 75, 77
  WPO 46–9, 52–3, 61, 74, 76, 77
  writers 179–80, *180*, 202
  see also Bloom, Valerie; Thomas, Odette
Women's International Democratic Federation (WIDF) 73, *73*, 74, 75–7, 78
Women's Political and Economic Organization (WPEO) 45–6
Women's Press 179
Women's Progressive Organization (WPO) 46–9, 52–3, 61, 74, 76, 77
Wong, Ansel 103, 104
Wood, Gertie 25–6
workers
  immigrant workers, life in Britain 78, 80, 81–2
  indenture system 32, 40, 188
  labour rebellions (across the West Indies, 1930s) 10–11, 99–100

women 25–6, 29, 30, 75, 77
  see also trade unions
Working People's Alliance (WPA) 191, 195
Workmen's Compensation Ordinance 77
World Trade Union Conference (TWTUC) 27
World War II 27–8, 100
Worrall, W.O.R. 67
WPA *see* Working People's Alliance (WPA)
WPEO (Women's Political and Economic Organization) 45–6

WPO (Women's Progressive Organization) 46–9, 52–3, 61, 74, 76, 77

Yale University Press 179
You Can't Cut Down a Green Heart Tree With Just a Grand Idea (Eric Huntley) 205
young people
  delinquency in British Guiana (1955–1957) 77
  see also Black Youth; children's literature; education system (Britain)